THE DYNAMICS OF PRAYER
IN THE LATINO PENTECOSTAL COMMUNITY

THE DYNAMICS OF
PRAYER
IN THE
LATINO PENTECOSTAL COMMUNITY

Mireya Álvarez

Cherohala Press
Cleveland, Tennessee

To my mother,
María Adela Reina,
who has lived a life dedicated to prayer
ever since I can remember.

The Dynamics of Prayer in the Latino Pentecostal Community
Published by Cherohala Press
900 Walker ST NE
Cleveland, TN 37311
USA
email. cptpress@pentecostaltheology.org

ISBN: 978-1-953358-18-9

TABLE OF CONTENTS

ACKNOWLEDGMENTS

I want to acknowledge my mentors at New York Theological Seminary who took the time to listen to my concerns as a Latina Pentecostal and wholly encouraged my academic journey. Wanda Lundy directed our diverse class with vitality and urged us to believe in ourselves. Keith Russell paid attention to my thoughts on prayer and supported my ideas and gave me biblical direction on the Gospel of Luke and Acts. My Latino mentors, Humberto Alfaro and Pablo Diaz, were a source of encouragement by affirming and understanding my cultural values. I made friends with classmates, who were all people of color, and in a way, we shared similar worldviews. My educational experience opened my eyes to people who minister in a city like New York, and it also helped me to understand the problems and challenges they face. Through social media, our cohort kept in touch by posting about our ministry endeavors.

Pastor Rodney Vickers in Azalea Garden Church of God was the gatekeeper for my project in the Latino congregation church in Virginia Beach. Members of the church were supportive of the research through discussions, and personal interviews at every stage: Marian Maye, Gladys Ashmore, Bill Holcomb, Mae Garcia, Frank Allen, and Domingo Mora.

My pastoral and missionary involvement with people in Honduras, the Philippines, Ecuador, and Latinos in New York, New Jersey, Maryland, Washington, D.C., Pennsylvania, and Virginia provided me with rich cross-cultural insights that continue to influence my life.

I want to recognize the encouragement of my extended family, who have celebrated every steppingstone of my life. I could have never embarked on this journey without the support of my husband Miguel and our five children, Daniel, Michelle, Enoc, Miguel Jose, and Mariadela Belle. To God be the glory.

INTRODUCTION

MY LIFE STORY AND PRAYER

Prayer throws faith on God and God on the world. Only God can move the mountains, but faith and prayer move God. [1]

Ministry Background

For the past thirty-five years, my life as a female Pentecostal minister has been a time of intense service. I was born in Central America in the mountainous city of Tegucigalpa, Honduras. I was raised in a close-knit family of four daughters. My parents were God-fearing Catholics who took us to church on Sundays. My mother was an entrepreneur who sustained a successful shop for about 30 years. I will never forget how she kneeled down, expressing gratitude to God every evening when closing her shop. She read portions of Psalms and Proverbs in her Bible often. However, we were not introduced to the experience of 'accepting Jesus in our heart' until about 1975, when my mother received healing from glaucoma at a small Pentecostal church in Tegucigalpa.

It was in that small church where I received my first teachings and guidance as a new Christian. I recall the day I responded to an altar call and gave my life to Jesus. The environment at the altar was one of vociferous prayers, crying, singing, and laying of hands. The small congregation gathered in a small house, and eventually it was established in 1979 as a Church of God (COG) in a suburban neighborhood called *Colonia Alameda,* in Tegucigalpa. The church is known

---

[1] Edward M. Bounds, *The Necessity of Prayer* (Grand Rapids, MI: Baker Book House, 1983), p. 10.

today as the Iglesia de Dios Familia de la Fe, an influential congregation that emphasizes evangelism, worship, and social outreach.

As a young convert, I felt called to ministry and was involved in
evangelism, worship, and youth ministry. I was baptized in water in
August 1975 and ten days later I received the baptism of the Holy
Spirit and spoke in tongues during a Tuesday night prayer service. I
married Miguel Alvarez, a young Honduran pastor, perhaps not
knowing what pastoral ministry would entail. I became immersed in
carrying out pastoral duties, teaching, preaching, and leading
women's ministries in the church. In order to enhance the finances
at home, I also taught English classes at the National University of
Honduras from 1979 until 1991.

In 1992, Miguel was appointed to be the president of a COG seminary in Manila, Philippines. We arrived in Manila in October 1992
with our children, ages 14, 12, 4, and a three-month-old baby. Our
foster son, Enoc, who was 12, stayed behind due to legal documents
and all the required paperwork since he was a minor. He joined us
later in 1997 and studied at the seminary. I must say that relocation
to Asia was not easy at first, yet the cross-cultural experience was very
valuable to each family member, including our five children. We were
involved in seminary education, pastoral ministry, and missionary
training during the nine years that we lived in Manila. We left Manila
in 2001 for the USA in order to work with a missionary agency established in Virginia Beach.

In Virginia, we were able to plant a Latino/Hispanic congregation
in a COG called Azalea Garden. Pastor Aubrey Maye let us use a
trailer in the church parking lot on Saturday afternoons. Soon after,
the church gathered in the new fellowship hall on Sunday mornings,
with an average attendance of 75. Miguel also taught missions courses
at Regent University, and I enrolled at Old Dominion University for
a Masters Certificate in Teaching English as a Second Language. I
also enrolled in a doctoral program in education in 2005. I took these
moments as an opportunity to study since my children were grown.
I finally had the time to invest in my lifetime dream of a doctoral
education.

In 2004, Miguel and I were appointed to work with Latino
churches in the Northeast region of the USA, which consisted of a
total of 200 churches across seven states. It was a time to be in touch
with our Latino roots. It was enlightening to encounter Mexicans,

Central Americans, Dominicans, Puerto Ricans, and South Americans in many towns and cities in the northeastern states. The *hermanos and hermanas* were warm-hearted and hospitable. It was my first encounter with Latino communities, and I got to observe firsthand how they adapted yet preserved their cultural ways. Those years involved intense ministry work. Administrative bishops become involved in educational programs, church planting, conflict resolution, and many other ecclesiastical duties.

In 2010 we moved to Quito, Ecuador, to head a COG seminary and to pastor a church. The pastoral role was intense. Miguel and I had planted previous churches, but this was an established church where leaders were used to specific routines and dynamics. Many people in the congregation were hurting and confused. The church environment was less Pentecostal than what we were used to. We emphasized prayer and ministry at the altar. It was amazing to see conversions every Sunday and also some miraculous healings.

At the seminary, teachers gravitated around certain theological viewpoints. I believe I never understood the pulse of the faculty, who were all graduates of the seminary themselves. They deeply respected one of the founders of the seminary, and one of their principal mentors is known as an eloquent speaker. Our work ethos was questioned, and we were not embraced by the seminary faculty. On the other hand, the simple brothers and sisters of the local church were at all times supportive of our ministry until we left Ecuador in 2012.

In 2013 Miguel and I were appointed to lead the Latino and Hispanic churches in the state of Virginia. This assignment was uncomplicated since we were comfortable relating to Central and South Americans, Mexicans, Dominicans, and Puerto Ricans. It was an agreeable time to plan educational conferences and visit the churches. It was during that time period that I enrolled at NYTS and worked on my doctoral project in the Latino churches of Virginia.

Role of Prayer in Ministry Settings

Prayer has played a pivotal role in each stage of my personal ministry involvement. Ministry opportunities bring about great opportunities but also difficult circumstances. It was during our missionary assignment (1992-2001) that I became more committed to a life of prayer as I raised our children in a diverse cultural setting. I kept a prayer journal where I expressed my thoughts and feelings to God. It brought a sense of peace and inner strength to my life. Journaling was a safe place not only to write my prayer requests but to convey my thoughts, doubts, and complaints to God. Writing was a way to stay focused in a dialogue with God and to follow up on answers to prayer.

Whenever I experienced heaviness of heart, seeking a time of solitude brought peace and encouragement to my inner being and to my perspective on life. I also wanted to experience a fruitful ministry, and I knew that, in my own strength, all attempts would only be human endeavors. I understood prayer from the perspective of Rom. 8.26- 27:

> In the same way, the Spirit helps us in our *weakness*. We do not know what we ought to pray for, but *the Spirit himself intercedes for us through wordless groans*. And he who searches our hearts knows the mind of the Spirit, because the Spirit intercedes for God's people in accordance with the will of God.[2]

Indeed, many times I found myself at a loss for words to express what I was going through. My heart and mind cried out to God in situations of decision-making and unanswered questions. In a classical Pentecostal approach, I made use of my prayer language: 'For anyone who speaks in a tongue does not speak to men but to God ... he utters mysteries with his spirit' (1Cor. 14.2). I prayed both during times of need and when overflowing with gratitude to God. In my personal experience, using a prayer language brought peace as I expressed myself beyond words, 'sighs too deep for words'. The Apostle Paul explained that 'He who speaks in a tongue edifies himself, but he who prophesies edifies the church' (1 Cor. 14.2, 4). My mind and heart were set free from carrying heavy burdens. These were times of refreshment, as described in Isa. 28:11: 'With ... strange tongues God will speak to this people ... This is the resting place, let the weary rest ... This is the place of repose'.

Reading Scripture or meditating on the *Lord's Prayer* brought hope and greater faith to my life. I was hungry and thirsty for God (Mt. 5.6). I cried out for a heart to serve others in a spirit of love. I wanted to manifest the fruit of the Spirit in my words and actions. I prayed

---

[2] Quotations of Scripture are taken from the New International Version.

for wisdom to guide and instruct my children. I prayed for my husband to exercise visionary leadership. I aimed to provide an atmosphere of trust and security for my children at home. It was through daily prayer and Scripture reading that I developed a greater dependency on God's leading. I knew that a branch separated from the vine would not produce fruit (Jn 15.5).

Because of this great commitment to prayer during our missionary experience, I realized that many Christians and many churches live in a state of prayerlessness. According to E.M. Bounds:

> True prayer must be *aflame*. Christian life and character need to be all on fire. Lack of heat creates infidelity…The fiery souls are those who conquer in the day of battle, from whom the kingdom of heaven suffereth violence, and who take it by force. The citadel of God is taken only by those who storm it in dreadful earnestness, who besiege it, with fiery, unabated zeal … This flame is not mental vehemence, nor fleshy energy. It is Divine fire in the soul, intense, dross- consuming, the very essence of the Spirit of God. [3]

I have observed prayerlessness in the individual lives of Christians, in churches, and in Christian educational circles. The work of the kingdom of God can only be carried out in prayer. Persistent prayer keeps our mission in focus. We are called to declare the Word of God to those who are alienated from the redemptive message of reconciliation (2 Cor. 5.19-20). It is an awesome responsibility for Christians to take the gospel message to the people we encounter on a daily basis.

I also see how church politics places men in positions of authority and power. The regrettable result is that administrative and church ministries are not carried out in a spirit of servanthood. Instead, egos are exalted, and competition provokes division and even conflict. Christians operate in bitterness and unforgiveness. It would seem that prayerlessness keeps the presence of the Holy Spirit away from a fuller manifestation in Christian circles.

It has been said that prayer is the oxygen of the soul. During times of prayer, believers make themselves available for the Holy Spirit. It takes time to submit to his will. People come not knowing how to

---

[3] Bounds, *The Necessity of Prayer,* pp. 49-50.

pray but the Spirit intercedes for them *through wordless groans*. The Holy Spirit helps them in their weakness by interceding in accordance with the will of God. The Apostle Paul visualized that the whole creation groans as a woman in labor (Rom. 8.22) awaiting a new day when there will be no more tears, no more pain, and no more injustice.

Jesus explained to his disciples that their prayers would be answered: 'Whatever you ask in my name, this I will do, that the Father may be glorified in the Son ... Ask, and it will be given to you' (Jn 14.13; Lk. 11.9). Christians may not realize all the good things God has in store for those who seek Him: 'No eye has seen, no ear has heard, no heart has imagined what God has prepared for those who love Him. But God has revealed it to us through the Spirit. The Spirit searches all things, even the deep things of God' (1 Cor. 2.9-10). The Spirit searches into the depths of God, and the Spirit reveals what God has planned for us. And has not the Holy Spirit been hovering since Creation?

> God wants warm-hearted servants. The Holy Spirit comes *as a fire* to dwell in us; we are to be baptized with the Holy Spirit and with fire. Fervency is warmth of Soul. A phlegmatic temperament is abhorrent to vital experience. If our religion does not set us on fire, it is because we have frozen hearts. God dwells in a flame; the Holy Spirit descends in fire.[4]

Prayer opens the way for the Holy Spirit of God to manifest the presence of Jesus among Christians: His mercy, grace, healing, forgiveness, joy, peace, courage, and love. The presence of God may be found through waiting in prayer: 'You, God, are my God, [early will] I seek you; I thirst for you, my whole being longs for you, in a dry and parched land where there is no water' (Ps. 63.1). Men and women must pray. The church must pray.

---

[4]E.M. Bounds, *The Complete Works of E.M. Bounds on Prayer* (Grand Rapids, MI: Baker Book House, 2002), p. 35.

1

PRAYER AS EMPHASIZED IN LUKE–ACTS

Relevance of Luke–Acts for Latino Pentecostals

The emphasis on prayer and the infilling of the Holy Spirit are two distinguishing features among Pentecostals today. Luke–Acts is a significant foundation for Pentecostals.

> Pentecostals read their Bibles in faith as the inspired and infallible Word of God, even if they may never have heard of these terms. The earliest Pentecostals at the turn of the twentieth century came mostly from the Holiness movement and carried over their commonsense realist approach to the Scriptures. Pentecostals read Acts not merely as history but as salvation history, that is, not merely as a historical document about what happened but as a literary-theological document about what may and even should happen.[1]

The discussion of Luke–Acts on prayer and the infilling of the Holy Spirit is relevant for Pentecostals. The Pentecostals stress the significance of prayer and use many terms for seeking God and the power of the Holy Spirit. Specifically, Pentecostals in Latin America live and move within societies ravaged by violence that seem to sink deeper into poverty. They manifest a sense of reliance on the Holy Spirit. The practice of *vigilias* (all night prayer vigils) is common, as are *el ayuno and la oración* (fasting and prayer). When needs arise, Pentecostals refer to *hay que orar* (we must pray) and *pídale a Dios* (ask God).

The presence of the Holy Spirit moving among the congregation is acknowledged as *el Espíritu se movió* (the Spirit moved), *la presencia de*

---

[1] Amos Yong, 'Reading Scripture and Nature: Pentecostal Hermeneutics and Their Implications for the Contemporary Evangelical Theology and Science Conversation', *Perspectives on Science and Christian Faith* 63. 1 (March 2011), pp. 3-15, https://www.asa3online.org/asa3.org/ASA/PSCF/2011/PSCF3-11Yong.pdf

Dios se sintió (we felt the presence of God), and *cayó el poder de Dios* (the power of God fell). *Hermanos* and *hermanas* can also exemplify the in-filling of the Holy Spirit in their lives. For example, *predicó con poder* (she/he preached with power), *Dios la usó*, (God used her). Prayer and fasting usually go hand in hand, and believers anticipate God will move in miraculous ways such as healing and deliverance. Pentecostals stress the work of the Holy Spirit in the lives of believers and the church.

The book of Acts reflects the experience of migration of the early believers when under persecution. Early Christians carried out the proclamation of the gospel in the villages and cities where they were displaced. Pentecostals today also carry the gospel message as they cross cultures. Latinos have migrated to the U.S., fleeing violence in their countries. As Latino immigrants arrive in the U.S., they seek other believers or churches as a point of stability and identity. Churches offer hospitality to migrants. Latino churches are truly places of refuge where immigrants can use their native language and find support in prayer circles. Just as the early believers migrated under persecution, Latinos escape conditions of oppression, violence, and poverty. Although they are labeled as 'illegals' and live in the shadows, they do not hesitate to engage in evangelism, church planting, and missions. They are outcasts of society, 'strangers and exiles' (Heb. 11.13), yet hold on to their faith in God.

The Latino/Hispanic population continues to grow in the US and so are evangelical and Pentecostal churches all over the nation.[2] The growth of Hispanic churches is closely tied to the immigrant experience.[3] According to Elizabeth Dias, Latino evangelicals are one of the fastest growing segments of America's churchgoers. Rick Warren, pastor of Saddleback Church, observed the Latino church growth is happening mostly among the Pentecostal or charismatic churches.[4] Venues for Latino churches are found in Anglo church buildings, storefronts, and even small living rooms.

Relevance of Luke–Acts

---

[2] Elizabeth Dias, 'The Rise of Evangélicos', *Time*, April 4, 2013. http://nation.time.com/2013/04/04/the-rise-of-evangelicos/ (accessed April 24, 2014).

[3] Dias, 'The Rise of Evangélicos'.

[4] Dias, 'The Rise of Evangélicos'.

Luke and Acts represent the biblical foundation for the tangible manifestations of the Holy Spirit that occurred in several parts of the world in the early twentieth century.

Pentecostals designate their spiritual heritage on the event that occurred while the disciples engaged in prayer in Jerusalem waiting for the promise of the Father. Luke reveals the work of the Holy Spirit as the one who initiates, empowers, and directs the church in its eschatological and worldwide mission.[5]

Peter boldly prophesies on the Day of Pentecost, as established in Joel's promise of the Spirit. The Old Testament indicated the Spirit's coming. Among the Israelites, God put His Spirit on the 70 elders, and they prophesied (Num. 11.25). When the Spirit of God came upon Saul, he also prophesied along with a group of prophets (1 Sam. 10.9, 10). Samuel anointed David in the presence of his brothers, and the Spirit of the Lord came mightily upon David (1 Sam. 16.13). David spoke prophetically about Christ, the Messiah (2 Sam. 23.1, 2; cf. Acts 2.29-30).

Luke's distinctive contribution is to emphasize the Spirit's role in empowering believers to be witnesses in order to expand the mission of the Church of the Lord Jesus Christ. Through the coming of the Spirit, the diversity of tongues signals the universal offer of salvation in Christ. The Spirit in Luke–Acts empowered believers to speak and perform notable actions that would otherwise lay beyond their abilities.[6] Luke's accurate description of supernatural demonstrations evidenced the active presence of the Holy Spirit amidst the community of believers.

Luke's theological interpretation of the life and ministry of Jesus and the story of the early church was not just history.[7] Luke's intention was both historical and theological. Luke writes to 'present an orderly account' (Lk. 1.3) of events and to enhance the power of the Holy Spirit manifested in the life of Jesus and in the lives of the early Christians. The book of Acts mentions the Holy Spirit in more than

---

[5] John Michael Penney, *The Missionary Emphasis of Lukan Pneumatology* (Sheffield, UK: Sheffield Academic Press, 1997), p. 15.

[6] J.R. Michaels, 'Luke Acts', in Stanley M. Burgess and Gary B. McGee (eds.), *Dictionary of Pentecostal and Charismatic Movements* (Grand Rapids, MI: Zondervan, 1988), pp. 544-61.

[7] French Arrington, *The Spirit-Anointed Jesus: A Study of the Gospel of Luke* (Cleveland, TN: Pathway Press, 2008), p. 23.

fifty references.[8] Luke believed the infilling of the Holy Spirit gave the Apostles and the early believers the power for the proclamation of good news. The early believers participated in teaching, healing, and acts of compassion. Luke wrote what his eyes witnessed and the result of the infilling of the Holy Spirit among believers. Through the years Pentecostal believers have interpreted the manifestations of the Holy Spirit in Luke–Acts as the basis for their distinctive view of the baptism of the Spirit.[9]

The expansion, growth, and strengthening of the modern Pentecostal movement is undeniable. Since the beginning Pentecostals have been characterized by their passion for the word of God, an emphasis on a sanctified life, Christ-centered preaching, exuberant worship, and an evangelistic devotion.[10] The early disciples went forth as Pentecostal witnesses 'to the ends of the earth'. Luke encouraged his readers to maintain their confidence in the power of God and to remain faithful to the Gospel.

The charismatic power and work of the Holy Spirit were manifested throughout the ministry of Jesus, and subsequently the Church carried out its evangelistic mission by the power of the same Spirit. Once anointed by the Spirit, Jesus endued the disciples with power from on high by pouring out His Spirit so they could carry an evangelistic mission (Lk. 2. 33). The Spirit linked the ministry of Jesus to the ministry of the church. As a result, the early disciples went forth as Pentecostal witnesses 'to the ends of the earth'. Luke encouraged his readers to maintain their confidence in the power of God and to remain faithful to the Gospel. Scholars, both in mainstream Protestantism and Pentecostalism have stressed the 'missionary empowerment aspect of Spirit-baptism in Luke–Acts'.[11]

Overview of Luke–Acts

Throughout the centuries, the Gospel of Luke and the book of Acts were considered two separate books written by the same author. However, it was in 1927 that Henry Cadbury wrote *The Making of*

---

[8] Arrington, *The Spirit-Anointed Jesus*, p. 31.
[9] Arrington, *The Spirit-Anointed Jesus*, p. 23.
[10] Grant McClung, (ed.), *Azusa Street and Beyond: Pentecostal Missions and Church Growth in the Twentieth Century* (South Plainfield, NJ: Bridge Publishers, 1986), p. 25.
[11] Penney, *The Missionary Emphasis of Lukan Pneumatology*, p. 13.

Luke–Acts in which he discussed their literary style and unity.[12] Since then, biblical scholars consider Luke–Acts as a single continuous work written by the same author. Both books have a cohesive theological theme: that God brought salvation to Israel and continues to bring salvation to unbelievers through Jesus Christ.

Prayer is one of the distinguishing motifs of Luke–Acts. Records of prayer materials in Luke's Gospel are rich and unique[13] and Luke is referred to as 'the evangelist of prayer'.[14] Luke–Acts presents a vivid portrait of the early church whereby the most significant redemptive-historical acts of God are rendered as developing in a context of prayer. At times important events are revealed in advance to someone praying or they occur as God's response to the prayers of his people. Luke shows that prayer was an integral and vital part in the daily life of Jesus and in key moments of his ministry.[15] The disciples themselves recognized the significance of prayer to Jesus and one day asked to teach them to pray.

A close association exists between the infilling of the Holy Spirit and prayer in Luke–Acts. The Gospel highlights the life of the 'Spirit-anointed Jesus'.[16] The Holy Spirit descended while Jesus prayed during his baptism (Lk 3.21). Jesus was anointed to carry out his ministry to the afflicted, brokenhearted, captives, and prisoners (Lk. 4.18; Isaiah 61.1-2). Jesus told his disciples to wait for the promise of the Father. The disciples would be filled 'with power from on high' (Lk. 24.49). The Holy Spirit initiated and empowered the church in its mission to the Jews and Gentiles.

The church began its post-resurrection life in prayer (Acts 1:4). The disciples followed the example of Jesus and continued to attend the temple during the hours of prayer (Acts 3.1; 21.27; 22.17). The disciples were empowered to carry the gospel message among the Jews and Gentiles (Acts 1.8). In their gatherings, they offered thanks when breaking bread *before* a meal, like Jesus did (Acts 2.46 b; Acts

---

[12] Henry J. Cadbury, *The Making of Luke–Acts* (London: Methuen, 1927), p. 29.

[13] Kyu Sam Han, 'Theology of Prayer in the Gospel of Luke', *Journal of the Evangelical Theological Society* 43.4 (December 2000), pp. 675-93.

[14] Steven F. Plymale, *The Prayer Texts of Luke–Acts* (New York: Peter Lang, 1991), 2. See also Oscar Cullman, *Prayer in the New Testament* (Minneapolis: Fortress Press, 1995), p. 112.

[15] Lindell O. Harris, 'Prayer in the Gospel of Luke', *Southwestern Journal of Theology* 10.1 (1967), pp. 59-69.

[16] Arrington, *The Spirit-Anointed Jesus*, p. 59.

2.7; 27.35). Prayer was carried out and accompanied by the laying of hands-on new believers and praying for the baptism of the Holy Spirit (Acts 8.15, 17). The Apostles laid hands on Stephen for his commissioning (6.6) and on those who needed healing (9.11; 28.8).

Both Luke and Acts have parallel patterns and theological themes.

1. They begin with a preface (Lk. 1.1-4; Acts 1.1-5).

2. Prayer and the manifestation of the Holy Spirit are present both in the life of Jesus during his baptism (Lk. 3.21-23), and upon the disciples on the day of Pentecost (Acts 2.1-13).

3. Jesus faces conflict with the religious leaders (Lk 5.29-6.11) and so do the apostles as they preach the gospel (Acts 4.1-8.3).

4. Luke and Acts include missionary journeys to the Gentiles to preach the good news (Lk. 10.1-12; Acts 13-20).

5. Jesus heads to Jerusalem, where he is arrested on false charges (Lk. 9.51-19.28) and Paul is arrested in Jerusalem, where Hellenist Jews stirred the crowds against him (Acts 21.27-28).

Authorship and Date of Luke–Acts

In Luke–Acts, the author does not identify himself. However, it remains generally agreed that the third Gospel and Acts were written by the same author due to similar prefaces, literary style and theological perspective.[17] The author was well-educated but had not been an eyewitness to the ministry of Jesus. Luke was probably a second-generation Christian (Lk. 1.1-4) and a native from Antioch in Syria. Luke must have traveled along with Paul in his second and third journeys and the final trip to Rome. In the narratives known as the 'we' passages (Acts 16.8-18; 20.5; 21.18; 27.1-18), the author shifts from third-person narration to first person: 'we' and 'us'.

It is widely accepted that Luke, a physician and a traveling companion of Paul, wrote Luke–Acts which reviewed a historical span of about thirty years, approximately from the thirties to the early sixties.[18] The earliest sources to confirm Lucan authorship for both books come from the Muratorian Canon (170 CE) and the Anti-Mar-

---

[17] Arrington, *The Spirit-Anointed Jesus*, p. 20.
[18] I. Howard Marshall, *The Acts of the Apostles* (Sheffield, UK: Sheffield Academic Press, 1992), p. 17.

cionite Prologue (160-180 CE). Irenaeus of Lyons (180 CE) identified Luke as a physician, a disciple of the apostles, and an associate of Paul until his death.[19] The early Church Fathers Clement of Alexandria, Tertullian, and Eusebius also referred to Luke as the author. The Anti-Marcionite Prologue described Luke as a Greek from Antioch in Syria, and a companion of Paul. Luke died in Bithynia at the age of 84.

The dating of Luke's work varies, and suggestions range from the 60s to the early second century. There are generally three views for the date: early (60s CE in Paul's lifetime), intermediate (80-90 CE), and late (110-120 CE). Scholars who emphasize the eyewitness character of its content favor an early date and thus assume that the book has historical reliability. Furthermore, Luke does not mention the results of Paul's trial or the destruction of the Temple by the Roman army in the 70 CE. Those who favor an intermediate date argue that Luke shows the influence of Josephus who published his book Antiquities in 93 CE. Scholars who support a late date question the historical value of Acts. Marshall concludes that the majority of scholars favor a date between the 60s to the 90s. [20]

The Purpose of Luke–Acts

Luke's two-volume history about the origin and spread of Christianity is the longest book of the New Testament and the most carefully designed book in the New Testament due to common motifs in the literary structure:

(1) beginning narratives;
(2) introductory narratives describing events manifesting the gift of the Holy Spirit;
(3) accounts of miracles;
(4) travel narratives; and
(5) trial narratives.[21]

Luke begins by addressing his narrators to Theophilus (Lk. 1.3, Acts 1.1) and expresses his concern for writing 'an orderly account' (Lk. 1.1). Luke distinguishes him as 'most excellent' [*kratistos*], a term

---

[19] Arrington, *The Spirit-Anointed Jesus*, p. 20.
[20] Marshall, *The Acts of the Apostles*, p. 17.
[21] Roger Stronstad, *The Prophethood of All Believers: A Study in Luke's Charismatic Theology* (Cleveland, TN: CPT Press, 2010), p. 1.

that was used for someone of a higher social class and was appropriate when addressing government officials. The same term is used on three occasions, as seen in:

(1) the letter of Lysias, the Roman commander [*chiliarch*], directed to the governor Felix (Acts 23.26);

(2) the speech of Tertullus in his charges against Paul before Felix (Acts 24.3); and

(3) Paul's speech before Festus (Acts 26.25).

Some biblical interpreters conclude that Theophilus must have been a Roman political figure, while others contend that Theophilus was a pagan Roman ruler impressed with Christianity. Luke's intention, then, was largely apologetic, trying to persuade Theophilus about the truth of the gospel and a more detailed understanding of the doctrines of the faith:

> Many have undertaken to draw up an account of the things that have been fulfilled among us, just as they were handed down to us by those who, from the beginning, were eyewitnesses and servants of the word. With this in mind, since *I myself have carefully investigated everything from the beginning, I too decided to write an orderly account for you, most excellent Theophilus* (emphasis added, Lk. 1.3).

Theophilus may have contributed to make the production of the books possible[22] or he may have supported Luke while he wrote the Gospel and Acts. Luke also had in mind that these narratives would be read by the Christian communities. They would add to the public proclamation of the Gospel as Christians met together for worship.

Because Luke explicitly mentions that he wrote 'an orderly account for you, most excellent Theophilus, so that you may know the certainty of the things you have been taught' [*katēchēthēs*, catechized, instructed] (Lk. 1.3, 4) a few commentators believe Theophilus was not a pagan.[23] Luke refers to the fact that Theophilus had undergone basic instructions within the early Christian communities (1 Cor. 14.19; Gal. 6.6). The term was also used in reference to Apollo who was instructed [*katēchēmenos*] by Priscilla and Aquila (Acts 18.25). The term *kata-echeo*, meaning 'by way of echo', suggests a method of oral

---

repetition or 'repeat after me'.[24] The Gospel message, as such, is handed down with fidelity to each generation of believers: 'For I received from the Lord what I also passed on to you' (1 Cor. 11.23).

The Lucan narrative also emphasizes the events on the day of Pentecost and continually refers to the role of the Holy Spirit in the expansion of the church. The principal verse that summarizes the book is, 'But you will receive power when the Holy Spirit comes on you; and you will be my witnesses in Jerusalem, and in all Judea and Samaria, and to the ends of the earth' (Acts 1.8).[25] Luke narrates how the Holy Spirit was present in the life of the first disciples within the Christian communities. Luke's primary intent was to present the life of Jesus as the Spirit-anointed Messiah and the work of the Holy Spirit directing and empowering the church in its worldwide eschatological mission.[26]

---

[24] Reardon, 'Most Excellent Theophilus', p. 1.
[25] Bradley P. Holt, *Thirsty for God: A Brief History of Christian Spirituality* (Minneapolis, MN: Fortress Press, 2005), p. 50.
[26] Penney, *The Missionary Emphasis of Lukan Pneumatology*, p. 13.

2

Prayer Narratives in the Gospel of Luke

Prayer Narratives in Luke

The Gospel of Luke comprises material about prayer, the prayers of Jesus, and the teachings of Jesus on prayer more than the other Gospels.[1] Scholars note that Luke is the New Testament author that mostly considers the place of prayer in the ministry of Jesus and the early church.[2] Jesus was depicted as praying not only in times of spiritual revelation but also in times of crisis and suffering (Lk. 3.21-22; 9.28-32; 5.16; 6.12). Luke implies that Jesus was praying in the wilderness when he was tempted by the devil as he also fasted (Lk. 4.2).

The inferences about prayer in Luke have become widespread in biblical studies and have received more attention during the last fifty years.[3] Luke establishes prayer as vital to the unfolding of the divine plan of salvation and it highlights the role it plays at the center of salvation history.[4] Two Greek words translated for prayer are used total of twenty-two times in Luke's gospel: the verb *proseuchomai* (I pray, pray for, offer prayer), and its noun form *proseuché* (prayer to God, a place for prayer).[5] Luke also employs the noun, *deésis* (supplication, petition) in several instances (Lk. 1.13; 2.37; 5.33; 10.2; 21; 22.32).

---

[1] Lindell O. Harris, 'Prayer in the Gospel of Luke', *Southwestern Journal of Theology* 10 (1967), pp. 59-69.

[2] David Crump, *Jesus the Intercessor: Prayer and Christology in Luke -Acts* (Grand Rapids, MI: Baker Book House, 1992), pp. 1-2.

[3] Crump, *Jesus the Intercessor*, p. 2

[4] Arrington, *The Spirit-Anointed Jesus*, p. 36.

[5] Han, 'Theology of Prayer in the Gospel of Luke', p. 675.

During crucial events in the life of Jesus, God guides the unfolding of redemptive history through prayer. For example, Luke includes the praise and prayer responses of three individuals surrounding the events of Jesus' birth: Mary (Lk. 1.46-55), Zechariah (Lk. 1.68-79), and Simeon (Lk. 2.29-32).

Jesus engaged in prayer during several events:

1) at His baptism (Lk. 3.21),
2) before He chose the Twelve (Lk. 6.12),
3) at the Transfiguration (Lk. 9.29),
4) upon the Cross (Lk. 23.46).

Only Luke writes of Jesus praying for Peter in his hour of testing (Lk. 22.32). Satan had demanded to sift Simon Peter like wheat, but Jesus prayed that his faith would not fail. Although Peter acted cowardly by denying he was one of the disciples, he kept his faith in Jesus and was able to strengthen the followers of Christ (Lk. 22.31-32).

Through the parables and the teachings of Jesus, Luke highlights the universality of the Good News of Jesus Christ, i.e., the Good Samaritan, the Prodigal Son, the Pharisee, and the Tax Collector. Women are also prominent in Luke's Gospel. Jesus' birth is told from Mary's perspective. He includes the story of Martha and Mary. Luke writes about women who accompanied Jesus: Mary Magdalene, Joanna, whose husband was the manager in Herod's court, Susanna and many other women who used their own financial means to support Jesus' ministry (Lk. 8.1-4).

On the Mount of Olives, Jesus told the disciples to pray so that they would not enter into temptation (Lk. 22.40). Jesus himself prayed about his impending death just before his arrest (Lk. 22.41-46). Jesus never prayed for revenge for his persecutors. Luke takes notice that the proper response to suffering and persecution is not the desire to escape or seek revenge on the oppressors. Instead, as Jesus exemplified, his followers are to remain faithful, praying, and seeking to be filled with the Holy Spirit. Jesus admonished the disciples to pray in order to remain faithful in their walk with God. From the cross, Jesus says his last prayer with a loud cry as he commits his spirit into the hands of his Father (Lk. 23.46).

The main significance of prayer in Luke's thought is that it serves to guide the course of redemptive history.[6] Christ in the center of redemptive history.[7] Jesus is involved in constant prayer in events that point to the divine plan of salvation. Luke considers that prayer is the important means by which God guided the ministry of Jesus and the progression of the early church.

Jesus prayed in public and in private The important turning points in Jesus' ministry are closely linked with prayer.[8] He spent his time in prayer at ordinary moments (Lk. 5.16; 11.11); at pivotal moments in his ministry (Lk. 9.18, 28-29); with all of his disciples (Lk. 9.18; 11.1); with some of his disciples (Lk. 9.28-29) and at times when the disciples were not around (Lk. 5.16; 6.12). Jesus also prayed in the presence of the general public (Lk. 3.21-22). He engaged in extended prayer (Lk. 6.12) and in shorter prayer (Lk 9.18); in the wilderness (Lk. 5.16) or on the mountains (Lk. 9.28-29). Luke records how the disciples perceived Jesus' steadfast moments of prayer which led them to ask, 'Lord, teach us to pray' (Lk. 11.1), and Jesus responded with guiding words in what is called the Lord's Prayer (Lk. 11.1-4).

Steven Plymale advocates that Luke presented a three-phase view of God's redemptive activity.[9] The first stage, the age of Israel, was represented by several characters who awaited the fulfillment of God's promises. Luke recorded the prayers of Zacharias and Elizabeth for a son (Lk. 1.13); the prayers of thanksgiving for the promised Messiah by Simeon and Anna (Lk. 2.26-38). Paul represented an obstinate Judaism working against the Messiah while Gamaliel represented those Jews who took time to consider the possibility of Jesus as the anointed one foretold in the Hebrew Scriptures.[10]

The second phase of redemption history referred to the time of Christ, a time of glory for Israel and a light for the Gentiles. Jesus was the fulfillment of the old and the unfolding of the redemptive

---

[6] O.G. Harris, "Prayer in Luke–Acts: A Study in the Theology of Luke' (PhD diss., Vanderbilt University, 1966), p. 221.

[7] Hans Conzelmann, *The Theology of St. Luke* (New York: Harper and Row Publishers, 1961), p. 79.

[8] S. John Roth, 'Jesus the Prayer', *Currents in Theology and Missions* 33.6 (December 2006), pp. 488-500.

[9] Steven F. Plymale, *The Prayer Texts of Luke–Acts* (New York: Lang, 1991), p. 103.

[10] Plymale, *The Prayer Texts of Luke–Acts,* p. 103.

plan preached in the new age. The third phase was the time of the church, as depicted in the book of Acts.

It is interesting to note that Luke began and concluded his gospel with occurrences of prayer. In Lk. 1.10, 'all the assembled worshippers were praying outside' just before an angel announced the birth of John to Zechariah. Luke ended his gospel with a description of Jesus' followers 'continually at the temple, praising God' (Luke 24.53).

The fact that Luke highlighted prayer during decisive turning points in salvation history has been largely accepted in New Testament scholarship.[11] Prayer, conceived as an instrument through which God is able to act historically, allows an individual to become properly aligned with God's predetermined action and thus able to participate obediently with God's appointed plans.[12]

Luke's Theology of Prayer

Luke presented Jesus as a model of true discipleship because Jesus persevered through prayer.[13] Prayer revealed Jesus as the Son in a unique relationship with the Father. While Jesus prayed, God the Father addressed him as 'Son' (Lk. 3.22; 9:35); and Jesus addressed God as 'Father' (Lk. 10.21; 22.42; 23.34, 46). Jesus continually taught about prayer and practiced prayer as witnessed by his disciples (Lk. 11.1). Luke portrayed Jesus as an Intercessor in his mission as Savior.[14]

Jesus prayed for his disciples to remain strong under temptation (Lk. 22.31) and to keep them safe from the evil one (Jn 17. 15b). Jesus prayed for Peter (Lk. 22.31), for the selection of his disciples (Lk. 6.12), and for laborers to be sent to the harvest (Lk. 10.2). Jesus is referred to as an Advocate (1 Jn 1.21) who restores the believers' fellowship with the Father when they sin. He is called the great high priest (Heb. 4.14) who provides grace in times of need. Jesus promises his disciples that the Father will answer the prayers done in his name (Jn 16.23).

Luke's 'theology of prayer' is an evident theme in Luke–Acts. Prayer is linked to salvation history, and it is offered as a didactic

---

[11] Crump, *Jesus the Intercessor*, p. 6.
[12] Crump, *Jesus the Intercessor*, p. 6
[13] Crump, *Jesus the Intercessor*, p. 8.
[14] Crump, *Jesus the Intercessor*, p. 20.

model for the church.[15] Jesus gave his disciples a model to follow when teaching them how to pray in what is known as the Lord's prayer [16] (Lk.11.2-14). Luke instructed believers to be assured that God would hear their prayers. After receiving the Holy Spirit, the disciples 'devoted themselves to the apostle's teaching and fellowship, to the breaking of bread and the prayers' (Acts 2.42). Prayer is God's way to guide and implement the realization of His will.[17]

Prayer was a common element in the revelation stories of Luke and Acts. The individual who received a revelation was frequently praying when it occurred, as shown in the following examples:

Lk. 1.10: A crowd of people was outside the Temple when an angel appeared to Zechariah.
Acts 9.11-12: Saul of Tarsus had a vision of Ananias
Acts 10.2: Cornelius had a vision
Acts 11.5: Peter had a vision in Joppa
Acts 12.5-13: The church praying for Peter
Acts 13.2: Church leaders at Antioch
Acts 22.17: Paul's vision in Jerusalem

Luke's theology of prayer is that prayer is communication with the divine in spite of the words being said.[18] Prayer places the individual in the ideal position to receive whatever God may have to give.[19] Prayer makes communication between the earthly and the divine possible. As seen in Jesus' life, prayer opens up a doorway between earth and heaven. Heaven was opened when Jesus prayed which allowed him to speak to the Father and at the same time made him receptive to the communication of God's will.

Prayer was at the center of the history of divine salvation in Jesus' life: his baptism, his transfiguration, his agony, and his crucifixion. The new age of the Spirit was initiated in an environment of prayer (Acts 2.1-4). Luke opens and closes his gospel with instances of prayer. In Lk. 1.10, people are praying outside of the temple during Zechariah's priestly duty. The angel Gabriel appears to Zechariah, bringing the announcement of the birth of a son. The last verse of

---

[15] Han, 'Theology of Prayer in the Gospel of Luke', p. 676.
[16] Plymale, *The Prayer Texts of Luke–Acts*, p. 5.
[17] Plymale, *The Prayer Texts of Luke–Acts*, p. 105.
[18] Crump, *Jesus the Intercessor*, p. 115.
[19] Crump, *Jesus the Intercessor*, p. 115.

the gospel shows a scene of Jesus' followers at the temple continually offering prayers to God (Lk. 24.53).

The life of Jesus reveals that he was continually involved in prayer. Prayer narratives in the Gospel of Luke occur in crucial moments and these served to confirm that Jesus proceeded in the right direction. Moments of special revelation strengthen him to complete his mission. The following texts portray Jesus' prayer life associated with the cross and discipleship.[20]

Prayer at the Baptism of Jesus (Lk 3.21)

Jesus arrived at the Jordan River to be baptized and as Jesus was praying, the Holy Spirit descended upon him in the form of a dove. The Spirit's descent upon Jesus marked the beginning of the Spirit-filled public ministry of Jesus[21] (Lk. 4.1, 14, 18-19). The people that were being baptized were filled with messianic expectation in response to John the Baptist's preaching of repentance for the forgiveness of sin. They wondered if John was the Messiah, but John pointed out that one who was more powerful than him, would baptize with the Holy Spirit and fire (Jn 3.15-17).

Luke narrates not just the baptism of Jesus but also prayer during the event. Luke understood prayer as an avenue through which spiritual insight, or revelation, was received. While Jesus prayed, the heavens opened, the Holy Spirit descended in bodily form, and a voice came from heaven. The scene included both a visible and audible event. The voice of God out of heaven said, 'You are my Son, whom I love; with you I am well pleased' (Lk. 3.22). The coming down of the Holy Spirit as a dove affirmed the promise: 'I will put my Spirit upon him' (Isa. 42.1). The voice signaled him out as the Son of God, the true King of Israel (Ps. 2.7). He was the beloved Son of God (Jn 3.16; Lk. 10.21, 22). By undergoing baptism by John, Jesus identified with the people he came to save as the Suffering Servant (Isa. 53). The Spirit equipped Jesus for his ministry of preaching, teaching, and healing.

The anointing of the Spirit imparted at his baptism continued throughout Jesus' ministry. Jesus was 'full of the Spirit' and was 'led

---

20 Han, 'Theology of Prayer in the Gospel of Luke', p. 679.
21 Arrington, *The Spirit-Anointed Jesus*, p. 92.

by the Spirit' into the wilderness (Lk. 4.1). He returned to Galilee in the 'power of the Spirit' (Lk. 4.14). People began to follow Jesus and 'all tried to touch him, because power was coming from him and healing them all' (Lk. 6.19). After His resurrection, two of his disciples on the road to Emmaus declared, 'He was a prophet, powerful in word and deed before God and all the people' (Lk. 24.19). In the book of Acts, Peter declared how 'God anointed Jesus of Nazareth with the Holy Spirit and power, and how he went around doing good and healing all who were under the power of the devil, because God was with him' (Acts 10.38). Jesus also empowered His disciples for their ministry of teaching, preaching, and healing (Lk. 9.1-6; 10.1, 17-21). It was the disciples who continued Jesus' Spirit-anointed ministry after his Ascension into heaven[22] (Acts 1.9). Jesus' baptism was the starting of his public mission and at the same time it also anticipated his death and resurrection.[23]

Jesus in Habitual Prayer (Lk. 5.16)

The phrase 'But Jesus often withdrew to lonely places and prayed' (Lk. 5.16) describes Jesus retreating to pray after the healing of the leper and prior to his first major encounter with the scribes and Pharisees. Crowds had gathered to hear Jesus teach by Lake Gennesaret. Jesus sat on a boat that belonged to Simon Peter. When he finished speaking, Jesus told the group of fishermen who had not caught fish all night to let down their nets. Simon Peter and the other fishermen were astonished to see the great catch. Peter and his companions gathered at the shore and left everything to follow Jesus. Jesus told Peter he would now become a fisher of people (Lk. 5.10, 11).

In a nearby town, Jesus healed a leper and commanded him not to tell anyone but to present himself before the priest as Moses established. The healing of the leper gave witness that the power of God was working through Jesus.[24] Stories about the miracles of Jesus continued to spread. As an inevitable result more crowds sought him to receive miracles and healings.

---

[22] Arrington, *The Spirit-Anointed Jesus*, pp. 91-93.
[23] Oscar Cullman, *Baptism in the New Testament* (Naperville, IL: Alec R. Anderson, 1950), p. 19.
[24] Arrington, *The Spirit-Anointed Jesus*, p. 111.

The context of Luke 5 shows that Jesus was anointed with the Spirit, the power of the Lord (v.17), to teach and heal. His popularity with the people kept on growing. His fame and ministry extended throughout every village of Galilee, Judea and Jerusalem. Such signs and wonders were within the context of his times of prayer. Jesus also prayed in preparation for the impending struggles, including the hostility and hatred from the religious leaders.[25]

Luke presented Jesus as the anointed deliverer surrounded by prayer in his successfully progressive ministry.[26] Crowds were in expectation of Jesus' miracles, but he continually withdrew to pray. For Jesus, prayer was a pattern of customary behavior. He refused to be carried away with the popular favor and demand. For Luke, prayer explains how Jesus' ministry demonstrated the power of the Spirit to teach and to heal (v.17). The crowds continued to acclaim him wherever he went, and prayer kept Jesus in close communion with his Father as he carried out God's plan.

Luke did not reveal the content of Jesus' words during solitary prayer. It seems, though, that Luke was offering an insight into the routine of Jesus and made a note of the regularity of Jesus' prayer life. Jesus also retreated to restore his physical strength. He experienced a constant drain of his human energy due to constant demands for his sympathy and compassion. Luke showed that the efficacy of Jesus' teaching and healing ministry was enveloped in prayer. Luke was using this instance to indicate Jesus' desire to spend time with God before he was to face any sort of opposition.

The Choosing of the Twelve (Lk. 6.12)

Luke narrated how the Pharisees and teachers of the law observed Jesus perform miracles in order to find a way to accuse him of blasphemy. They were outraged when Jesus forgave the sins of the paralytic (Lk. 5.21). At Levi's house, he was criticized for eating with tax collectors and sinners (Lk. 5.30). The Pharisees accused Jesus of violating the law when he healed a man on the Sabbath. The hostility against Jesus intensified, and the Pharisees and the teachers of the law began to plot against him (Lk. 6.11).

---

[25] Crump, *Jesus the Intercessor*, p. 143.
[26] Crump, *Jesus the Intercessor*, p. 144.

As the hostility of the religious leaders increased, Jesus withdrew to the mountainside and spent a whole night in prayer (Lk. 6.12). Luke highlights how important prayer was to Jesus. Now he faced a critical decision, the choosing of twelve men whom he would instruct to engage in ministry at his side. Jesus was preparing leaders who would continue the work he began. Luke stresses the importance of God's guidance through prayer in the selection of the Twelve.[27]

Jesus chose twelve disciples from a larger group of disciples (Lk. 6.13). The number of the chosen disciples is significant. It is the number associated with the twelve patriarchs of Israel and the twelve tribes.[28] The Twelve represented the New Israel, the new people of God, established by Jesus. They were also designated as Apostles and called to preach the kingdom of God, to cast out demons, and to heal the sick (Lk. 9.1-2). Jesus guided and taught them for they would eventually lead the followers of Jesus and consequently the church. These men became the main witnesses to the ministry of Jesus and his resurrection (Acts 1.21, 22).

Jesus chose to work through ordinary people. Most of the twelve apostles were fishermen (e.g. Peter, Andrew, James, and John), and Matthew was a despised tax collector.

Simon, the zealot, belonged to a group dedicated to the violent resistance of Rome. Jesus also chose Judas, who would betray him. The fall of Judas teaches that a person with great spiritual blessings can forfeit them through sin. By praying all night before choosing his twelve disciples, Jesus was making himself available to hear the voice of the Father.

Peter's Confession (Lk. 9.18-27)

Jesus' fame had extended as he traveled throughout Galilee and Judea to proclaim the kingdom of heaven. Herod also heard about the miracles of Jesus and wondered who he really was. He heard some people say that John had been raised from the dead. Others said Elijah had come back to life, and still others thought Jesus was a prophet from long ago. Herod, who had beheaded John, was confused yet curious about the identity of Jesus and wanted to see him (Lk. 9.9).

---

[27] Crump, *Jesus the Intercessor*, p. 145.
[28] Arrington, *The Spirit-Anointed Jesus*, p. 112.

On one occasion, Jesus withdrew with his disciples to Bethsaida; however, the crowds followed him to hear his teachings and to receive his miracles. Jesus showed compassion for the crowds who had followed him to a remote place and fed more than 5000 with five loaves of bread and two fish. Once again, as was customary for Jesus, he retired from the crowds to pray. On this occasion, Luke mentions that the disciples were close to Him, but it did not seem they were necessarily praying along with him or taking part in praying.

Jesus took time to probe the disciples about their views of his ministry. He asked them what people said about him. Both Herod's and the crowd's perceptions about Jesus were similar. Herod listened to different opinions yet did not understand who Jesus was and he had no one close to him to explain Jesus' identity.[29] The crowds also had mixed reviews about Jesus' identity—saying he was John the Baptist, Elijah, or one of the ancient prophets who had come back to life. The religious leaders opposed Jesus because they considered him a blasphemer when he forgave sins (Lk. 5.21-25), and he associated with the lowest class of people in society (Lk. 15.1-2).

Luke is the only author to introduce the narrative of Peter's confession, with Jesus praying before he asked the disciples about his true identity. Jesus asked them, 'But what about you? Who do you say I am?' Jesus was clearly rejecting the crowd's opinion and expecting a new indication from his close followers. Up to this moment, there had been different levels of messianic expectation. The crowds showed an expectant perception of Jesus, but they did not think of him as the Messiah. The disciples still lacked an adequate messianic understanding of Jesus.

Peter spoke on behalf of the rest of the disciples when he answered who Jesus was: 'The Christ of God' (Lk. 9.20). Peter confessed Jesus as the Anointed One, the Savior that God has promised to send, and the One Israel has been looking for so long.[30] Peter's perception of Jesus as the Messiah revealed a greater spiritual depth than that of Herod's and the crowds. He warned them not to tell the revelation to no one as he pointed to details about his imminent death.

---

[29] Crump, *Jesus the Intercessor*, p. 28.
[30] Arrington, *The Spirit-Anointed Jesus*, p. 383.

The Father provided a revelation through the prayers of Jesus.

Peter's confession brought about a modification in Jesus' teaching to his disciples. For the first time he told them about his approaching rejection by the religious leaders. He began to prepare the disciples for his death on the cross and his resurrection. Jesus explained to them the cost of discipleship and taught them about self-denial and spoke to them of another cross that must be taken up daily by his followers (Lk. 9.23-26). The cross his disciples would carry is not literal, but it would be the cross of self-denial. For Christian disciples, taking up the cross is voluntary and calls for self-denial.[31]

Jesus commanded the disciples not to tell anybody that he was the Messiah to avoid a misunderstanding of his mission among the people of Judah. The term Messiah was associated with a political and military leader who was expected to deliver the Jews from Roman domination. Before Jesus' identity became public information, he wanted his disciples to understand what kind of Messiah he was.

The disciples had not associated the concept of the Messiah with a sacrificial death. It was not easy for them to understand this aspect of his mission. The harsh reality of his death caused them to be confused and grief-stricken. They abandoned Jesus during his crucifixion. It was after the Resurrection that the disciples understood he had to suffer many things (Lk. 24.13-36) and they eventually understood His Kingdom and his purpose for coming.

The Transfiguration (Lk. 9.28-36)

Luke described the transfiguration as taking place eight days after Peter's confession of Jesus as Christ (Lk. 9.20). On this occasion, Jesus sought solitude in the mountain to pray along with Peter, James, and John (Lk. 9.28). Luke records that while Jesus was praying, his appearance changed, and his clothes became radiant 'as bright as a flash of lightning' (Lk. 9.29). During the Transfiguration God revealed the glory of His kingdom. Through the Transfiguration, Jesus received encouragement from the Father[32] since he would soon make his way

---

[31] Arrington, *The Spirit-Anointed Jesus*, 383.
[32] Crump, *Jesus the Intercessor*, p. 41.

to face opposition in Jerusalem and his death at the Cross. The Transfiguration experience encouraged Jesus along the new phase of his ministry that would lead to his death (Lk. 9.21-27).

The epiphany witnessed by the disciples confirmed Jesus' intimate fellowship with the Father and it anticipated the glorification of Jesus. The divine glory would be a reminder to his disciples that true glory and the cross would go together.[33] Once again, Luke does not reveal the content of Jesus' prayer. Luke describes this moment of Jesus in communion with God through which he received the Father's encouragement.[34]

The disciples witnessed this event within an environment saturated with prayer. It was during Jesus' communion with the Father that he was transfigured. 'Prayer is the appropriate posture for a divine revelation, although here the revelation is not to the One praying but to the accompanying disciples'.[35] Two visitors, Moses and Elijah, representing the law and the prophets, appeared next to Jesus and both men reflected glorious splendor. They spoke with Jesus about his soon departure to be fulfilled at Jerusalem. The disciples were very sleepy, but they saw the glory of Jesus and recognized the two men standing with him.

Peter suggested building three shelters, one for Jesus and one for each of the two visitors. Luke makes a reference to Peter not knowing what he was saying (Lk. 28.33). As Peter finished speaking, a cloud appeared, signifying the presence of God. It covered the disciples, and they were terrified. The voice of God was heard, which further revealed the true identity of Jesus. The voice was mainly directed to the three disciples, commanding them to obey Jesus: 'This is my Son, whom I have chosen; listen to him' (Lk. 28.35). This phrase provided a more complete revelation to the disciples about Jesus. It confirmed Peter's confession of Jesus as the Messiah (Lk. 28.20). Jesus was greater than who the disciples thought he was. He had the authority to speak for God. He was the chosen prophet, greater than Moses, to whom they must listen (Deut. 18.15.) He was the suffering servant (Isa. 42-53) who would be rejected and killed (Lk. 9.22).

---

[33] Arrington, *The Spirit-Anointed Jesus*, p. 175.
[34] Crump, *Jesus the Intercessor*, p. 41.
[35] I. Howard Marshall, *The Gospel of Luke: A Commentary on the Greek Text* (Grand Rapids, MI: Eerdmans, 1978), p. 383.

The disciples received a new revelation into the true meaning of the person and ministry of Jesus. Later, Peter would describe:

He received honor and glory from God the Father when the voice came to him from the Majestic Glory, saying, 'This is my Son, whom I love; with him I am well pleased'. We ourselves heard this voice that came from heaven when we were with him on the sacred mountain (2 Pet. 1.17-18).

The Transfiguration provides a preview of his majesty when he returns to the earth 'with great power and glory' (Lk. 12.27).

Prayer after Mission of the 70 (Luke 10.21-24)

Jesus sent seventy disciples by pairs to the different towns and villages and commanded them to preach the kingdom of God and heal the sick (Lk. 10.8-9). This narrative is similar to the passage of the seventy elders set apart by Moses who received the Spirit and prophesied in the desert (Num. 11.16-17). When asked, Moses responded that he longed for God to pour out his Spirit on all people so they could be prophets (Num. 11.29). The mission of the seventy is an allusion to a future worldwide outpouring of the Holy Spirit and mission.[36]

The disciples returned with good reports of their task. In this occurrence, Luke records the lengthiest of Jesus' personal prayer as he rejoiced and thanked God for hearing his prayers. It is the only occasion in the New Testament where Jesus is said to rejoice.[37] Jesus was 'full of joy through the Holy Spirit' (Lk. 10.21). The spiritual revelation that the Father gave the disciples was as an answer to his prayer (Lk. 10.24). God the Father had revealed the identity of the Son to the disciples through Peter's confession and through the Transfiguration. Jesus reminded his disciples that more important than signs and wonders was for their names to be written in heaven (Lk. 10.20).

The disciples were compared to little children, who trusted in God, compared to those who had the wisdom of the world yet could not discern spiritual realities. The disciples had been chosen as recipients of divinely bestowed insight into the character and nature of Jesus by virtue of his prayers.[38] Their mission was fruitful, and the

---

[36] Penney, *The Missionary Emphasis of Lukan Pneumatology*, p. 51.
[37] Crump, *Jesus the Intercessor*, p. 49.
[38] Crump, *Jesus the Intercessor*, p. 67.

prayer of Jesus confirmed that his disciples would bring God's harvest to completion. Through this text Luke shows that prayer is the lifestyle of those who will enter the kingdom.

The Watchful Prayer (Lk 21.36)

Luke 21.36 is an exhortation from Jesus to always be on guard in relation to prayer: 'Be always on the watch, and pray that you may be able to escape all that is about to happen, and that you may be able to stand before the Son of Man'. Once again, Jesus teaches that his children need to be involved in persistent prayer, as the word 'always' stresses.

Jesus had been teaching about the end times, which suggests that this verse has an eschatological significance because one day every person will stand before the Son of Man (v. 36). Prayer for the believer involves a vision of the eternal over the temporal and carnal. In this manner, believers can avoid temptation, worldly sins, and the cares of life. Thus, Christian believers are free to dedicate their lives to the service of God. Believers are to be on the watch and thus vigilant. They need to be wise to discern the signs of the times (Lk. 21.27, 31; 1 Chron. 12.32).

The text of Luke 22.31-32 reveals that Jesus was an intercessor for his disciples. He presented the disciples' needs before the Father. On this occasion, Jesus and his disciples were gathered for the Passover supper. Jesus told Peter that Satan had demanded to sift him like wheat. But Jesus confirmed that he had prayed for Peter and the disciples.

Jesus knew the instability of Peter's nature and had considered it as a matter for prayer. He repeats Peter's old name twice: 'Simon, Simon' (Lk. 22.32), thus emphasizing the seriousness of the matter. Satan had placed a demand to sift the disciples like wheat. This indicated that Peter would revert to his old nature temporarily.[39] The passage parallels the court scene where Job and his belongings were given over to the Devil's hands (Job 1.12; 2.6). The enemy is not only an opponent of Jesus' but also of his followers. Satan comes to accuse God's people before the throne, but unlike Job's situation (Job 9.33) there is now an advocate to plead on their behalf.

---

[39] Harris, 'Prayer in Luke–Acts', p. 63.

The final intention of the adversary is the destruction of the disciples' faith. Satan had asked to sift the disciples, but Jesus the Intercessor prayed to counteract Satan's intent and for Peter to persevere in the faith (Lk. 22.31-32). 'But I have prayed for you, Simon, that your faith may not fail. And when you have turned back, strengthen your brothers' (Lk. 22.32).

The Enemy does not have unlimited authority to harm God's people.[40] Peter had an advocate who by prayer came to his defense before the heavenly throne. Jesus knew that Peter would reveal the weakness of his character. Jesus prayed for Peter to persevere in the faith and the Father answered this prayer. Peter's failure was temporary, and he was restored in the Lord. Peter was able to return and comfort the disciples. The ultimate focus of Jesus' intercessory prayer was Peter´s ministry to others. The times of testing for believers will not achieve what the Enemy wants to accomplish. Although Peter lost courage and denied that he knew Jesus, his faith was not destroyed.

Peter did not realize the serious implications of Jesus' cautionary words. In his impulsive manner, he claimed to be ready to go into prison or die with Jesus. Peter's audacity might seem admirable as he drew his sword to defend Jesus from the soldiers during his arrest (Lk. 22.50, Jn 18.10). However, trials and temptations cannot be overcome by human strength (1 Cor 10.12-13). Just a few hours later, Peter cowardly denied knowing Jesus to escape persecution. Peter recognized the contradictions of his own nature and became better prepared to encourage the other disciples.

The resurrected Lord Jesus requested from Peter to 'feed my sheep' (Jn 21.17). On the day of Pentecost, Peter delivered a bold message in which 3000 people repented and proclaimed faith in Jesus Christ (Acts 2.41). Peter became an encouraging voice for the disciples and the early believers (Acts 2).

Jesus Prays on the Mount of Olives (Lk 22.39-44)

The passage about the Mount of Olives is saturated with images of a praying Jesus. Luke begins and ends this passage with Jesus urging the disciples to 'Pray that you will not fall into temptation', (22.40,46). This is a narrative in which Jesus engaged in a prayer of supplication

---

[40] Arrington, *The Spirit-Anointed Jesus*, p. 363.

for himself. His praying posture stood in contrast with that of the sleeping disciples, who did not pray or did not totally comprehend the adversity of the moment. Luke mentioned the Mount of Olives several times as the place where Jesus spent the nights during his final week (Lk. 19.29, 37; 21.37). Luke narrates Jesus' anguish as He prayed in anticipation of the cross (Luke 22. 39-44). According to Luke, Jesus was the supreme example of a prayer.

At the Mount of Olives, Jesus withdrew a little further from his disciples to pray. Jesus was aware that his enemies would not delay the time of his arrest. Luke presents Jesus praying on his knees with his heart open to God. His words are recorded as: 'Father, if you are willing, take this cup from me; yet not my will, but yours be done' (Lk. 22.42). This was a profound and intense moment of agony for Jesus. He referred to the cup that would symbolize the sacrifice for the sin of humankind (Ps. 75.7-8; Isa. 51.17). The scene was similar to the moment Abraham was getting ready to sacrifice Isaac (Gen. 22.9-12). Jesus was about to become the Passover lamb, taking on the punishment for sin and allowing his blood to be shed for the sin of humanity. The Bible does not discuss more details, but one must wonder if God the Father was suffering as intensely as Jesus. Jesus continued to struggle in prayer throughout the lonely night. At the Supper, Jesus told his disciple that his blood was the new covenant between God and humanity. His sweat fell to the ground like great drops of blood (Lk. 22.44) as though he were already beginning to shed his blood.

Scripture does not give ample details of Jesus' great anguish. Jesus always demonstrated courage and determination in the most adverse circumstances. He might have begun to experience the distress of spiritual death. Soon all of the sins of the world would bear weight upon him on the cross at Calvary. The divine plan was about to be totally fulfilled (Isa. 53.10). He was made sin for the world (2 Cor. 5.21). No matter what circumstances Jesus encountered, he never relinquished his obedience to the Father. He submitted in loving obedience to God's will: 'Yet not my will, but yours be done' (Lk. 22.42). Jesus is ready to face death for the fulfillment of the plan of salvation.

In the meantime, the disciples were sound asleep. It was probably past midnight, and they were worn out from sorrow (Lk. 22. 45). The disciples did not realize the struggle Jesus had gone through. They had slept through one of the most difficult moments of their Lord's life. Jesus woke them up and reprimanded them, 'Why are you sleeping? Get up and pray so you will not fall into temptation' (v.46). Even in the distress of facing death, Jesus exemplified prayer to those around him.

Amidst Jesus' intense struggle an angel appeared to strengthen him. Jesus continued to pray. The appearance of angels was a consistent motif in Luke–Acts as seen in the birth and post-resurrection narratives[41] (e.g. Zechariah, Mary, Jesus in the wilderness, the empty tomb). The angelic presence depicted by Luke indicates the relationship between prayer and spiritual realities.[42] The angel from heaven did not lift the struggle but assisted Jesus to go through the agony. Jesus was strengthened and able to persevere in obedience to the will of God.

Luke portrays how Jesus and the disciples faced the moments of trial in different ways and with different outcomes.[43] Jesus had prayed during the darkest hour and was able to withstand the test and face the Cross. Meanwhile the disciples lacked spiritual strength. They would face the coming trials with the limitations of their own human abilities.

As the mob approached Jesus, the disciples attempted to resist by using their swords (Lk. 22.49). They were relying on physical power and the display of force. Matthew wrote that the disciples deserted Jesus and fled (Lk. 26.56). Luke was teaching the church that they could only resist temptation through the divine strength available through prayer. This holds true for believers today.

Jesus' Prayer on the Cross (Lk. 23.34, 46)

The Lucan passion narrative includes two of Jesus' prayers on the Cross in the place called the skull. During the crucifixion, a few individuals nearby received spiritual illumination into the true nature of the person of Jesus.[44] Two other men were crucified next to Jesus. Luke refers to them as criminals and Matthew and Luke call them robbers (Mat 27.38; Mk. 15.27): 'he was numbered with the transgressors' (Isa. 53.12). Jesus prayed on the cross in trust and surrender

---

[41] Crump, *Jesus the Intercessor*, p. 119.
[42] Crump, *Jesus the Intercessor*, p. 119.
[43] Crump, *Jesus the Intercessor*, p. 168.
[44] Crump, *Jesus the Intercessor*, p. 76.

to the Father (Lk. 23.34, 46). One of the criminals hurled insults at Jesus but the other one was convinced of the innocence of Jesus and demonstrated repentance and confession (v.41).

Crucifixion was a dreadful form of capital punishment practiced by the Romans. It was also a public event. The culmination of Jesus' suffering took place at the cross. Jesus prayed for those who crucified him and pleaded for God to forgive them because they acted out of ignorance. Even while on the cross, Jesus was concerned for the lost and those who were blind to spiritual realities. The soldiers cast lots to divide his clothes, and the rulers and the soldiers mocked him. They crucified the Son of God without realizing the brutality of their actions. Jesus asked the Father to forgive everyone—the Jews and the Gentiles—who added to his suffering. Following the Lord's example, Stephen later prayed for those who did him wrong (Acts 7.60).

The religious leaders belittled Jesus' power and authority since he took on punishment and did not save himself. They disdained him as 'the Christ, the Chosen One' (Lk. 23.35). Their theology of the Messiah, the Anointed One, was one who would act with power to destroy His enemies. They lacked a revelation of the Suffering Servant, (Isa. 52.13-53.12). Their Messiah would not come to suffer and die shamefully on a cross. Suffering had no place in their convictions of the Messiah.[45]

Luke narrates how darkness covered the earth for about three hours. The curtain in the temple was torn in two. Just before his agony ended, Jesus expressed his trust in God and cried out to the Father with a loud voice: 'Father, into your hands I commit my spirit' (Lk. 23.46, Ps. 31.5). At this moment of death, Jesus handed himself over to the Father. He spent his entire ministry doing good, trusting God every step of the way. At the cross, Jesus gave himself to death with assurance and trust in God the Father. Jesus completed his mission and became the offering for the forgiveness of sin.

Jesus' prayer and his death provoked an effect on those who were watching. The onlookers beat their breasts and departed from the scene. They left saddened and grieved, realizing that wicked men had crucified an innocent person (Lk. 23.48; Acts 2.22-24). The Roman centurion, responsible for the execution of Jesus, expressed a prayer of confession. He was moved to glorify God and declared, 'Surely

---

[45] Arrington, *The Spirit-Anointed Jesus*, p. 381.

this was a righteous man' (Lk. 23. 47). Friends and followers of Jesus watched the events from afar (Lk. 23.49). Their standing at a distance highlighted the loneliness of the Savior during his sacrificial death. In the hour of his greatest suffering, even his friends stood aloof, frightened, and even embarrassed by what was happening (Isa. 53.2-4).

Jesus was aware the kingdom of God had begun by giving his life as a ransom for many (Lk. 10.45). There were two conversions at the cross, and they occurred when the criminal and the centurion confessed Jesus' true identity. Both individuals saw and heard events that transformed their hearts to Jesus as their Lord and Savior. Jesus had completed his mission to seek and save the lost (Lk. 19.10).

Jesus Teaches About Prayer Through Parables

The following section will discuss the passages in which Jesus taught about prayer. These passages include the Lord's Prayer (Lk. 11.1-4); parable of the midnight friend (Lk. 11.5-13); and the parable of the unjust judge (Lk. 18.1-8). When the disciples asked Jesus to teach them to pray, he responded with what is now labeled the Lord's Prayer. A more in-depth discussion of the Lord's Prayer will follow the review of the Parables of the Midnight Friend and of the Unjust Judge.

Parable of the Midnight Friend (Lk. 11.5-13)

In this parable Jesus emphasized the spirit of urgency that is needed in prayer.[46] The underlying theme is that God is faithful to hear prayer and He is also faithful to work his own good will. Jesus taught that sinful parents would not give their children stones for bread, serpents for fish, or scorpions for eggs. If evil human beings give good things to their children, how much more will God give good things to those who ask Him?

Luke specifies this good thing to be the Holy Spirit (Lk. 11.13). Jesus was anticipating the promise that the Father would certainly give the Holy Spirit to those who would ask. Luke indicates that prayer is not a guaranteed means of acquiring whatever one asks for. Prayer is a means by which God gives what he determines to be good. The parable teaches that God does answer prayer, but it also cautions

---

[46] Harris, 'Prayer in Luke–Acts', p. 67.

of the dangers inherent in believing that prayers offered often enough will invariably be answered as and when requested.[47]

Luke was guided by the conviction that prayer was a channel through which God would reveal his will to his children. Jesus' prayer life was seen to be effective because he always prayed according to the will of His Father (Lk. 10.21-22). True prayer involves listening and learning from God more than just asking God.[48]

Jesus stressed the spirit of urgency that should lie behind prayer. God cannot answer prayer in response to a half-hearted desire on the part of the supplicant. Just as the persistent friend would eventually receive what he asked for, so too will the persistent praying person receive when he asks, seeks, and knocks (Lk. 11.10).

Parable of the Unjust Judge (Lk. 18.1-8)

This parable was another story that Jesus used to teach about the persistence of prayer. A widow who sought justice against her adversary was persistent in pleading with a judge who had no concern for her and refused to help her. Eventually, the judge agreed to make sure she received justice in order for her nagging to cease. The story teaches that God answers those who pray persistently.

The defenseless widow had no influential friends, or enough money to give the judge. However, she continued to petition him for the compensation of her grievances. The judge answered her petition in order to silence her. But God is concerned to answer prayer from the highest motive of love even though there may be a delay.[49] Believers should keep on praying even in moments where there are delays in the answers.

Both parables point out that believers should pray habitually and faithfully. God longs to help his children who pray to him with sincerity and patience. Jesus taught that prayer is designed to bring God's children into agreement with His will. He was teaching that men ought to pray and not lose heart.

The Lord's Prayer

Jesus was praying one day, and one of his disciples asked Him to teach them how to pray (Lk. 11.1). Jesus replied with a prayer directed to the Father:

---

[47] Crump, *Jesus the Intercessor*, p. 132.
[48] Crump, *Jesus the Intercessor*, p. 134.
[49] Harris, 'Prayer in Luke–Acts', p. 68.

When you pray, say, 'Father, hallowed be your name, your kingdom come. Give us each day our daily bread. Forgive us our sins, for we also forgive everyone who sins against us. And lead us not into temptation' (Lk. 11.2-4).

The Lord's Prayer presents a vision of the ideal way to approach God. Men and women can easily stray from God and fail in their walk with God. Forgiveness is necessary. 'To pray is to acknowledge human need, lack, and weakness'.[50] Prayer can be messy due to a vast diversity of events and unforeseen circumstances in daily human existence. Yet, at the same time prayer is grounded on trust in God's goodness. The simplicity of the Lord's Prayer is based on the certainty that God hears our requests and will answer our prayer in accordance with the goodness of God's character.

The petitions in the Lord's Prayer are divided into two parts. The first ones are addressed to God the Father. The second half of the prayers make references to the ongoing personal needs or interests people have in life. Those who pray the Lord's Prayer 'immerse themselves in the tradition of two thousand years of Christian prayer'.[51]

Father

'Father' was the way Jesus addressed God. In the Old Testament individuals did not use the term 'Father' to speak or address to God.[52] However, Jesus taught his disciples to pray to God as a loving Father who is accessible to His children. The Old Testament makes references to the paternal qualities of God, but in the literature of ancient Palestinian Judaism, 'my Father' does not appear as a way to address God.[53] Jesus presented the paradigm of a new relationship with God. Christians have access to a more personal relationship with God through the life of Jesus. 'Father', in Luke makes prayer more intimate and it stands in contrast to 'Our Father' in Matthew.[54] The

---

[50] Kate Dugdale, 'Understanding the Lord's Prayer as a Paradigm for Prayer', *The New Zealand Journal of Christian Thought and Practice* 19.3 (September 2012), pp. 30-37.

[51] James D.G. Dunn, 'Prayer', in Joel B. Green, Scot McKnight and I Howard Marshall (eds.), *Dictionary of Jesus and the Gospels* (Downers Grove, IL: IVP, 1992), p. 662.

[52] James W. Kinn, *The Spirit of Jesus in Scripture and Prayer* (Oxford: Sheed and Ward, 2004), pp. 118-119.

[53] Joachim Jeremias, *The Prayers of Jesus* (Philadelphia: Fortress, 1978), p. 29.

[54] Harris, 'Prayer in Luke–Acts', p. 65.

phrase points to qualities of trust, intimacy, and familiarity with the Father.

Hallowed be thy name

The first petition, 'hallowed be thy name', asks that God be recognized as holy or treated in a holy way (Lk. 1.49). When prayer takes place, this request involves adoration or praise of God as the Creator. God's name is separate from all human limitations and imperfections. Yet God, the Creator, is near His children as a loving Father. He will reign where He is known, and His people will honor Him for who He is. His people submit to His name. Because His children respect His name, they can also become 'holy and blameless in his sight' (Eph. 1.4). God's people were called to be holy from the beginning, as God the Father designated them to be a kingdom of priests and a holy nation (Exod. 19.6).

Judaism strived to maintain the holiness of God's name, and Jewish people would not dare to pronounce his name out loud. Isaiah 57.15 proclaims: 'This is what the exalted One says-- I live in a high and holy place, but also with the one who is contrite and lowly in spirit'. The God of Israel told his people, 'You shall be holy, for I the Lord your God am holy', (Lev. 19.2). Human beings need to acknowledge that because God is holy, their lives are to pay him honor. In this way, they have access to enjoy communion with Him in heart and soul.

Thy Kingdom Come

The second request in the Lord's Prayer, 'thy kingdom come', mainly refers to the final coming of the reign of God through Christ's return. The kingdom was one of the motifs Jesus taught about. Jesus was aware that the coming of the kingdom of God was taking place during his public ministry. Jesus said, 'The kingdom of God is within you', (Lk 17.21). The very presence of Jesus was a sign that the kingdom had come. Paul described the kingdom of God as 'righteousness and peace and joy in the Holy Spirit' (Rom. 11.17). In their longing to see His kingdom come, Christians will be dedicated in action, thought, and word to see justice and peace in their world and in culture. Christians are urged to carry out the mission of the church in a wholehearted manner. Yet, the establishment of the kingdom is a divine prerogative and will not be established by humans.[55]

Give Us Each Day Our Daily Bread

This request changes its focus from the holy character of God and His kingdom to the basic concerns of human existence. Through this petition, Christians can ask God for immediate everyday concerns. 'Give us ... our daily bread' expresses an ongoing dependence on God for his daily provision of physical and material needs. The phrase 'Give us', expresses the trust of children who look to their Father for their sustenance and provision. The phrase highlights the goodness of God. Jesus reminds the disciples they can trust God as their Father: 'Ask and it will be given to you; seek and you will find; knock and the door will be opened to you' (Lk. 11.9). The goodness of God does not compare to the nature of human beings: 'If you then, though you are evil, know how to give good gifts to your children, how much more will your Father in heaven give the Holy Spirit to those who ask him' (Lk. 11.13).

'Our bread' signals the nourishment the Father provides for His children, both material and spiritual. Jesus wants his disciples to trust in God the Father for their needs instead of worrying about tomorrow. God's providence and mercy extend to all of His creation. 'Consider the ravens: They do not sow or reap; they have no storeroom or barn; yet God feeds them. And how much more valuable you are than birds' (Lk. 12.24).

The Father will make provision for our needs if we 'seek first his kingdom and his righteousness' (Lk. 11.33). The provision of bread is a reminder of hunger among many people in the world. Christians are called to exercise compassion for others who undergo suffering and oppression (Mic. 6.8). The kingdom of God brings in the Spirit of Christ, implying the establishment of holiness on different levels: personal, social, and economic.

People in the world experience another kind of hunger. 'Man shall not live on bread alone' (Lk. 4.4) is a phrase that points to a famine among people in the world. 'There is a famine on earth, not a famine of food or a thirst for water but a famine of hearing the words of the Lord' (Amos 8.11). The Christian has received empowerment from the Holy Spirit to proclaim the Word of God to the ends of the earth.

---

[55] Dugdale, 'Understanding the Lord's Prayer', p. 34.

Forgive Us Our Sins

Jesus himself is the epitome of forgiveness in action. At the greatest point of suffering on the cross, he prayed, 'Father, forgive them, for they do not know what they are doing' (Lk. 23.34). 'Forgive us our sins', points to the need of the human heart to be delivered from the enslavement of sin. Since the fall of Adam and Eve, human beings have been separated from God. The Jews had a sacrificial system for the covering of their sins. The psalmist recognized that the true sacrifices of God are a broken spirit: 'A broken and contrite heart, O God, thou wilt not despise' (Ps. 51.17). If Christians hold on to sin, they will remain separated from God. Asking the Father for forgiveness removes any trace of self-righteousness, e.g., the Pharisee and the Publican (Lk. 18.9). The tax collector who humbled himself said, 'God, have mercy on me, a sinner', and he went home justified before God (Lk. 18.13, 14).

The second part of this request indicates that Christians need to ask for forgiveness and, at the same time, release any injustices committed against them. As God grants forgiveness, those who receive it have the responsibility to forgive others. The two elements are necessary in the transaction of forgiveness for sins. The tax collector presented himself humbly before God. But the Pharisee prayed, 'God, I thank you that I am not like other people—robbers, evildoers, adulterers—or even like this tax collector'. No human being can stand up for his own justice before God. Only in Jesus can 'we have redemption through his blood, the forgiveness of sins, in accordance with the riches of God's grace', (Eph. 1.7).

Forgiveness must flow out of the heart toward those who offend us. His mercy will be poured upon the hearts of those who ask for forgiveness, and at the same time, as they forgive others,

> Whoever claims to love God yet hates a brother or sister is a liar. For whoever does not love their brother and sister, whom they have seen, cannot love God, whom they have not seen. And he has given us this command: Anyone who loves God must also love their brother and sister (1 Jn 4.20-21).

If Christians refuse to forgive their fellow believers, their hearts can become bitter and hardened. Unforgiveness blocks the flow of God's mercy. God's grace is manifested in the human heart when sins are confessed.

When Jesus washed His disciples' feet, He reminded them, 'A new command I give you: love one another. As I have loved you, you must love one another. By this, everyone will know that you are my disciples if you love one another' (Jn 13.34). It is not easy to completely forget an offense or for feelings of hurt to surface. Even when the followers of Jesus suffer injustice, they must pray for their oppressors: 'Love your enemies, do good to those who hate you' (Lk. 6.27-36). With the help of the Holy Spirit, the human heart can be set free and released from darkness (Isa. 61.1, Lk. 4.18).

In the book of Acts, Stephen prays to the Father as they stoned him to death. Forgiveness is the highest point of Christian prayer. When the act of forgiveness takes place, the heart becomes open to receiving God's grace. Jesus reminded his disciples, 'If your brother sins, rebuke him, and if he repents, forgive him. If he sins against you seven times in a day and seven times comes back to you and says, "I repent," forgive him' (Lk. 17.3-4).

Lead Us Not Into Temptation

The petition 'lead us not into temptation' creates awareness that the disciples of Jesus will come to a place of testing and temptation. Jas. 1.13-15 explains:

> When tempted, no one should say, 'God is tempting me'. For God cannot be tempted by evil, nor does he tempt anyone; but each person is tempted when they are dragged away by their own evil desire and enticed. Then, after desire has been conceived, it gives birth to sin, and sin, when it is fully grown, gives birth to death.

Testing can come in the form of suffering, persecution, or temptation to sin. Christians need to discern whether their faith is being tested or if they are facing the temptation to sin. Prayer is important in these moments so that a Christian can be strengthened in their faith. There is no guarantee that Christians will never face trials and temptations, but God promises to strengthen His children to endure such moments.

> Though now, for a little while, you may have had to suffer grief in all kinds of trials. These have come so that the proven genuineness of your faith—of greater worth than gold, which perishes even though refined by fire—may result in praise, glory, and honor when Jesus Christ is revealed (1Pet. 1.6-7).

Christians need to pray in order to be protected in circumstances that may weaken their trust in God. Jesus told his disciples, 'Watch and pray so that you will not fall into temptation. The spirit is willing, but the flesh is weak' (Mt. 26.41). The worries, riches, and pleasures of life can lead believers away from a life of discipleship (Lk. 8.13-14). Such testing can result in strengthening the faith of believers. 'We must go through many hardships to enter the kingdom of God' (Acts 14.22). On the other hand, temptation leads to sin and death (Jas 1.14-15). Discernment unveils the falsehood of temptation that appears to be 'pleasing to the eye and also desirable'.

Christians can endure temptation because Jesus, the high priest, understands human weaknesses. He was tempted in every way yet did not sin (Heb. 4.15). God provides a way for His children to endure trials and temptations (1 Cor. 10.13). Victory over trials and temptations can only be achieved through prayer. Jesus was able to overcome the tempter when he prayed in the wilderness at the onset of his public ministry (Mt. 4.1-11). Jesus prayed intensely at the Garden of Gethsemane before his trial and crucifixion (Mt. 26.36-44). Prayer contributes to a state of vigilance for our hearts and those among the community of believers.

Conclusion

Luke presents Jesus as praying before or during many crucial events of his life and ministry. Luke draws attention to Jesus' dependence on God and the Spirit. Jesus prayed at His baptism (Lk. 3.21); before choosing his disciples (Lk. 6.12); and before announcing his approaching suffering and rejection (Lk. 9.18-23). Luke narrates Jesus praying at the transfiguration (Lk. 9.28); for Peter and the disciples at the Last Supper (Lk. 22.32); during his agony in the Mount of Olives (Lk. 22.41); and during His crucifixion (Lk. 23.46). Luke emphasizes Jesus being driven, inspired, and empowered by the Spirit. Luke's message for believers today is to depend on the Holy Spirit and to continually recognize our need to pray, as Jesus modeled prayer throughout his life and ministry.

3

PRAYER IN THE ACTS OF THE APOSTLES

The Acts of the Apostles was a sequel to the Gospel of Luke. It is significant because it emphasizes the continuity of Old Testament biblical history with early Christian history. Jesus, the Messiah and Lord, left a legacy for the Apostles to follow, as narrated in the book of Acts. The Spirit empowered the praying disciples on the Day of Pentecost, and they became bold witnesses of the gospel.

Luke speaks of different manifestations of the Spirit. In the Acts of the Apostles, the Holy Spirit initiated the early community of believers, conducted the gospel from Jerusalem to Rome, and reached the receptive Gentile world in place of the Jewish nation.

Historical Details

The book of Acts is characterized by its accuracy in historical details. The account reviews a period of about 30 years and elaborates on events from Jerusalem to Rome. Luke's narrations occurred in different settings, such as Jerusalem, Antioch, Ephesus, Athens, Corinth, and Rome. He referred to people of diverse social backgrounds, including government officials.

Luke was objective in the accounts he presented by recording the failures as well as successes in the early communities. For example, he noted the ethnic conflict between the Grecian Jews and the Hebraic Jews in relation to the distribution of food among their widows (Acts 6.1). He also recorded the discord between Paul and Barnabas (Acts 15.39, 40). There were divisions and differences between the Judaizers and the first Gentile converts (Acts 15.1, 2; 21.20, 21).

Luke skillfully used speeches that contributed to the drama of his narrative. He included the speeches of Peter, Stephen, Paul, and a number of other individuals. These can be classified into (1) evangelistic (Acts 2.14-40; 3.12-26; 4.8-12; 5.29-32; 10.34-43; 13.16-41); (2) apologetic (Acts 7.2-52; 22.1-21; 26.2-23; 20.18-35); and (3) exhortatory (20.18-35).

Luke, 'the beloved physician' and companion of Paul (Col. 4. 14; 2 Tim. 4.11; Phlm. 24) was the only New Testament writer that refers to the events at Pentecost. It would seem that the author's intent was not merely a historical account but to inform about the work of the Holy Spirit. Luke and the other Gospel writers are considered editors who not merely put together stories and traditions but carefully arranged the material they collected.[1] They were creative with their particular theological concerns and viewpoints Thus, Luke was considered not only a historian but a theologian:

> Luke is both historian and theologian … The best term to describe him is 'evangelist', a term which, we believe, includes both of the others … As a theologian Luke was concerned that his message about Jesus and the early church should be based upon reliable history.[2]

Through the use of historical details, Luke was informing Theophilus of the certainty of what had happened but also about the significance of those events for the Christian believer. Luke referred to 'receiving the Spirit', being 'filled with the Spirit', and being 'baptized in the Spirit'. The Book of Acts narrates the Apostles engaging in 'signs and wonders' (Acts 5.12) or supernatural experiences such as healings, prophecy, exorcism, speaking in tongues, discernment, laying of hands, and tongues of fire.

For Pentecostals, these manifestations of the Spirit that occurred among the early Christian believers are still a reality. Pentecostals believe these signs contribute to the realization of the divine plan in history. Luke reported these events to teach Christian believers about the reality of the work of the Holy Spirit in their own lives and communities.

---

[1] J.R. Michaels, 'Luke–Acts', in Stanley M. Burgess and Gay B. McGee, (eds.), *Dictionary of Pentecostal and Charismatic Movements* (Grand Rapids, MI: Zondervan Publishing House), pp. 544-562 (p. 545).

[2] Marshall, *The Gospel of Luke,* pp. 8-19.

The Pentecost event or baptism in the Spirit is a pivotal episode in the book of Acts. Prior to His ascension Jesus instructed His disciples to wait in Jerusalem until they received *power:* 'I am going to send you what my Father has promised; but stay in the city until you have been clothed with power from on high'. The infilling of the Holy Spirit upon the one hundred twenty disciples gathered in the Upper Room occurred within the Feast of Weeks (Exod. 23.14-17; Deut. 16.16). According to the Temple Scroll from Qumran other Pentecost celebrations included a Feast of New Wine occurring fifty days after the Feast of New Grain.[3] The speaking in tongues by the disciples was considered as a result of engaging in the Pentecost festivities and drinking 'too much wine' (Acts 2.13).

Luke's intention was to show his readers that the message they had heard concerning Jesus was trustworthy. Luke establishes a connection between the events before and after the Resurrection. The account begins with the ascension of Jesus in Jerusalem and concludes with the arrival of Paul in Rome. Luke weaved together several themes as he related the establishment of the early Christian church: prayer, the infilling of the Holy Spirit, life in the community of believers, miracles, preaching, teaching, suffering, persecution, service, martyrdom, and expansion of the early church.

Luke upheld that readers could be certain that God's salvation as promised in the Old Testament was fulfilled in the life, ministry, death, and resurrection of Jesus.[4] He emphasized the significance of the twelve apostles, and that God´s salvation in Jesus was a fulfillment of the ancient hopes of the twelve tribes of Israel (Joel 2.28, Isaiah 32.15; 44.3–5; Ezekiel 11.19-20; 36.26, 27; 37.1–14; 39.29; Zechariah 12.10). Luke established that Jesus was the expected Messiah.

The risen life of Jesus and the infilling of the Holy Spirit as prophesied in the Old Testament had occurred and become part of the lives of believers in Jesus Christ. Luke, then, was writing to reassure his readers that Jesus' teachings did not contradict God´s message but that Jesus was the fulfillment of God´s dealings with Israel. Luke bridged the gap between his readers and the story of salvation in Jesus and the coming of the Holy Spirit.

---

[3] Joseph A. Fitzmyer, *The Acts of the Apostles: A New Translation with Introduction and Commentary* (New York: Doubleday, 1998), p. 32.

[4] Graham H. Twelftree, *People of the Spirit: Exploring Luke's View of the Church* (Grand Rapids, MI: Baker Academic, 2009), p. 9.

Luke portrayed several characters as bold witnesses of the Gospel. Those early followers were empowered by the Holy Spirit and spoke words inspired by the Holy Spirit.[5] Some of those early laborers in the work of the church were Cornelius, Barnabas, Timothy, John Mark, Apollos, Lydia, Phoebe, Priscilla, and Aquila. Luke highlights the influential role of Peter, Stephen, Philip, Barnabas, Agabus, and Paul as Spirit-filled prophets in the spread of the Gospel.

The first twelve chapters of Acts describe events in the life of Peter and the beginnings of the Christian community in Jerusalem. The remaining chapters focus on the life of Paul and the expansion of the gospel message from Antioch to Rome. Paul's story was considerably different than the other disciples, yet Luke established similarities between Peter and Paul thus contributing to establish Paul's credentials as an authentic apostle. Both Peter and Paul were filled with the Spirit (Acts 2.4; 4.8, 31; 9.17; 13.9, 52) and led by the Spirit (Acts 10.19; 13.2-4; 16.6-7). Both carried out signs and wonders (Acts 5.12; 14.3) including healing the lame (Acts 3.1-10; 14.8-10) and raising the dead (Acts 9.36-43; 20.9-12).

Luke abounds in references to prayer in the gospel and in the book of Acts. It is important to note that Luke placed emphasis on prayer in the lives of the disciples, just as he depicted Jesus praying in his gospel. For example, Luke reported that Jesus spent the whole night in prayer before he chose the twelve disciples (Luke 6.12-17). In the same manner, Luke mentioned that Peter and the disciples met behind closed doors in Jerusalem to pray (Acts 1.12-14). The apostles prayed before the election of Matthias. After praying for ten days, the Holy Spirit descended upon the one hundred twenty believers. Such an event was a life-transforming experience for the apostles and the spread of the gospel.

The life of the early believers was described as 'devoted to prayer' (Acts 2.42) even amidst situations of conflict and persecution. Peter and John were arrested for healing a lame man at the Temple Gate (Acts 3.1-10) and upon their release, they returned to the community of believers. As they gathered to pray, the place where they were meeting shook, and they all were 'filled with the Holy Spirit and spoke the word of God boldly' (Acts 4.31). Stephen was described as being

---

[5] Roger Stronstad, *The Prophethood of All Believers: A Study in Luke's Charismatic Theology* (Cleveland, TN: CPT Press, 2010), p. 81.

full of the Holy Spirit and carrying out great signs and wonders among the people (Acts 6.8). His preaching infuriated the religious leaders of the Sanhedrin. Stephen continued to pray as he was stoned to death (Acts 7.59).

Many other instances of prayer in Acts seem to enhance the manifestations of the Spirit. For example, in Acts 10, Cornelius is described as a man of prayer. Peter had a vision as he went up to the rooftop to pray. God prepared him to meet Cornelius through a vision. He saw a sheet with all kinds of animals and heard the message, 'Do not call anything impure that God has made clean' (Acts 10.15). The Holy Spirit was guiding the apostles to break racial barriers in order to reach the Gentiles with the gospel message. Both the infilling of the Holy Spirit and the dedication to prayer among the believers of the first century were vital to the spread of the gospel in the Mediterranean world.

The Book of Acts and the Holy Spirit

The work of the Spirit is palpable throughout the narration of the book of Acts. It has been said that the appropriate title should be 'Acts of the Holy Spirit' since it provided accurate descriptions about the early Christian community and the manner in which the disciples were baptized, filled, and led by the Holy Spirit. The action of the Holy Spirit plays a dominant role in this book like in no other book in the Bible. Pentecostals highlight the person of the Holy Spirit In Luke–Acts, as a tangible reality and identifiable in physical evidence.[6] The Spirit in Luke–Acts enabled believers to understand, speak, and accomplish actions in ways beyond their abilities. The manifestations of the Holy Spirit were 'seen' and 'heard' in the homes and streets of Jerusalem. The visions, words, and deeds were 'the evidences of the Spirit's active presence'.[7] Luke asserted that he 'investigated everything' in order to write an 'orderly account' to establish the certainty of the teachings of the Christian Way (Lk. 1.1-4).

The forty days between the resurrection and the ascension of Jesus was a period of transition and preparation for the upcoming work

---

[6] Michaels, 'Luke Acts', pp. 544-561.
[7] Michaels, 'Luke Acts', pp. 560.

for the apostles.[8] The disciples gathered to pray and waited in anticipation for the power promised to them through the Holy Spirit (Acts
1.8). The last chapter of the Gospel of Luke describes the apostles
after the Ascension returning to Jerusalem with 'great joy ... [and
that] they stayed continually at the temple, praising God' (Lk. 24.53-
54).

There are a number of stories and references to post-resurrection
events in the New Testament, but only Luke referred to the events
of Pentecost.[9] Luke described how the disciples, on the feast of Pentecost 'were filled with the Holy Spirit' (Acts 2.4). The term 'filled'
(Greek, *pimplēni*) was used by Luke to refer to a person consumed
with the Spirit and speaking boldly in intimidating circumstances.[10]
Peter spoke boldly to the religious leaders of the Sanhedrin when
filled with the Spirit (Acts 4.8). Peter and John were filled with the
Spirit and proclaimed the word of God with boldness (Acts 4.31).
Luke also wrote people were filled with wonder and amazement (Acts
3.10). For Luke, to be filled with the Holy Spirit meant 'to be overcome, overwhelmed or consumed with God's Spirit in a way that
dominated the feelings or emotions and controlled the activity of the
person. Quite often...the result was inspired speaking ... but also
included performing miracles'.[11]

Luke contrasted the significance of Pentecost for the disciples
with the Holy Spirit descending upon Jesus at his baptism (Luke
3.22). On both occasions, during the baptism of Jesus and during
Pentecost, the Spirit descended from heaven (Lk. 3.21; Acts 2.2).
There was also a visionary experience, that is, in Jesus' baptism, the
Spirit descended in bodily form like a dove (Lk. 3.22) and on Pentecost, there was a sound like a rushing wind, and tongues of fire appeared over each one (Acts 2.2-3).

In both events, at Jordan and Pentecost, the participants were
characterized as receiving power (Lk. 4.14; Acts 1.8). Jesus was 'full
of the Holy Spirit' and was led to the wilderness by the Spirit (Lk.
4.1). The disciples were also 'filled with the Holy Spirit' and spoke in
tongues (Acts 2.4). Jesus began his ministry by proclaiming, 'The

---

[8] Bruce M. Metzger, *The New Testament: Its Background, Growth, and Content* (Nashville, TN: Abingdon Press, 2003), p. 209.
[9] Twelftree, *People of the Spirit*, pp. 66-72.
[10] Twelftree, *People of the Spirit*, pp. 66-72.
[11] Twelftree, *People of the Spirit*, p. 72.

Spirit of the Lord is upon me' (Lk. 4.18, as stated in Isa. 61.1). Peter preached a bold message of repentance to the crowd on the day of Pentecost, and 3000 responded in repentance to the message of the gospel.

Luke reported the transformation of the disciples from frightened followers to Spirit-empowered Apostles.[12] Peter explained to the crowd who thought the disciples were drunk that 'this is what was spoken by the prophet Joel: 'In the last days, God says, I will pour out my Spirit on all people' (Acts 2.17). Luke interpreted Pentecost not so much as the birth of the Church, but as event of empowerment for mission.[13] Luke was signaling the beginning of a new age.[14] He emphasized that believers in Jesus Christ, who received forgiveness, would be filled with the Spirit, and begin a Spirit-based relationship with God:

> Repent and be baptized, every one of you, in the name of Jesus Christ for the forgiveness of your sins. And you will receive the gift of the Holy Spirit. The promise is for you and your children and for all who are far off—for all whom the Lord our God will call (Acts 2.38, 39).

This new empowerment was not simply an ecstatic experience but gave boldness and power to perform signs and wonders, including prophesying and miracles. Such manifestation would allow believers to undertake a universal mission of witnessing to the resurrection.

The empowerment by the Spirit was a dynamic and multi-faceted experience. Thus, it could not be simplified to one single term to explain its meaning. Luke described the empowering experience of the disciples in various terms such as: clothing (Lk. 24.49); baptizing (Acts 1.5); coming upon (1.8); filling (2.4); pouring out (2.33); receiving (2.38); and falling upon (11.15).[15] The disciples experienced 'an intensity of the Spirit beyond what they had experienced during the earthly ministry of Jesus'.[16] The essence of the Pentecostal experience throughout the book of Acts was a manifestation of the presence and power of God.[17]

---

[12] Stronstad, *The Prophethood of All Believers*, p. 1.
[13] Twelftree, *People of the Spirit*, p. 75.
[14] Twelftree, *People of the Spirit*, p. 83.
[15] Arrington, *The Spirit-Anointed Jesus*, p. 17.
[16] Arrington, *The Spirit-Anointed Jesus*, p. 17
[17] Arrington, *The Spirit-Anointed Jesus*, p. 17.

Through the empowerment of the Spirit, God's people are able to carry out the mission of the Church. Luke portrays the Spirit as the source of guidance and power to believers. They witnessed boldly to the saving grace of Christ. The early believers were able to engage in the actions, teachings, and experiences of Christ due to the empowerment of the Holy Spirit. Luke presented Jesus as the Spirit-anointed Christ, and the disciples became the Spirit-anointed community on Pentecost.[18] The significance of the Day of Pentecost was that the same Holy Spirit that came from God upon Jesus now descended upon the disciples. The believers became a Spirit-anointed community as heirs of the charismatic anointing that Jesus received. The outpouring of the Spirit at Pentecost was 'the pivotal pattern for the continuing charismatic activity of the Spirit among God's people'.[19]

The coming of the Spirit was essential to Luke. 'For John baptized with water, but in a few days you will be baptized with the Holy Spirit' (v. 5). The coming of the Spirit on the day of Pentecost was for Luke, 'the eschatological event that marks the beginning of a new age'.[20]

Prayer in the Book of Acts

The Book of Acts presents the disciples as persevering in prayer as Jesus instructed them to wait for the promise of the Father in Jerusalem (Acts 1.4-5). While they were gathered in prayer (Acts 1.4, 13), Peter requested to choose a replacement for Judas (Acts 1.26). Among the one hundred twenty disciples were Mary, and Jesus' brothers. For Luke, prayer was a vital way by which God guided the course of redemptive history and made known the divine plan of salvation.[21]

It is important to observe that the early converts to the gospel message of repentance continued to practice some of their Jewish devotional traditions after Pentecost. The community of the early believers participated in the apostles' teaching, fellowship, the breaking of the bread (in the temple and in homes), and prayer (Acts 2.42, 46). They met to pray in Solomon's Porch at the temple, worshiping

---

[18] Arrington, *The Spirit-Anointed Jesus*, pp. 17-18.
[19] Arrington, *The Spirit-Anointed Jesus*, p. 18.
[20] Twelftree, *People of the Spirit*, p. 83.
[21] Harris, 'Prayer in Luke–Acts', p. 59.

the one true God through His Son (Acts 2.46; 3.1). Each day, more people were added to the fellowship of the believers, where they all shared their belongings and met daily in the breaking of bread, 'praising God and enjoying the favor of all the people' (Acts 2.47). Houses in Jerusalem became places of prayer and worship as they shared food and goods and were united as a praying community.

In the book of Acts, the early believers now prayed in a Christocentric manner. Jesus was identified as the Savior (4.12); the author of life (3.15; 5.31); the one who would provide forgiveness and salvation (5.31; 2.17-39); and the coming judge (10.42). The church had been bought through his blood (20.28). Jesus received the promise of the Holy Spirit, and now he pours out the Spirit (2.33).

The Spirit of prophecy (Joel 2.28) was now dispensed on all disciples, enabling visions, dreams (Acts 7.55; 9.10-18; 10.10; 16.9-10; 18.9-10), and prophetic wisdom (Acts 10.19; 13.2; 6.9; 16.7; Lk 21.15). The Spirit has now directed and empowered the church. The Spirit allowed new possibilities for prayer (Acts 2.4; 10.46; 19.6).

At almost every important point in the narrative of God's redemptive plan, there was a mention of prayer. For example, the disciples prayed for the choice of Matthias to replace Judas (Acts 1:24). Peter and John prayed before the Samaritans (the first Gentile converts) could receive the Spirit (Acts 8.14-17). Prior to his healing Paul was described as praying and receiving a fresh vision (Acts 9:11). While the Antioch church was in prayer and fasting, the Spirit indicated they should set aside Paul and Barnabas for a mission to Galatia (13.2-3).[22]

An early conflict erupted for the disciples as they went to the temple to pray. The Sadducees, responsible for the maintenance of the Temple in Jerusalem, had been the priests who secured the crucifixion of Jesus. However, the enthusiasm of the new Jewish sect threatened their prestigious position of power. The Sadducees arrested Peter and John because they taught that Jesus was the author of life and that He had risen from the dead (Acts 3.15). The Sadducees forbade them to teach in the name of Jesus (Acts 4.13-18).

---

[22] M.M.B. Turner, 'Prayer in the Gospel and Acts', in D. A. Carson (ed.), *Teach Us to Pray: Prayer in the Bible and the World* (London: Baker Book House, 1990), pp. 73-74.

Peter and John were imprisoned shortly after because the Sadducees considered them dangerous (Acts 5.17, 18). However, Luke narrated that on this occasion, they were freed from jail by an angel of the Lord. The religious leaders were sent to jail for them, but the apostles were no longer there. They were found teaching in the temple courts. The high priest demanded that they stop preaching in the name of Jesus and keep silent. But the apostles responded boldly: 'We must obey God rather than human beings'! (Acts 5. 29). The apostles were flogged and released (Acts 5.41, 42). Amidst persecution, the apostles continued the proclamation of the gospel. When they faced conflict and persecution, they joined together to pray. In spite of enduring hardships, hostility, riots, and imprisonment, the gospel continued to be proclaimed in many places. When the Apostles gathered to pray, manifestations of the Holy Spirit were tangible (Acts 5.12, 15, 16).

Prayer and the ministry of the Word became the obligations of the twelve disciples as the number of believers increased (Acts 6.4). Prayer was carried out when commissioning laborers, including Stephen and Phillip (Acts 6.6), Saul and Barnabas (Acts 13.3), and elders in the churches (Acts 14.23). The Samaritans received the Holy Spirit through prayer (Acts 8.15, 17). The Holy Spirit directed the actions of believers gathered in prayer (Acts 8.29). Peter raised Tabitha from the dead (Acts 9.40) and Paul healed Publius' father and others who were sick in Malta (Acts 28.7, 8).

In several instances, the revelation of God's messages through dreams and visitations of angels among the early Christian communities was associated with prayer. Through a vision Ananias was asked to pray for Saul of Tarsus (Acts 9.11). An angel appeared to Cornelius as he prayed (Acts 10.4). An angel of the Lord freed Peter from prison while the church prayed (Acts 12.5, 12). The early church turned to prayer when making important decisions (Acts 1.24). The twelve disciples gave priority to 'prayer' and ministry of the word (Acts 6.4). For the Apostles, prayer was just as important as the ministry of the word or preaching of the Gospel.[23]

Prayer references in the last chapters of Acts indicate God's consent in the universal mission carried out by Paul. Paul and his com-

---

[23] Plymale, *The Prayer Texts of Luke–Acts*, p. 8.

panions carried out Jesus' commands to pray vigilantly without ceasing. As Paul faced opposition, persecution, and suffering he continually prayed for himself and for the believers in the churches in the Gentile world as the epistles demonstrate. The prayers of the early believers stood in continuity with the Jesus' movement and its Israelite beginnings.[24]

---

[24] Turner, 'Prayer in the Gospel and Acts', p. 83.

4

THE RELEVANCE OF THE BOOK OF ACTS TO PENTECOSTALS

Pentecostals will refer to their spiritual heritage, not as based on the Azusa Street revival but as one that occurred in the Upper Room in Jerusalem. The modern Pentecostal movement interpreted Luke–Acts as a basis for the power and tangible manifestations of the Holy Spirit that occurred in several parts of the world around the beginning of the twentieth century.

> Humble believers of the twenty-first century—gathering for worship in the favelas of Sao Paulo, in the shantytowns of Nairobi, or in secret meetings across China's rural village—may never visit Los Angeles, but they have traveled hundreds of times back to Jerusalem's Day of Pentecost in the collective memories of their songs, stories, and sermons ... Jesus Christ revealed to his disciples that the gift of the Holy Spirit was coming from the Father and was indispensable—even to the point of commanding them to stay in Jerusalem (Lk 24.49; Acts 1.4-5) until they received 'power from on high' as the necessary equipping for witnessing to 'the ends of the earth' (Acts 1.8).[1]

Scholars, both in mainstream Protestantism and Pentecostalism have stressed the 'missionary empowerment aspect of Spirit-baptism

---

[1] Grant McClung, 'Waiting on the Gift: An Insider Looks Back on One Hundred Years of Pentecostal Witness', *International Bulletin of Missionary Research* 30.2 (April 2006), p. 64.

in Luke–Acts'.[2] Luke presents the work of the Holy Spirit as the one who initiates, empowers, and directs the church in its eschatological and worldwide mission.[3] The book of Acts mentions the Holy Spirit in more than fifty references.[4] The charismatic power and work of the Holy Spirit were manifested throughout the ministry of Jesus, and subsequently the Church carried out its evangelistic mission by the power of the same Spirit. Once anointed by the Spirit, Jesus endued the disciples with power from on high by pouring out His Spirit so they could carry an evangelistic mission (Acts 2.33). The Spirit linked the ministry of Jesus to the ministry of the church. As a result, the early disciples went forth as Pentecostal witnesses 'to the ends of the earth'. Luke encouraged his readers to maintain their confidence in the power of God and to remain faithful to the Gospel.

The Spirit in Luke–Acts manifested power 'enabling believers to see, speak words they would otherwise be unable to speak, and perform mighty deeds that would otherwise lay beyond their abilities'.[5] Luke made accurate descriptions of supernatural manifestations as evidence of the active presence of the Holy Spirit amidst the community of believers.

Luke's theological interpretation of the life and ministry of both Jesus and the story of the early church was not just to present 'an orderly account' (Lk. 1.3) of events. He wrote to enhance the power of the Holy Spirit as manifested in the lives of Jesus and the early Christians. Luke believed the infilling of the Holy Spirit gave the Apostles and the early believers the power for the proclamation of good news and for teaching, healing, and acts of compassion. Luke wrote about what his eyes witnessed and the consequences of the infilling of the Holy Spirit among believers.

Pentecostal believers have through the years interpreted the manifestations of the Holy Spirit in Luke–Acts as the basis for their distinctive view of the baptism of the Spirit.[6] The expansion, growth, and strengthening of the modern Pentecostal movement which began in the early 20th century is undeniable.

---

2 Penney, *The Missionary Emphasis of Lukan Pneumatology*, p. 13.
3 Penney, *The Missionary Emphasis of Lukan Pneumatology*, p. 15.
4 Arrington, *The Spirit-Anointed Jesus*, p. 31.
5 Michaels, 'Luke Acts', pp. 544-61.
6 Arrington, *The Spirit-Anointed Jesus*, p. 23.

The Pentecostal Movement and Women

It is important to note that the growth of the modern Pentecostal movement is attributed to the mobilization of women in the ministry.[7] Prior to the Pentecostal revival, the holiness movement strengthened women´s rights in public ministry since they pointed to biblical equality for men and women. Three theological themes were emphasized in the preaching of the holiness movement which contributed to greater freedom for women in the church. First, the theme of biblical equality in Galatians 3.28 erased gender differences and opened the way for women to have access to ministry. Second, the redemption argument meant that women were no longer under the curse associated with the Fall since Jesus Christ provided salvation for all. Lastly, the outpouring of the Spirit on men and women indicated that both were equally empowered for ministry.[8]

In the early twentieth century, several women started Pentecostal denominations. Florence Crawford established the Apostolic Faith Mission in Oregon. Aimee Semple McPherson founded the International Church of the Foursquare Gospel (ICFG). Two African-American women, Magdalena Tate and Ida Robinson, planted churches and were ordained bishops in their Pentecostal denominations. Several women went out from the Azusa Street to work as evangelists and missionaries to different places within the United States and around the world: Africa (Liberia) and Asia (India).[9]

In 1901, Agnes Ozman, a former Methodist affiliated with the Assemblies of God, was the first to experience baptism with the Holy Spirit with the manifestation of speaking in tongues. She was a student at Charles F. Parham's Bethel Bible College in Topeka, Kansas. The event affirmed the doctrine that the manifestation of the Spirit baptism was speaking in tongues. Although in many Pentecostal-Charismatic circles today, the centrality of speaking in tongues as ev-

---

[7] Allan Anderson, *An Introduction to Pentecostalism: Global Charismatic Christianity.* (Cambridge: Cambridge University Press, 2004), p. 273; McClung, *Azusa Street and Beyond*, p. 76.

[8] Vinson Synan, *The Century of the Holy Spirit: One Hundred Years of Pentecostal and Charismatic Renewal* (Nashville, TN: Thomas Nelson, 2001), p. 238.

[9] Estrelda Alexander, 'Introduction', in Estrelda Alexander and Amos Yong, (eds.), *Philip's Daughters: Women in Pentecostal-Charismatic Leadership* (Eugene, OR: Wipf and Stock, 2009), p. 4.

idence of the Spirit baptism is refuted by some, it is pertinent to establish that a woman generated the doctrine of Spirit baptism among early Pentecostals. Agnes Ozman recalled the experience years later: 'Mary the mother of Jesus was present ... and received the Holy Spirit. That is a great encouragement to us women today. We know God who gave the women the languages spoken in them also is giving today.'[10]

The Azusa Street Revival highlighted the importance of the empowerment of the Spirit for the work of the church and missions. The participation of women in evangelization, prophesying, ministering, and praying at the altar was the acceptable standard because it embraced the promise, 'your sons and your daughters shall prophecy' (Joel 2.28; Acts 2.17). During this initial stage, the evidence of the power of the spirit in the life of a believer was the proof for ministerial service.

Holiness churches interpreted the Scriptures in a way that allowed a greater participation of women in ministry. During the abolition movement, women spoke, preached, and debated in the public arena on behalf of the slaves. The ideas put forth challenged the ideas of predestined roles based on skin color or gender.[11] This contributed to a new approach to biblical interpretation leading to a more accurate reading of the text. Abolitionists argued on the basis of scriptural principles and proof-texting began to lose credibility as a way to establish doctrine. This new approach required that passages be understood in their legitimate contexts. Galatians 3.28 was used as the focal theological point for equality of women: 'There is neither Jew nor Gentile, neither slave nor free, nor is there male and female, for you are all one in Christ Jesus'.

In general, the Pentecostal movement placed emphasis on the power of ministry to do missions and the work of the church. In the early 1900s, Pentecostals viewed ministerial authority as rooted in the Spirit. Instead of 'women should remain silent in the churches' (1 Cor. 14.34) the central scripture was 'Your sons and daughters will prophesy' (Joel 2.28). Women were involved in praying for the evangelization of the world and for the repentance and conversion of the unsaved.

---

[10] McClung, *Azusa Street and Beyond*, p. 77.
[11] Synan, *The Century of the Holy Spirit*, p. 237.

In spite of women praying and prophesying, not all Pentecostal churches made a way for women to gain ministerial credentials for ordination. Inadvertently, Pentecostals moved away from an exclusive qualification of ministry based upon the Holy Spirit and added other qualifications for ministry.[12] As the credentialing process was established in many churches, women were denied or limited to basic credentials. For example, the first General Overseer of the Church of God, A.J. Tomlinson wrote, 'that the good sisters sit in perfect freedom to preach the Gospel, praying for the healthy and the sick, testify, call, etc., but respectfully stay away from taking positions of governmental affairs'.[13] In 1914 the Assemblies of God agreed that women could be ordained as evangelists and missionaries, but not in positions of ecclesiastical authority.

The participation of women continues to be widespread in Pentecostalism. Harvey Cox argued that women, more than men, were the principal carriers of the Pentecostal gospel to many parts of the world.[14] Early Pentecostals affirmed the same Spirit who was poured out on men also empowered women. In North American Pentecostalism, a hierarchical male clergy and a high degree of institutionalism still prevail.[15] On the other hand, Pentecostalism in Latin America seems to have the potential to bring about societal transformation since women have been granted or assigned to positions of authority previously for male bishops only.[16]

In the context of the global society of the 21st century, the bias toward exclusive male leadership in the church and against women has overtones of inequality. Normally, women make up more than 50% membership in many local churches. Some Pentecostal churches seem to perpetuate inequality towards women because they lack an

---

[12] Gaston Espinosa, 'Third-class Soldiers: A History of Hispanic Pentecostal Clergywomen', in Estrelda Alexander and Amos Yong, (eds.), *Phillip's Daughters: Women in Pentecostal-Charismatic Leadership* (Eugene, OR: Wipf & Stock, 2009), pp. 95-111.

[13] Lisa P. Stephenson, 'Prophesying Women and Ruling Men: Women's Religious Authority in North American Pentecostalism', *Religion* 2.3 (August 2011), pp. 410-426.

[14] Harvey Cox, *Fire from Heaven: The Rise of Pentecostal Spirituality and the Reshaping of Religion in the Twenty-First Century* (Cambridge, MA: De Capo Press, 1995), pp. 124-125.

[15] Cheryl Bridges Johns, *Pentecostal Formation: A Pedagogy Among the Oppressed* (Sheffield, UK: Sheffield Academic Press, 1993), p. 19.

[16] Anderson, *An Introduction to Pentecostalism*, p. 271.

official review of how the interpretation of biblical texts and cultural standards have negatively affected women in ministry. A more in-depth study of the tradition against women in ministry is greatly needed in order to catalyze changes in favor of the inclusiveness of women in ministry.

Influence of Feminism in the Evangelical Church

It is undeniable that the rise of the feminist movement in the twenti-eth century had a great effect on the social and cultural role of women. Gender studies have concluded that 'women continue to face a range of multiple challenges relating to access to employment, choice of work, working conditions, employment security, wage par-ity, discrimination, and balancing the competing burdens of work and family responsibilities'.[17]

The importance of discussing feminism is due to the fact that many Pentecostal denominations did not endorse feminism, as done by other conservative churches. Lawless observed that Pentecostal female pastors, in their independent and outspoken manner, must not give the impression that they deny their role as a good wife and mother.[18] Most of the Pentecostal women she interviewed criticized the feminist movement and did not identify themselves as feminists. Latina women in the Assemblies of God generally reject the militant feminist movement because of its support of a liberal agenda.[19] In the same manner, many Pentecostal women do not consider them-selves feminists in spite of advocating greater inclusion of women in the church.[20]

David Roebuck discusses how the Church of God denomination promoted the role of woman as a wife and mother after World War II.[21] It was a time when feminist concepts seemed to threaten the

---

[17] Asian Development Bank, 'Women and Labour Markets in Asia: Rebalanc-ing for Gender Equality', 2011, pp. 1-56, http://www.adb.org/sites/de-fault/files/pub/2011/women-labor-markets.pdf (accessed January 14, 2015).

[18] Elaine Lawless, *Handmaidens of the Lord: Pentecostal Women Preachers and Tradi-tional Religion* (Philadelphia: University of Pennsylvania Press, 1988), p. 64.

[19] Espinosa, 'Third-class Soldiers', 109.

[20] Chery Johns, personal communication, October 1, 2012.

[21] David Roebuck, *Limiting Liberty: The Church of God and Women Ministers 1986-1996* (PhD dissertation, Vanderbilt University, Nashville, TN, 1997), pp. 171-172.

domestic role of women and the integration of family life. The leadership of women was curtailed as a stance against feminist ideals of gender equality.[22]

In the United States, the Women's Suffrage Movement of the early 20th century had a tangible effect in establishing the legal status of women. As societal and cultural changes in favor of women began to occur, women in ministry also questioned the established denominational structures that kept them restricted under the 'stained glass ceiling'.[23] Influential feminists in the Catholic Church argued that Christian history and theology had been mostly written from a patriarchal perspective.[24] Within Evangelical circles, male and female theologians expanded on the church's discriminatory practice toward women and sought to eradicate biblical language that fostered male dominance.[25]

In the same manner, several authors attempted to recover the voice of women writers and other references to women throughout church history. Elizabeth Clark researched female writings from the early church and other documents where women are mentioned.[26] Ruth A. Tucker and Walter L. Liefeld wrote an extensive history on the contributions of women in different time periods of the church.[27]

The modern feminist movement in the U.S. has been divided into three historical periods or 'waves'. First-wave feminism aimed to establish that women are human beings and should not be treated like property. Women engaged in social and political activism associated with the suffrage movement in the late nineteenth and the early twentieth century.[28] Leaders of this period included those who had campaigned for the abolition of slavery, such as Elizabeth Cady Stanton,

---

[22] Mark Chaves, *Ordaining Women: Culture and Conflict in Religious Organizations* (Cambridge, MA: Harvard University Press, 1997), p. 159.

[23] Susie Stanley, 'Shattering the Stained-Glass Window', in Reta Halteman and Kari Sandhaas (eds.), *The Wisdom of Daughters: Two Decades of the Voice of Christian Feminism* (Philadelphia: Innisfree Press, 2001), pp. 83-86.

[24] Mary Malone, *Women and Christianity: The First Thousand Years* (Maryknoll, NY: Orbis, 2000), pp. 17-18.

[25] Nancy Hardesty, *Women Called to Witness* (Knoxville, TN: University of Tennessee Press, 1999), pp. 57-65.

[26] Elizabeth A. Clark, *Women in the Early Church* (Collegeville, MN: Liturgical Press, 1983), pp. 204-245.

[27] Ruth Tucker and Walter L. Liefeld, *Daughters of the Church: Women and Ministry from New Testament Times to the Present* (Grand Rapids, MI: Academie Books, 1987), c.f.

[28] Chaves, *Ordaining Women*, pp. 45-46.

Lucrecia Mott, and Susan B. Anthony. Based upon their Quaker principles, these women upheld that men and women were equal before God. The first-wave feminism ended with the passing of the Nineteenth Amendment for women's right to vote (1919). In several Latin American countries women gained the right to vote in the 1940s to the 1950s.

In 1949 Simone de Beauvoir wrote The Second Sex, in which she discussed the inferior treatment of women throughout history. Her book is regarded as an influential work of feminist philosophy and the starting point of the second phase of feminism also known in the 1960s as the women's liberation movement.[29] The main thrust of this period was to campaign for the social, legal, political, and economic equality for women. In addition, several societal and cultural shifts altered women's role. For example, labor saving devices (gas stove, washing machine, and refrigerator) freed women from domestic chores. Birth control allowed women greater participation in the labor force. The Equal Rights Amendment (ERA), the National Association for Women (NOW), and other feminist endeavors helped to guard women against discrimination based on gender.

By the early 1990s, a new movement arose as a response to the perceived failures of some of the initiatives of second-wave feminism. Third-wave feminism assumed a critical stance toward the previous feminist movement, maintaining it had included only the concerns of middle class white women from Western Europe and North America.[30] This feminist movement emphasized how gender inequality interacted with racism, gay and lesbian issues, and colonization as a structure of domination.[31] Also known as post-structural feminism, the tendency of third-wave feminism is to examine the experiences among women of different races, cultural backgrounds, and sexual orientation.[32]

---

[29] Heather W. Reichgott, 'What is Feminist Theology?' Voices of Sophia [blog], http://voicesofsophia.wordpress.com/what-is-feminist-theology (accessed February 10, 2015).

[30] Reichgott, 'What is Feminist Theology?'

[31] Patricia Hill, *Black Feminist Thought: Knowledge, Consciousness, and the Politics of Empowerment* (New York: Routledge, 2000), pp. 23, 69.

[32] Carol Gilligan, *In a Different Voice: Psychological Theory and Women's Development* (Cambridge, MA: Harvard University Press, 1982); see also, Astrid Henry, *Not my Mother's Sister: Generational Conflict and Third-Wave Feminism* (Bloomington: Indiana University Press, 2004), pp. 128-140.

The feminist movement in general has influenced all sectors of society in most parts of the world. Feminism was also discussed in theological circles. During the 1980s feminist theologians began to reconsider the traditions, practices, and scriptures from a feminist perspective.[33] Some of the aims of feminist theology have been to: (a) reinterpret the male-dominated language about God; (b) increase the participation of women among clergy; and (c), promote a biblical basis for a gift-based rather than a gender-based ministry.[34] Currently, two basic views on the ministry of women prevail among Evangelicals: the complementarian, and the egalitarian.

In the 1980s, the Evangelical and Ecumenical Women's Caucus (EEWC) embraced a pro-choice stand and defended gay and lesbian rights. Women who were doctrinally conservative departed from the EEWC. Two groups were eventually formed, currently known as complementarian and egalitarian. Both are theologically conservative, and members do not necessarily refer to themselves as feminists.

Complementarians believe men and women are equal in value but have different roles: men are to lead, and women are to submit to the leadership of men. The Council on Biblical Manhood and Womanhood constitutes the complementarian organization. Complementarians advocate male priority and female submission. Some complementarian authors include Wayne Grudem, Tim Keller, John MacArthur, John Piper, and Elisabeth Elliot.

By contrast, egalitarians advocate a ministry based on the individual´s spiritual giftedness and not on gender, socioeconomic class, or race. They conclude that women can exercise leadership in the church. Furthermore, they support the ordination of women and the roles of mutual respect and submission in marriage. The egalitarian organization Christians for Biblical Equality promotes the biblical rationale for equality. Egalitarian authors, such as Gilbert Bilezikian, Catherine Clark Kroeger, Gretchen Gaebelien Hull, and Janette Hassey, advocate the full participation of women in church ministry.

The tension between egalitarians and complementarians is the frequent complementarian critique that egalitarians have followed radical feminism. Haddad asserts that egalitarians are not secular femi-

---

[33] Tucker and Liefeld, *Daughters of the Church*, pp. 445-446.
[34] Mimi Haddad, 'Egalitarian Pioneers: Betty Friedan or Catherine Booth?' *Priscilla Journal Papers* 20.4 (Autumn 2006), p. 53.

nists but are linked to the first wave of feminists who defended Scripture, participated in missions, and labored for the abolition of slavery.[35]

In relation to the ordination of women, there is a broad spectrum of opinion among Evangelical churches. Churches have generally ordained male ministers. However, during the last century more Evangelical churches ordained women partly based on the Protestant ethos of priesthood of all believers. Some churches claim there are no examples of ordained women in the New Testament and continue to defend ordination for males only.[36] For Mark Chaves, women's ordination was mostly generated by external pressure on denominations from the equal rights movement in the mid- twentieth century.[37]

Churches such as the Presbyterian, Methodist, Lutheran, Southern Baptist Convention, and Episcopal Church granted female ordination beginning in the 1950s. However, denominations that do not yet ordain women have a different approach, as in the case of several Pentecostal and Holiness groups. For these conservative groups, ordination is considered a part of the liberal agenda, and consequently, these denominations show not only resistance to female leadership but also to modernity. Churches may have members who are committed to an egalitarian view, but it is up to the governing boards of each denomination to decide in favor of or against the ordination of women.

In relation to women preparing as leaders in seminary, Hardesty discusses the different stages they may undergo.[38] Many women begin theological training unaware of the issues they will face in the church. A phase of conscientization takes place when women come to the realization of the existing gender barriers. However, with increased women enrollment, some positive changes have taken place. Seminaries have begun to appoint women faculty, professors have started to use inclusive language, and courses of women in ministry have been added to the curriculum. Women become aware that there will be difficulties and may face ministry battles. Younger students may not be as zealous about gender issues because they have experienced

---

[35] Haddad, 'Egalitarian Pioneers', p. 53.

[36] Chaves, *Ordaining Women*, p. 47.

[37] Chaves, *Ordaining Women*, p. 47.

[38] Nancy Hardesty, 'Women and the Seminaries', *The Christian Century* 96, (February 7, 1979), pp.122-123.

a more egalitarian treatment in society. Seminaries may have different levels of acceptance to women in ministry.

In her book, Closing the Leadership Gap, Marie Wilson concludes that barriers to women's leadership continue as long as they are denied access to positions of authority.[39] The world has witnessed the vital importance of women in business, education, and government, as more power sharing has taken place.[40] Many women provide an 'enabling and engaging' leadership style. [41] Female leaders advise other women to take on leadership roles in order to counterbalance macho culture.[42]

In the case of Latin American nations, terms of gender equality have also impacted society and more women are participating in politics.[43] In several Latin American Countries about 50% of women integrate political positions of legislature (lower house), mayor, and council offices. In the religious sphere, Pentecostal women were known for exerting influential leadership as preachers, teachers, and missionaries. The political context of gender inclusiveness and the stimulus generated in thriving Pentecostal congregations may probably exert influence on women pastors to engage in leadership.[44] As church leaders, women can most likely become agents of change as seen in women in the corporate world and women in impoverished settings.[45]

---

[39] Marie Wilson, *Closing the Leadership Gap* (New York: Penguin Books, 2007), p. 32.

[40] Wilson, *Closing the Leadership Gap*, p. 137.

[41] Sarah Mullaly, 'More Women Leaders Will Help to Counteract Macho Culture', *Nursing Standard* 23.13 (December 2008), p. 8.

[42] Ibid.

[43] Kristen Sample, 'No Hay Mujeres: Latin American Women and Gender Equality', *Open Democracy* (February 2009), https://www.opendemocracy.net/article/idea/no-hay-mujeres-latin-america-women-and-gender-equality (accessed December 2014).

[44] Erik Tryggestad, 'As Churches Mature in the Global South, U.S. Christians Find Supporting Roles', *The Christian Chronicle* (2009), christianchronicle.org/ article/as-churches-mature-in-the-global-south-u-s-christians-find-supporting-roles (accessed November 29, 2014).

[45] Cynthia Lee Andruske, 'Self-Directed Learning Projects of Women on Welfare as Political Acts', *Adult Learning*, 14 (2003), 13-16. See also, 'Gender Equality and Development', *World Development Report 2012*, http://siteresources.worldbank.org/INTWDR2012/Resources/7778105-1299699968583/7786210-1315936222006/Complete-Report.pdf (accessed January 2015).

Sadly, many Pentecostal churches still operate in a structure in which women are not full participants in leadership capacities. Even though Latina Pentecostals have contributed with solid and spiritual leadership in their churches, there are still obstacles to overcome in order for them to gain equality in leadership with their male counterparts in the church. Women have learned to navigate a system that does not give them full opportunities, yet they advance in leadership and contribute to the edification of their churches and, consequently, the kingdom of God.

Latinas are making history and will continue to make history within their denominational circles. There are stories of female ministers who lead effective ministries. For example, in Honduras, Pastor Ana R. Díaz has a church of more than 2000 members. Women are setting examples for the younger Hispanic women who will walk closely in their footprints. Latinas are indeed hard-working, courageous, and engaged in raising the consciousness of gender equality in the church.

Women as Members of the Community of the Spirit in Luke–Acts

Women are mentioned in Luke's Gospel more than in any of the books of the New Testament. Luke displayed Jesus' attitude towards women who were included among those who were disadvantaged and oppressed.[46] In spite of the objections and suspicions that could arise, Jesus was willing to teach them (Lk. 10.38-42), and to admit them as His followers (Lk. 8.2-3). Luke showed how Jesus was considerate and supportive of women in distress women in distress by forgiving them (Lk. 7.36-50) and healing them (Lk. 13.10-17). Women were present at His crucifixion, and they followed those who laid His body in the tomb. Women were the first witnesses of His resurrection (Lk. 24) and they carried the news to the apostles (Lk. 24.9).

Luke made references to the examples of women in the life and teachings of Jesus. The annunciation showed Mary responding in gratitude to God (Lk. 1.36-38). Elizabeth was filled with the Holy

---

[46] Mark Allan Powell, *What Are They Saying About Luke?* (Mahwah, NJ: Paulist Press, 1989), p. 93.

Spirit (1.40-45). Anna rejoiced and prophesied over Jesus (Lk. 2.26-38). A woman was healed on the Sabbath (Lk. 13.10-17). There is a reference to a woman who lost a coin (Lk. 15.8-10). Luke made a list of women who followed Jesus (8.1-3). In the story of Mary and Martha (Lk. 10.48-52), Luke portrayed Jesus as defending Mary by affirming the right of women to learn the word as men do. The Kingdom of God was likened to a woman working with leaven (Lk. 13.20-21). Mary, the mother of Jesus, was portrayed as an ideal disciple (Lk. 1.38). She underwent the test of discipleship (2.35), persevered in her faith, and became part of the apostolic community (Acts 14).

The Book of Acts portrayed women in a new light. Women were not excluded from baptism, the sign and seal of the covenant of grace (Acts 8.12; 16.15). After the ascension, the apostles gathered together to pray, with the women and Mary, the mother of Jesus (Acts 1.14). The Holy Spirit also descended upon them, and Peter expounded that the prophecy of Joel about the outpouring of the Holy Spirit included women: 'Your sons and daughters will prophesy' (Joel 2.28; Acts 2.18).

As the number of Jewish Christians grew in Jerusalem, women were mentioned. Acts 5.12-15 refers to the men and women' who believed in the Lord and were added to the growing number of disciples. Hellenist widows were mentioned due to a conflict in the community of believers. They had been neglected when the number of disciples was increasing, and the distribution of food took place (Acts 6.1-7).

Tabitha (Dorcas) lived in Joppa and is described as doing good and helping the poor (Acts 9.36). She was either a widow or an unmarried virgin who worked for a living and was devoted to doing good works. Mary, the mother of John Mark seemed to be a wealthy widow who had a house large enough for people to gather in prayer (Acts 12.12). Priscilla was an artisan, a tentmaker, along with her husband Aquila. They were a couple on the move who carried the Gospel wherever they traveled as artisans. They were teachers who explained the 'way of God' more accurately to Apollos in Ephesus (Acts 18.24-26). Priscilla was presented as expounding the Scriptures more accurately than Apollo (Acts 18.26). Paul mentioned her name as a co-worker and an important woman in the work of mission (1 Cor. 16.9; Rom. 16.3; 2 Tim. 4.19). She seems to be a woman for whom marriage poses no obstacle to the totality of her work in ministry.[47]

When Paul looked for a place to pray in Philippi, he found a group of God-fearing women by the riverside. These women accepted the gospel message, including Lydia, a merchant of purple cloth (Acts 16.13, 14). In Berea, Paul taught at the Jewish synagogue where among those who believed were a good number of prominent Greek women (Acts 17.12). In Athens, Paul spoke in the meeting of the Areopagus to Stoic and Epicurean philosophers (17.22). When Paul left the council, several followed him and became believers, including a woman named Damaris who was associated with the Areopagus (17.34) and was probably a philosopher.[48]

Richter Reimer notices that many pagan women felt attracted to the Christian faith because it gave them hope amidst the brutality of the political system of their day.[49] Luke referred to Phillip's four unmarried daughters in Caesarea who had the gift of prophecy (Acts 21.9). The daughter's names were not given. However, the male prophet who foretold of Paul's arrest in Jerusalem was identified as Agabus (Acts 21.10).

Luke presented women in surprising way as they prayed alongside men, prophesied, and engaged in good deeds. According to Donald Guthrie, Luke's intention was to show that the followers of Jesus were a community of the Spirit and that new opportunities were open to women.[50] Women were portrayed as playing a significant part in the spread of the Gospel.

A leading part of the spread of the gospel was undertaken by women; sometimes in public or semi-public, as in the work of Priscilla, a Lydia, a Phoebe, a Syntyche; and sometimes in the women's quarters of the home or at the laundry. The opportunity of finding faith where they could be given an equality of status, and a real sphere of service must have helped many women to put their trust in Jesus as Lord.[51]

---

[47] Ivoni Richter Reimer, *Women in the Acts of the Apostles: A Feminist Liberation Perspective* (Minneapolis: Fortress Press, 1995), p. 219.

[48] Reimer, *Women in the Acts of the Apostles*, p. 247.

[49] Reimer, *Women in the Acts of the Apostles*, p. 247.

[50] Donald Guthrie, *New Testament Introduction* (Downers Grove, IL: Intervarsity Press, 1970), p. 91.

[51] Michael Green, *Evangelism in the Early Church* (Grand Rapids, MI: William B. Eerdmans, 1970), p. 118.

Luke attempted to convey the inclusiveness of the gospel message to both men and women, Jews, and Gentiles, in order to stress equality for all in God's plan of redemption and their equal importance to the new community of the Spirit. Women in the biblical text of Luke–Acts were indeed prayers.

Persecution

At times, Pentecostals look at the early church in the book of Acts as an ideal and trouble-free church. However, Luke reported considerable conflicts among the early Christian communities. The church of the twenty-first century also faces hostile environments, and in many regions of the world, Christians undergo persecution. The world witnessed shocking videos of the massacre of Egyptian Christians in February 2015.

The Islamic State of Iraq and Syria or ISIS orchestrated and filmed the dramatic mass killing of African Christians who refused to deny their faith. Western agencies use the term ISIS to refer to a terrorist group, once affiliated with Al Qaeda, but rebranded as ISIS around 2013. It is estimated that the group has up to 30,000 fighters including local supporters. Security officials affirm that more than 3000 individuals have left their homes in the West to join ISIS or other terror groups. The shocking news caused fear of future massacres, but it also led to Egypt's largest Bible tract distribution of more than 1.5 million copies.[52]

Throughout the Book of Acts, there are instances where the early believers experienced increasing opposition and hostility. Yet those believers demonstrated a daily consciousness of the dynamic presence of the Holy Spirit. They had received the infilling of the Holy Spirit and had witnessed the miraculous manifestations of God's power. The Holy Spirit guided and comforted them as they carried out the proclamation of the Gospel. Through the Holy Spirit, Christians were strengthened and encouraged (Acts 9.1), set apart for service (13.2), guided in their deliberations (15.28), and appointed as pastors (20.28).

---

[52] See, Jayson Casper, 'How Libya's Martyrs are Witnessing to Egypt', *Christianity Today* (February 23, 2015).

For the early believers, the baptism of the Spirit was a dynamic reality in their daily lives, enabling them to face external adversities and to deal with conflicts in the church. Luke urged his readers to have confidence in the Spirit's power and His guidance. Christians were encouraged to maintain unity in the church and to live as Christians in an unbelieving and unfriendly world.

When Mary and Joseph brought Jesus to the Temple, Simeon broke out in joyous praise for God. Then Simeon told Mary that the child was destined to cause the rise and fall of many in Israel' (Lk. 2.34) and that he would be opposed. The opposition would come from his own people (Israel) and Mary would also suffer to see the rejection of Jesus. Simeon compared it to a sword that would pierce her soul (verse 35). Throughout the Gospel, Luke portrayed Jesus undergoing rejection and predicting his death (4.28-29; 9.52-56). Luke also developed the theme of suffering for the disciples of Jesus (Lk. 21.12-19).

The book of Acts also included stories of suffering and persecution for the followers of Jesus. Most probably Luke's readers were also undergoing similar suffering and Luke might have wanted to encourage his readers.[53] Peter and John underwent arrest by the Sanhedrin (Acts 4.1-22); later they were placed in prison (Acts 5.18). In Jerusalem, the disciples were scattered under persecution (Acts 8.1) and Saul dragged men and women to prison (Acts 8.1-3). Herod arrested some believers, then killed James with a sword and placed Peter in prison (Acts 12.1-3). Silas, Barnabas, and Paul also suffered persecution and imprisonment.

The martyrdom of Stephen was representative of the suffering of Jesus. The common elements in both their lives were the unjust trials, the scornfulness, the prophetic messages when facing death, the last prayers offering their spirits to God, and the prayers of forgiveness for their persecutors. Luke also compared the suffering of Paul and Jesus. They were both seized by gangs, struck, tried four times, jeered by the crowds (Lk. 23.18; Acts 22:22) and deemed innocent three times.

Luke emphasized the presence of the Holy Spirit among them amidst opposition (Acts 5.29-32). Peter and the other apostles, after

---

[53] Twelftree, *People of the Spirit*, p. 102.

a miraculous release from prison, defied the high priest and the Sanhedrin by declaring their obedience to God rather than men (v. 29). Persecution surfaced after the appointment of seven leaders who would assist the apostles. These seven men were filled with the Holy Spirit and wisdom (Acts 6.3). Stephen was the target of a new wave of opposition from certain members of the Jewish diaspora who were not able to stand up against his wisdom (Acts 6.10). They decided to stone him to death. Like Jesus, Stephen commended his own spirit to God (Acts 7.59), and he asked forgiveness for his tormentors (Acts 7.60). A great persecution broke out in Jerusalem against the church, and many believers were scattered throughout Samaria and Judea (Acts 8.1).

The book of Acts presents intense stories of rescue from persecution. Jesus promised wisdom and the help of the Holy Spirit when his disciples faced persecution for His name (Lk. 12.11-12; Lk. 21.15). Luke included vivid accounts of supernatural intervention for the rescue in the lives of Peter and John (Acts 5.17, 21; 12.6-11); Paul and Silas (Acts 16.25); and men and women persecuted by Saul of Tarsus (Acts 9.1-22).

At the same time, Luke did not withhold distressing stories or even martyrdom, as exemplified in the lives of Stephen, James, and even Paul. Luke's writing conveyed the message that his followers were not going to be exempt from persecution and sorrow for serving Jesus. But Luke also included stories about how God promised to intervene in the darkest hours and how his followers persevered in opposition. Jesus sent his disciples as 'lambs before wolves' (Lk. 10.3).

Persecution is a result of following the rejected Christ and being a follower of his name: 'Blessed are you when people hate you, when they exclude you and insult you and reject your name as evil, because of the Son of Man' (Lk. 6.22).

In a time where many Christians preach a gospel of prosperity, it is necessary to understand that the followers of Jesus will undergo suffering and persecution. Jesus prayed during the most difficult moments of his ministry. Stephen, the first Christian martyr, prayed to Jesus the Intercessor, whom he saw standing at the right hand of the Father (Acts 7.56). Christians are promised to receive help through the Holy Spirit. Jesus taught his disciples that authentic prophets of

God suffered rejection and persecution as they set out to enter Jerusalem.

> I must press on today, tomorrow, and the next day—for surely no prophet can die outside Jerusalem! Jerusalem, Jerusalem, you who kill the prophets and stone those sent to you, how often I have longed to gather your children together, as a hen gathers her chicks under her wings, and you were not willing (Lk. 13.33- 34).

Prayer and the presence of the Holy Spirit will strengthen the lives of believers under the fiercest circumstances of temptation, trials, and persecution.

Conclusion

Luke emphasized Jesus at prayer and narrated how the disciples followed his example. He emphasized the work of the Spirit for the advancement and establishment of the new people of God. He continued the story of Jesus' deeds and teachings through a second volume that offered the most comprehensive and inclusive narrative of the new people of the Spirit (Acts 1.1).

Both Luke and Acts belong together and are special due to the continuity of redemption history.[54] Luke presented Jesus as the fountain of Christianity,[55] along with his disciples, their converts, and their experience with the Holy Spirit. In the book of Acts, the major object of prayer was the gift of the Spirit.[56] Luke highlighted how the Spirit came according to God's determination to prayerful people.

---

[54] Conzelmann, *The Theology of St. Luke*, p. 17.
[55] Stronstad, *The Prophethood of All Believers,* p. 1.
[56] Graham H. Twelftree, 'Prayer and the Coming of the Spirit', *Expository Times* 11.7, pp. 271-76.

5

PRAYER IN PENTECOSTAL LATINO CHURCHES

Pentecostals as People of the Book

Pentecostals embrace Scripture in a literal sense and are often criticized for their 'pre-modern' approach to studying the Bible.[1] Whether in Africa, Asia or Latin America, Pentecostals value Scripture as the 'Word of God'. They place emphasis on hearing the Word, obeying the Word, and doing what the Word says. In the Catholic milieu of Latin America, new converts welcome the Bible as their source of instruction and guidance since many were hardly introduced to the study of Scripture. Latino Pentecostals are aware of the transformation in their lives and commit themselves to a life of obeying the Word of God.

Kenneth Archer observes that early Pentecostals engaged in a pre-critical, text-centered approach to Scripture.[2] They believe in 'plenary relevance' that the Bible contains all the answers to human questions and must simply be read, believed, and obeyed. Pentecostals see themselves as people of the book and their understanding of the

---

[1] Julie Ma, 'Pentecostal Evangelism, Church Planting, and Church Growth', in Wonsuk Ma, Veli-Matti Kärkkäinen, and J. Kwabena Asamoah-Gyadu (eds.), *Pentecostal Mission and Global Christianity* (Eugene, OR: Wipf and Stock, 2014), pp. 87-106.

[2] Bobby Lynch and Kenneth Archer, 'Listening to the South: Quichua-Ecuador Contributions to an Affective Pentecostal Hermeneutic', in Vinson Synan, Amos Yong and Miguel Alvarez (eds.), *Global Renewal Christianity: Latin America* (Orlando, FL: Charisma, 2016), pp. 111-119; see also, Kenneth Archer, *A Pentecostal Hermeneutic for the 21st Century* (London, UK: T & T Clark International, 2004), pp. 133-134.

book shapes their lives and their community experiences.[3] For Allan Anderson, Pentecostals approach Scripture with an inherent question, 'How does the Bible relate to our daily experiences?'[4] Thus, Pentecostals read or interpret Scripture in a way that applies directly to their lives and circumstances. The Bible is prayed, sung, danced, preached and prophesied amidst their communities.

During the last three decades, there has been a proliferation of Pentecostal scholars engaged in postmodern hermeneutical methodologies. Their writings consider their involvement with current issues in biblical and theological studies. Included in Pentecostal scholarship are theologians from Africa, Asia, and Latin America.

Latino Pentecostals

The Latino/Hispanic population continues to grow in the US and so are evangelical and Pentecostal churches all over the nation.[5] The growth of Hispanic churches is closely tied to the immigrant experience.[6] According to Elizabeth Dias, Latino evangelicals are one of the fastest growing segments of America's churchgoers. Rick Warren, pastor of Saddleback Church, observed the Latino church growth is happening mostly among the Pentecostal or charismatic churches.[7] Venues for Latino churches are found in Anglo church buildings, storefronts, and even small living rooms. Dias visited Latino churches and reported:

> All were fervent believers—they sang with hands high, danced during worship, and often brought their own tambourines and flags to Sunday services. They were charismatic and believed in miracles. They told me their stories over tamales and café con leche—how they converted, how God healed their physical illnesses, and how their churches became refuges from hunger and homelessness. To the mainstream American culture, and even

---

[3] Daniel E. Albrecht, *Rites in the Spirit: A Ritual Approach to Pentecostal / Charismatic Spirituality* (Sheffield, UK: Sheffield Academic Press, 1999), p. 246.

[4] Allan Anderson, *An Introduction to Pentecostalism: Global Charismatic Christianity* (Cambridge: Cambridge University Press, 2014), p. 244.

[5] Elizabeth Dias, 'The Rise of Evangélicos', *Time*, April 4, 2013. http://nation.time.com/2013/04/04/the-rise-of-evangelicos/ (accessed April 24, 2014).

[6] Dias, 'The Rise of Evangélicos'.

[7] Dias, 'The Rise of Evangélicos'.

other white evangelical churches, they were invisible. But they were hiding in plain sight.[8]

Traditionally two-thirds of the 52-million-plus Latinos in the US have been Catholic, but according to the Pew Forum on Religion and Public Life, that number could decrease to fifty percent by 2030, since many immigrants are joining evangelical Protestant congregations.[9] A good number of those who are joining evangelical churches are Catholic converts who have a desire for a more direct, personal experience of God.[10] The nation's religious landscape is being transformed by Hispanics in Pentecostal and charismatic traditions. More than ever, the renewalist movement continues to expand among Latinos.

According to Luis Lugo, director of the Pew Forum on Religion and Public Life, there is a rise among the Latino population in relation to the high numbers who practice Pentecostal-influenced beliefs.[11] About two-thirds of Latinos are in ethnic churches that include Hispanic clergy, Spanish-language services, and a majority of Hispanics in their congregation.

Latinos are bringing the 'fiesta spirit' to church.[12] The distinctive Pentecostal practices of speaking in tongues, divine healing, and prophesying are much more common among Hispanics, both Protestant and Catholic, than among other white Evangelical churches. Darío Lopez stated that during Pentecostal services there are moments of encountering the God of Life and these are characterized by spontaneity, joy, fellowship, mutual acceptance, and emphasis on the Word. All of these elements give services a taste of 'fiesta' where friends meet in a family context.[13] People who are marginalized in society find a place where they can openly express themselves through prayer, song, testimonies, and preaching. Pentecostal

---

[8] Dias, 'The Rise of Evangélicos'.

[9] Pew Hispanic Center, Pew Forum on Religion and Public Life 'Changing Faiths: Latinos and the Transformation of American Religion', 2007, http://www.pewforum.org/files/2007/04/hispanics-religion-07-final-mar08.pdf

[10] Pew, 'Changing Faiths: Latinos and the Transformation of American Religion'.

[11] Luis Lugo, 'Event Transcript', Pew Research Religion and Public Life Project, http://www.pewforum.org/2007/04/25/changing-faiths-latinos-and-the-transformation-of-american-religion/ (accessed April 15, 2014).

[12] Dario López, *La Fiesta del Espíritu: Espiritualidad y Celebración Pentecostal* (Lima, Perú: Ediciones Puma, 2006), p. 29.

[13] López, *La Fiesta del* Espíritu, p. 29.

communities generate the formation of new relationships where differences vanish. Those in the shadows become missionaries and visionaries that dream beyond their present circumstances.[14]

The population of Latino churches is mostly made up of first- and second-generation immigrants. New converts could profit from a scriptural foundation in prayer in order to cultivate a deeper relationship with God. As the Latino population continues to grow, church leaders must realize the importance of the practice of prayer. Hispanic immigrants must be aware of the relevance of prayer in their lives as they establish themselves in a new cultural milieu. Church leaders may need to model the essentiality of prayer. The criticality of prayer requires a concrete and practical response from the followers of Jesus Christ. Consequently, Hispanic immigrants can also be guided to establish solid prayer habits.

Hunger for Spirituality

Materialism and humanism have dominated Western thinking. Individualism and independence are highly valued, and reason is used as the primary way to understand reality. The Western worldview has placed God into a neat, predictable mold. Generally, Evangelicals have been driven by correct doctrinal assumptions. Charles Kraft stated there is a hunger for spirituality in Western societies.[15] Kraft concluded Evangelicals are beginning to sense that there must be more, and some may ask what is wrong with their powerless Christianity. Kraft considered that there is a reality beyond the rational, a spirit world that can be affected through prayer. By seeking the presence of God through prayer Christian disciples will receive the necessary power and authority to carry out ministry.

It would seem that modern Christians are embarrassed to preach a Gospel accompanied by power. Kraft relates how he underwent a paradigm shift, that is, from an Evangelical mindset to one who realized there was a spirit world.[16] The linear and rational characteristics of the western worldview practically do not sustain what cannot be

---

[14] López, *La Fiesta del* Espíritu, p. 34.

[15] Charles Kraft, *Christianity with Power: Your Worldview and Your Experience of the Supernatural* (Ann Arbor, MI: Servant Books, 1989), p. 7.

[16] Kraft, *Christianity with Power,* p. 34.

scientifically understood.[17] On the other hand, there is a hunger for spirituality that is palpable among the younger generations. In many cities, palm readers, spirit mediums, and New Age followers are alive and well.

While Evangelical churches have emphasized correct doctrine, Pentecostals have emphasized experience in their relationship with God. The emphasis on the supernatural in the Pentecostal-Charismatic tradition is relevant to helping those seeking a closer experience with God through prayer. The millennial generation (those born between 1984-2002) holds a greater openness to the supernatural than some of the previous generations. They have a genuine hunger for spiritual things, even though they may be hostile towards the church and organized religion.

Stanley Grenz pointed out that if we want to connect with a postmodern generation, the gospel message must consider that the goal of human existence encompasses more than the accumulation of knowledge.[18] Postmodern minds are turned off by metanarratives and by modernity's endeavors to reduce faith in God to a series of theological propositions. On the other hand, postmodernists are deeply attracted to the mystery of the God who cannot be understood with the rational mind alone. In summary, the emphasis on the supernatural in the Pentecostal-Charismatic tradition is relevant to those that are seeking a closer experience with God to prayer.

Russell Moore of the Southern Baptist Convention, a denomination of 16 million members, calls for a fresh approach to ministry in an increasingly post-Christian America.[19] About one third of older Americans identify as evangelicals; however, among younger Americans, the number drops to one in ten. Church leaders need to build community and engage with millennials in creative ways, for instance, through social media. It would seem that evangelicals no longer hold the 'Moral Majority' but instead are a minority in an increasingly secularizing America.

---

[17] Kraft, *Christianity with Power*, p. 25.

[18] Stanley Grenz, *A Primer on Postmodernism* (Grand Rapids, MI: Eerdmans, 1996), p. 171.

[19] Jan Crawford, 'Southern Baptist Leaders Calls for Fresh Approach', *CBS This Morning* (April 18, 2014).

Hispanics and Prayer

Hispanic churches are thriving amidst a secular, individualistic, and materialistic society. A great majority of these churches are composed of first, second, and third-generation Latinos. Generally, prayer and fasting are common spiritual disciplines in the ethos of Pentecostal churches in Latin America. A major concern is that as immigrants assimilate into a growing secularizing culture, the personal emphasis on prayer may decrease. Thus, Hispanic churches may need to intentionally seek greater understanding of the biblical, theological, and spiritual dimensions of prayer.

Hispanic churches have the capability to impact the religious landscape and the spiritual fabric of the American nation. For Samuel Rodriguez, President of the National Hispanic Christian Leadership Conference (NHCLC), the growing Hispanic community is able to provide the oxygen to the fire of Pentecost in America.[20] 'This community—full of purpose, passion and promise—carries the anointing to preserve biblical orthodoxy, ignite a righteousness-and-justice movement, strengthen the firewall of holiness and humility, and project a kingdom-culture, multi-ethnic demonstration of the gospel'.[21] The Holy Spirit has been moving amidst the Pentecostal explosion in the Latin American nations. The same Holy Spirit is moving amidst Hispanic congregations that may go unnoticed by many American Christians.

In order to keep the vitality of prayer alive in Hispanic churches, it is essential for Hispanic Pentecostals to be knowledgeable about the value of their prayer tradition. Churches also need to be aware of the significance of prayer in the life of Christ and in the early church, as described in the Book of Acts. It is beneficial for believers to have a biblical base for prayer and to comprehend how Jesus modeled prayer throughout his lifetime.

I propose that Hispanic churches and their accentuation on the practice of prayer can be a contribution to a secularized society and to the state of prayerlessness in Evangelical churches.

---

[20] Samuel Rodriguez, 'How God is Exploding Among Latinos', *Charisma Magazine* (December 2012). https://www.charismamag.com/anniversary/pages-from-our-past/15089-gods-latino-explosion (accessed May 10, 2015).

[21] Rodriguez, 'How God is Exploding Among Latinos'.

Pentecostalism in Latin America

Manifestations of the outpouring of the Holy Spirit occurred in many parts of the world during the early twentieth century including India, Los Angeles, Wales, Chile, Nicaragua, Guatemala, and Puerto Rico. At least half of classical Pentecostals in the world live in Latin America with an estimated 141 million adherents in the year 2000.[22] Pentecostalism in Latin America was not necessarily imported from North America, but had its own inception in Chile, Argentina, and Brazil.[23] Chilean Pentecostals and others referred to themselves as *criollo* (native) Pentecostals. This popular movement has transformed the religious landscape of the traditionally Catholic countries of Latin America. Edward Cleary observed that the Latin American soul is a Christian soul and Pentecostalism is one expression of this.[24]

Several factors have contributed to the 'Pentecostalization' of Latin America. Early studies concluded that churches grew because they were closely-knit communities that helped people cope with industrialization and urbanization. Pentecostal groups seem to offer people unique resources that enable them to cope with personal and family problems, e.g., alcoholism, poverty and illness.[25] People make changes in their ethical behavior, and they show an as increase in personal discipline. The gifts of the Holy Spirit are also meaningful and relevant in Pentecostal communities.

A second factor for the growth of Pentecostalism is the egalitarian tendency to open free social space for the marginalized poor of Latin America.[26] Interestingly, some authoritarian Pentecostal pastors have followed a paternalistic leadership style after the *hacienda* (plantation, or estate) power relations. Although Pentecostals have been labeled as politically conservative, politicians are trying to court them for

---

[22] Anderson, *An Introduction to Pentecostalism*, 63.

[23] Anderson, *An Introduction to Pentecostalism*, 76.

[24] Edward L. Cleary and Juan Sepúlveda, in Edward L. Cleary and Hannah W. Stewart-Gambino, (eds.), 'Chilean Pentecostalism: Coming of Age', *Power, Politics and Pentecostals in Latin America* (Boulder, CO: Westview), 1998, p.10.
Murray, Dempster and Byron D. Klaus, *The Globalization of Pentecostalism: A Religion Made to Travel* (Eugene, OR: Wipf and Stock), 1999, p. 135.

[25] Henri Gooren, 'The Pentecostalization of Religion and Society in Latin America', *Exchange* 39 (2010), p. 362.

[26]David Martin, *Tongues of Fire: The Explosion of Protestantism in Latin America* (Oxford: Blackwell, 1990), p. 278.

their votes in Guatemala, Nicaragua, Venezuela, and Honduras.[27] There is an influence of Pentecostal language and music on public religious meetings and political rallies.[28]

A third observation of the spread of Pentecostalism is the gradual influence on civil society. Pentecostalism has been called the largest self-organized movement of the poor in the world.[29] Radio, television, and mass meetings transmit prayers, Pentecostal music, and enthusiastic shouts of approval by the audience. David Martin observed that Pentecostalism has the potential to eventually erode the persisting colonial remnants in Latin American societies.[30]

Fourthly, it seems that there is an upward mobility among Pentecostals. A growing number of groups emphasize a prosperity gospel, that is, the belief that God's blessings will be poured on believers who lead a righteous life, give tithes to the church, and have a solid faith. A fifth factor that contributes to an increase in Pentecostals is the change in gender relations. The average Pentecostal church attendant is usually under thirty, more often female than male, and of a low to lower middle- class background. Women seem to become more independent in the home and in the public domain. Males shift away from drinking, gambling, and adulterous relationships.[31] Pentecostalism is considered a main social force against machismo.[32]

Pentecostal churches believe that the Holy Spirit empowers women because it is seen clearly in the New Testament: 'I will pour out my Spirit on all people. Your sons and daughters will prophesy' (Acts 2:17). Women participate in services and in Latin America quite a few women pastor growing churches. For example, according to the national Church of God Bishop in Honduras several female ministers are currently pastoring churches that average more than 200

---

[27] See, Roberto Zub, *Protestantismo y paricipación política* (Managua, Nicaragua: CIEETS/UENIC, 2002).

[28] Gooren, 'The Pentecostalization of Religion', p. 362.

[29] Raúl Zibechi, 'Pentecostalism and South America's Social Movements', *Americas Program*, Upside Down World, http://upsidedownworld.org/main/international-archives-60/1529-Pentecostalism-and-south-americas-social-movements (accessed March 10, 2014).

[30] Martin, *Tongues of Fire*, pp. 107-109.

[31] Stephen Offutt, 'The Transnational Locations of Two Leading Evangelical Churches in the Global South', *Pneuma: The Journal of the Society for Pentecostal Studies* 32 (2010), pp. 390-411.

[32] Elizabeth Brusco, '*The Reformation of Machismo: Evangelical Conversion and Gender in Colombia*' (Austin: University of Texas Press, 1995), pp. 28-29, 61-64.

members, and one female pastor has a church of more than 3000 members.[33] Several scholars agree that the participation of women has been widespread in Pentecostalism.

Pentecostal Spirituality

Currently Pentecostal churches represent the largest Protestant group in the world and their spirituality has influenced every branch of Christianity. Bradley P. Holt describes Pentecostal or charismatic spirituality as one that focuses on the love of God which is perceived to be present and active.[34] Steve Land defines spirituality as 'the integration of beliefs and practices in the affections which are themselves evoked and expressed by those beliefs and practices'.[35] Spirituality is the lived experience of 'the whole of one's spiritual...experience, one's belief, convictions, and patterns of thought, one's emotions and behavior in respect to what is ultimate, or God'.[36]

The trademarks of Pentecostal spirituality include religious practices, such as worship, prayer, missions, and individual religious experience such as Spirit baptism, and gifts of the Spirit. Pentecostal spirituality fosters a deep and mystical, piety that emphasizes the immanent sense of the divine.[37] The belief system accentuates an understanding of the 'gifts of the Spirit'. The 'Spirit baptism' appears and operates as normative in the life of Pentecostal churches.

For classical Pentecostals, the practice of speaking in tongues is experienced as an assurance of God's love and a form of surrender to God.[38] Answers to prayers for healing emphasize the presence of God amidst the congregation. Holt states that the traditional suspicion of education and intellectual endeavor in early Pentecostalism

---

[33] Pedro S. Guardado, interview by author, Tegucigalpa, Honduras, October 2014.

[34] Holt, *Thirsty for God*, p. 142.

[35] Steven J. Land, *Pentecostal Spirituality: A Passion for the Kingdom* (Cleveland, TN: CPT Press, 2010), p. 3.

[36] Anne E. Carr, *Transforming Grace* (San Francisco: Harper and Row, 1996), pp. 201-202.

[37] Daniel E. Albrecht, 'Pentecostal Spirituality: Ecumenical Potential and Challenge', *Cyberjournal for Pentecostal-Charismatic Journal*, http://www.pctii.org/cyberj/cyberj2/albrecht.html#N_4_ (accessed May 7, 2014).

[38] Holt, *Thirsty for God*, p. 142.

has diminished but 'there is still a sense that the anointing of the Spirit is more important than academic degrees for leadership'.[39]

There are key elements of Pentecostal spirituality or of a Pentecostal worldview that can be observed across many global contexts and denominational traditions. According to James Smith, a Pentecostal worldview has something powerful to say to the academy because Pentecostal spirituality is not just a compartmentalized way of being religious.[40] The practices of a Pentecostal spirituality carry over into the everyday life of believers in such a way that the Pentecostal faith involves not only 'speaking in tongues' but also 'thinking in tongues'.[41] For Smith, a Pentecostal spirituality is embedded within a Pentecostal worldview. For James Olthius, a worldview is a framework or set of 'fundamental beliefs through which we view the world and our calling'.[42] A worldview manages reality and judges what order is and what disorder is. It is the pivotal point on which a person's everyday thinking and behavior turns.

A Pentecostal worldview disposes its adherents to conceive or comprehend the world under a 'Spirit-charged construal'.[43] There are a variety of spiritual practices that carry within them an understanding of Pentecostal worship. During a service, it is common for people to raise their hands, clap, and dance. Amidst enthusiastic worship, congregants may sing, shout, walk or even run in the meeting space. Uplifted arms and hands are expressions of surrender to God. Many responses are unplanned and may occur spontaneously at any point in the service.

A Pentecostal worldview manifests a radical openness to God.[44] To have a deep sense of expectation of God doing something new is what lies at the heart of Pentecostal spirituality.[45] Pentecostal communities are characterized by an emphasis on the ministry of the Holy Spirit. A blog posted by Jackie Johns describes the signs of a

---

[39] Holt, *Thirsty for God,* p. 142.

[40] James K.A. Smith, *Thinking in Tongues* (Grand Rapids, MI: Eerdmans, 2010), p. 30.

[41] Holt, *Thirsty for God,* p. 25.

[42] James H. Olthius, 'On Worldviews', *Christian Scholar's Review* 14 (1985), pp. 155-156.

[43] Smith, *Thinking in Tongues,* p. 30.

[44] Smith, *Thinking in Tongues,* p. 12.

[45] Smith, *Thinking in Tongues,* pp. 33-34.

Spirit-filled church: exuberant praise, deep fellowship, unbounded love, devotion to the Word and sound doctrine.[46] For Jack Deere:

> The book of Acts is the best source that we have to demonstrate what normal church life should be like when the Holy Spirit is present and working in the church…a church that has a passion for God, is willing to sacrifice—even to the point of martyrdom—and is a miracle-working church.[47]

In practice, Pentecostal worship is shaped by an openness to surprise and to the working of the miraculous. A Pentecostal service makes room for God to be heard (in tongues, prophecy, and in the word of wisdom) and for God to work (to heal, to transform). Worshipers respond in different ways to the presence of the Holy Spirit of God in their midst. For Pentecostals, God's Spirit is free to move among them with signs and wonders.

In addition, Pentecostal spirituality considers a sense of the presence of the Spirit of God in culture and creation. It is marked by a deep sense of the Spirit's immanence.[48] There is sense that all creation—nature and culture—is 'charged with the presence of the Spirit'. In the same manner, Pentecostal spirituality is concerned with the presence in the world of other spirits. There is a sense of spiritual oppression caused by the work of supernatural forces. In order to overcome oppression, Pentecostals refer to prayer in the modality of spiritual warfare as stated in Ephesians 6:12: 'For our struggle is not against flesh and blood, but against the rulers, against the authorities, against the powers of this dark world and against the spiritual forces of evil in the heavenly realms'. Prayer and worship are considered ways to resist evil forces. Although North American Pentecostalism has neutralized this emphasis, spiritual warfare is a primary factor in the phenomenal growth of Christianity in Asia, Africa, and Latin America.[49]

A Pentecostal spirituality affirms the goodness of embodiment and materiality. For example, Pentecostals believe in healing of illness and disease, as a gift of the Holy Spirit. The message of Jesus was a

[46] Jackie David Johns, Facebook post, March 20, 2014, https://www.facebook.com/jackie.d.johns (accessed March 20, 2014).
[47] Jack Deere, *Surprised by the Power of the Spirit* (Grand Rapids, MI: Zondervan, 1993), p. 114.
[48] Smith, *Thinking in Tongues*, p. 40.
[49] Smith, *Thinking in Tongues*, p. 41.

message of liberation from sin, oppression, and poverty (Lk. 4.18-19). Sin and oppression can include illness and disease. Pentecostal spirituality values the whole person since God cares about our bodies.[50] For King, the affirmation of bodies and materiality is a deconstruction of fundamentalist dualism.[51] There is a sense that a Pentecostal worldview values the whole person, and it is concordance with God's affirmation of the goodness of material creation (Gen. 1.27).[52] Pentecostals are not just passive recipients but engage actively in worship.

Pentecostal spirituality is rooted in affective and narrative practice.[53] Pentecostals emphasize 'experience' in contrast to a rationalistic evangelical theology which cultivates an intellectual relation to God. Knowledge for Pentecostals is rooted in the heart. The affective is encountered in the narrative. Cheryl Johns proposes that the emphasis on the oral-narrative allows Pentecostalism to engage in a personal and social critique and at the same time allows the participation of everyone.[54] Pentecostals share testimonies from their personal encounters with the Spirit of God. The story serves as a hermeneutical approach, and it is a way to inform and explain the Pentecostal life.

Pentecostal Scholarship

In relation to scholarship, Pentecostals were criticized for not producing academic literature. Most early Pentecostal theologians did not have the benefits of formal academic theological training and were labeled as being anti-intellectual and opposed to learning.[55] Pentecostals criticized academic education because it could lead people away from the Bible. Yet Pentecostals established Bible training institutes in their denominations.

---

[50] Smith, *Thinking in Tongues*, p. 43.
[51] Smith, *Thinking in Tongues*, p. 43.
[52] Smith, *Thinking in Tongues*, p. 43.
[53] Smith, *Thinking in Tongues*, p. 43.
[54] Johns, *Pentecostal Formation*, pp. 9, 19, 58.
[55] See, Christopher A. Stephenson, *Types of Pentecostal Theology: Method, System, Spirit* (New York: Oxford University Press, 2013).

In 1956, Charles W. Conn, a Church of God historian stated: 'we have prayed, preached, fasted, and urged much, but have written little'.[56] Arlene Sánchez-Walsh stated that early Pentecostalism was considered 'anti-intellectual, anti-rational, ahistorical, and non-liturgical'.[57] It was even considered a religious subculture and morally dangerous due to the uninhibited responses during prayer and spiritual manifestations. Men and women fell to the floor in close proximity to one another, under the power of the Spirit, an experience referred to as 'slain in the Spirit'.[58] The alleged carnality of Pentecostalism was considered heretical. For example, a delegation of California evangelical ministers aimed to ban Aimee Semple McPherson from preaching in Britain arguing she could cause an outbreak of mental illness.[59]

Early Pentecostals depended on what the Holy Spirit did and were not concerned about producing systematic theology or studying biblical criticism. There was a sense that the Holy Spirit would lead to revelation and no books were needed besides the Bible. However, in the last 30 years there has been an emergence of Pentecostal scholarship.[60] The number of Pentecostal scholars has increased as well as the number of Pentecostal studies in the theological academy. There are a number of journals including Pneuma, academic societies, such as the Society for Pentecostal Studies, and institutions of higher education established among Pentecostals.[61]

Guided By The Holy Spirit

The Spirit baptism was central to the Pentecostal message and so was the emphasis on evangelism and missions. The belief on the imminent return of Christ moved the early Pentecostals to carry the Gospel to the ends of the earth. The missionary and evangelistic vision

---

[56] Charles W. Conn, *Pillars of Pentecost* (Cleveland, TN: Church of God Publishing House, 1956), p. 34.

[57] Arlene M. Sánchez-Walsh, *Latino Pentecostal Identity: Evangelical Faith, Self, and Society* (New York: Columbia University Press, 2003), p. 5.

[58] Sánchez-Walsh, *Latino Pentecostal Identity*, p. 5.

[59] Sánchez-Walsh, *Latino Pentecostal Identity*, p. 5

[60] Wolfgang Vondey and Martin William Mittelstadt, *The Theology of Amos Yong and the New Face of Pentecostal Scholarship* (Leiden, Netherlands: Brill, 2013), p. 5.

[61] Vondey and Mittelstadt, *The Theology of Amos Yong*, p. 5.

was essential in sending forth missionaries all around the globe.[62] According to Vinson Synan, as far as theology was concerned, Pentecostals did not necessarily form a unified doctrine. They had different emphases in their beliefs and theology ranging from Wesleyan-holiness, to Reformed, and Unitarian.[63]

Smith notes that the Pentecostal worldview is committed to ministries of empowerment and social justice with a preferential option for the marginalized.[64] Smith calls for Pentecostals to engage in a critical reflection on who they are and to a deconstruction to what they have become in order to regain an eschatological and prophetic vision. For Smith, Pentecostals cannot forget the poor and the weak of the world (1 Cor. 1.27).[65]

George O. Wood, the General Superintendent of the General Council of the Assemblies of God (AG) states that the baptism of the Spirit is for the empowerment of believers for life and service. For Wood, the enduring evidence of the Spirit baptism results in believers engaged in evangelism and outreach as in Acts 1.8. If believers do not demonstrate fruitfulness, they contradict the mission of the Holy Spirit.[66]

It is common in Pentecostal communities to allow the Spirit to guide believers in the understanding of the word. Kenneth Archer affirms that, 'Pentecostals require a hermeneutical strategy that involves an interdependent tridactic dialogue between Scripture, the Spirit and community resulting in a creative negotiated meaning'.[67] The role of the Holy Spirit is to lead and guide the community in understanding the pres2ent meaningfulness of Scripture. Pentecostals engage in a hermeneutical strategy that differs from both the Liberal and the Fundamentalists methodologies.[68]

---

[62] Vondey and Mittelstadt, *The Theology of Amos Yong*, p. 10.

[63] Vinson Synan. *The Holiness-Pentecostal Tradition: Charismatic Movements in the Twentieth Century* (Grand Rapids, MI: Eerdmans, 1997), p. 7.

[64] Smith, *Thinking in Tongues*, p. 45.

[65] Smith, *Thinking in Tongues*, 46.

[66] George Wood. 'What George O. Wood Really Thinks About Pentecostals Speaking in Tongues', *Charisma Magazine,* http://www.charismamag.com/spirit/church-ministry/20268-what-george-o-wood-really-thinks-about-Pentecostals-speaking-in-tongues (accessed April 25, 2014).

[67] Archer, *A Pentecostal Hermeneutics*, p. 191.

[68] Archer, *A Pentecostal Hermeneutics*, pp. 2-3.

Pentecostals and Participation in the Public Sphere

Amos Yong notes that Pentecostals in Latin America are increasingly participating in neighborhood organizations in order to improve the living conditions of their communities.[69] Guatemala had two Pentecostal presidents, Efraín Ríos Montt (1982-1983) and Jorge Serrano (1991-1993), and although both were removed from office, their participation in politics anticipated that more Pentecostals would participate in the public sphere. Many Pentecostals will undoubtedly run for public office, and many will be elected to government positions.[70] Pentecostals are voting, and this signals an emerging sociopolitical consciousness. For example, in Guatemala more Pentecostal churches are becoming involved in relief work.

For Yong, Pentecostalism in Latin America is not yet a politicized faith. Generally, Pentecostals are focused on eschatological salvation or on a gospel that God blesses the individual. Pentecostals are motivated by a fervent moralism, a conviction that God punishes the unjust, and they are aware of the images of the Old Testament of people struggling against injustice.[71] On the other hand, Bernardo Campos considers that Pentecostals can choose to become active players in civil society or politics.[72] He regards that Pentecostalism will contribute significantly to decision-making in the region's social system.[73]

Pentecostals and Prayer

The one common element for early Pentecostals was their emphasis on prayer since they believed that being in constant communion with God meant prayer and intercession for daily living. For example, the Latin American Bible Institutes founded in 1926 (California and Texas) included in their moral codes or Discipline: 'Every student

---

[69] Amos Yong, *The Spirit Poured Upon All Flesh: Pentecostalism and the Possibility of Global Theology* (Grand Rapids, MI: Baker Academic, 2005), p. 37.

[70] Rowan Ireland, *Kingdoms Come: Religion in Brazil* (Pittsburgh, PA: University of Pittsburgh Press, 1991), p. 107.

[71] Yong, *The Spirit Poured Upon All Flesh*, p. 37.

[72] Bernardo Campos, 'In the Power of the Spirit: Pentecostalism, Theology and Social Ethics', in Benjamin F. Gutierrez and Dennis A. Smith (eds.), *The Power of the Spirit: The Pentecostal Challenge to Historic Churches in Latin America* (Guatemala City, Guatemala: CELEP, 1996), p. 50.

[73] Campos, 'In the Power of the Spirit', p. 50.

must maintain communion with God'.[74] Prayer is essential in order to maintain a Pentecostal worldview.

Miller and Yamamori wrote:

> ... there is something personal and primitive about the prayers of Pentecostals. They tend to flow from the heart, expressing spontaneous feelings of praise as well as the deepest anguish of the heart. Sometimes these prayers are focused on an individual's needs, other times on those of loved ones, the congregation, the community, or the world. And, not infrequently, prayer is a potpourri of needs and thanksgiving, personal and public.[75]

For Pentecostals, prayer becomes a collective experience, and the needs of others are raised in prayer before the entire community. Prayer has an empowering quality since shared burdens are no longer individual struggles. The results are left to God. The believer is liberated to continue with the daily tasks of life.[76]

Charles Haavik concluded prayer may be a point of contact between Pentecostals and millennials or people with a postmodern worldview.[77] To the postmodern mind, the structured church service may represent a rigid and authoritarian institution. If the church tries to make everyone fit into a mold and to teach doctrinal precepts, the more will the church be rejected by a postmodern mindset. Millennials are seeking a deeper sense of intimacy with God.

The version of an aloof God or of Jesus in a vacuum does not attract the millennial generation.[78] They are seeking out a more authentic faith that is integrated into all areas of life and not compartmentalized. Hispanic churches also face the challenge of helping children and youth so they will remain in church during their adult years.

---

[74] Sanchez-Walsh, *Latino Pentecostal Identity*, p. 59.

[75] Donald Miller and Tetsunao Yamamori, *Global Pentecostalism: The New Face of Christian Social Engagement* (Los Angeles: University of California Press, 2007), p. 145.

[76] Miller and Yamamori, *Global Pentecostalism*, p. 145.

[77] Charles Elias Haavik, *Joyful in My House: Introducing Postmoderns to the Life of Prayer* (D. Min dissertation, Assemblies of God Theological Seminary, 2006), pp. 8-9.

[78] Barna Group, 'Three Spiritual Journeys of Millennials', *Barna Group*, May 9, 2013, https://www.barna.org/barna-update/millennials/612-three-spiritual-journeys-of-millennials.html#prodigals (accessed May 12, 2014).

In the U.S.A. almost 60 percent of millennials from a Christian background have dropped out of going to church and about 50 percent have been frustrated by their faith.[79]

It is significant that early Pentecostals rejected the rational modernity of the Enlightenment. Pentecostals exhibited a distrust of reason, secular rationalism, and ideologies that disregarded Scripture.[80] Pentecostals sought religious experience and were not interested in dogma: they spoke in tongues in the same way the Apostles had done on the feast of Pentecost. Pentecostals reached out to a transcendent God beyond the scope of words.

Harvey Cox states that the religious experience of Pentecostals filled a vacuum left by modernity's quest for reason.[81] While fundamentalists sought a rational or scientific control over faith, Pentecostals stressed inclusiveness, love, and compassion. Mainline denominations despised Pentecostals and their beliefs in miracles and gifts of the Spirit.[82]

According to Donald Miller and Tetsunao Yamamori, Pentecostals believe in healing and in deliverance or casting out demons as Jesus did.[83] In addition, they note that for a Western mindset or for people who operate on assumptions of empirical evidence, the tendency is to dismiss the reality of demons. Generally, Pentecostals believe they are in a spiritual battle and acknowledge that there are battles to be fought on different fronts, for different reasons, and with varying degrees of intensity. For Pentecostals spiritual battles are real, even though they cannot physically see the attacker. Besides spiritual battles, believers understand they face a worldly battle, and a battle within themselves.

Miller and Yamamori argue that Pentecostalism is ironically postmodern or post-Enlightenment.[84] Pentecostals are experience-oriented and suspicious of theological dogmas that substitute for direct

---

[79] Barna Group, 'Five Reasons Millennials Stay Connected to Church', *Barna Group*, September 17, 2013, www.barna.org/barna-update/millennials/635-5-reasons-millennials-stay-connected-to-church#.U3EimuZdWCI (accessed May 12, 2014).

[80] Pedro Moreno, 'Rapture and Renewal in Latin America', *First Things* 74 (June-July 1997), pp. 31-34.

[81] Cox, *Fire from Heaven*, 103-108.

[82] Karen Armstrong, *The Battle for God* (New York: Random House, 2000), pp. 180-182.

[83] Miller and Yamamori, *Global Pentecostalism*, p. 154.

[84] Miller and Yamamori, *Global Pentecostalism*, p. 154.

encounters with the holy. Pentecostalism encourages people 'to merge mind and body into a unified expression that honors emotional and physical expressions as integral elements of worship'.[85] Pentecostalism appeals to many people because it fills the void of the ecstasy deficit that characterizes contemporary life. Miller and Yamamori classify Pentecostalism as a renewal movement characterized by seeking a direct experience with the holy, breaking away from hierarchical authority, encouraging lay participation, and manifesting a preference for experience over theological dogma.[86]

Pentecostals follow the Spirit's leading in their church services. Instead of a structured liturgical service, a typical Latin American Pentecostal service includes singing, shouting, clapping, and dancing. As the service begins, the congregants become deeply immersed, their eyes closed, some crying, others singing at the top of their voice or 'speaking in tongues', and still others lifting faces and hands toward heaven.[87] Shouts of praise and clapping abound as the pastor preaches or as responses to testimonies and answered prayers. There is no clear beginning to the service, and usually there is no clear end.

For Haavik, Pentecostalism's focus on experience and authentic encounter with God is attractive to postmodernists.[88] The emphasis on the mystery of God that transcends human knowledge appeals to a generation weary of attempts to reduce spirituality to propositional truth. Many newcomers to a Pentecostal service appreciate the environment of openness to spiritual things, direct experience, and communally discovered truth.

Generally, among Hispanics, there is a much more open attitude toward public expression of emotions in comparison to white, middle-class American culture. For newly arrived immigrants, the church becomes one of the few places where they are free to laugh, cry, shout, and sing. These emotional expressions become evident at many points during a Pentecostal service. Tears often accompany the spontaneous prayers of congregants. People share their testimonies of being saved by God from drugs, alcohol, or depression.

---

85 Miller and Yamamori, *Global Pentecostalism*, p. 142.
86 Miller and Yamamori, *Global Pentecostalism*, p. 128.
87 Moreno, 'Rapture and Renewal in Latin America', pp. 31-32.
88 Haavik, *Joyful in My House*, pp. 8-9.

In a Pentecostal church, immigrants undergoing culture shock and racism can freely express their emotions loudly and physically without anybody looking down on them. These Latino churches have a welcoming environment and many times the pastors are from the same neighborhoods and socioeconomic backgrounds as the congregants, making them easier to approach and relate to.[89] In conclusion, Pentecostalism is less prone to the dry intellectual faith (theological formulas and creeds) than evangelical or mainline protestant churches. Services are more fluid as the participants anticipate listening to God's voice and to be 'led by the Spirit'.

Prayer and the Holistic Mission of the Church

Generally, Pentecostals are satisfied and comforted in prayer for their personal needs and for those in their communities. It can be said that Pentecostals have remained within the four walls of their church and have been very cautious about expressing their public opinion on political matters.[90]

The evangelical community in Latin America has approached sociopolitical issues with discretion. Both Evangelicals and Pentecostals considered that the preaching of the Gospel should not be mixed up with politics or that sociopolitical issues should not be mentioned from the pulpit.[91] Church leaders are aware of social inequalities and corruption in government; but Evangelical leaders discuss political matters among themselves and not in a public manner.

Pentecostals have not taken a critical stand on the role of the church and social responsibility. They might have social outreaches to help the poor, such as distribution of food or medical missions, but do not denounce injustice. Evangelicals and Pentecostals in Latin America have emphasized personal evangelism and personal piety. They have steered away from political activism or political participation. According to Eldin Villafañe, Pentecostals must see themselves

---

[89] Bruce Wallace. 'The Latino Pentecostals', *Drew Magazine* (Fall 2008). http://www.drewmagazine.com/2008/09/the-latino-Pentecostals/ (accessed May 12, 2014).

[90] Robert Davis, 'What About Justice?' *Transformation: An International Journal of Holistic Mission Studies* 26.2 (April 2009), pp. 89-103.

[91] Miguel Alvarez, 'A Century of Pentecostalism in Latin America', in Vinson Synan, Amos Yong and Miguel Alvarez (eds.), *Global Renewal Christianity: Latin America* (Orlando, FL: Charisma, 2016), pp. xiv-xix.

not just called to engage in personal liberation, but they must position themselves as a church for social liberation.[92] Beyond the *culto* (service) there are structures and institutions that must be confronted in the power of the Spirit to break the chains of hate, hostility, and injustice.[93]

In spite of a lack of involvement in the transformation of social structures, there is a generation of rising Pentecostal scholars who critically analyze the harsh reality of the Latin American nations. For instance, a book published in October 2015, *Pentecostals and Charismatics in Latin America and Latino Communities*, discusses the concerns and challenges faced among Latinos in the U.S. and in Latin America.[94] The writings of young academicians and practitioners reveal the difficulties and suffering of people in Latin American societies.

It is undeniable that prayer can empower Pentecostals to have greater compassion for the needs of those who suffer conditions of injustice. Evangelicals and Pentecostals are coming to the realization that 'the Lord calls the church to speak prophetically to society and work for the renewal and reform of its structures'.[95] In our era of increasing globalization Pentecostals can join efforts for peacemaking in regions of widespread violence. Isolation or separation from the sinful world is no longer possible. 'The illusion of a Christian life in a convent or hermitage has disappeared'.[96]

Prayer can be a catalyst for peaceful interventions without bitterness or anger. Christians must pray, 'Forgive us our sins, for we also forgive everyone who sins against us' (Luke 11:4). Both personal and systemic sin leads to alienation and poverty. 'Sin leads people to abuse, engage in corrupt acts, and misuse resources in a way that is hurtful to themselves, their families, and their communities'.[97] It is becoming more widespread for Evangelicals today to accept the notion that sin is not only attributable to individuals but also to social

---

[92] Eldin Villafañe, *Seek the Peace of the City: Reflections on Urban Ministry* (Grand Rapids, MI: Eerdmans, 1995), p. 200.

[93] Villafañe, *Seek the Peace of the City*, p. 200.

[94] See, Néstor Medina and Sammy Alfaro, *Pentecostals and Charismatics in Latin America and Latino Communities* (London: Palgrave McMillan, 2015).

[95] Davis, 'What About Justice?' p. 91.

[96] Davis, 'What About Justice?' p. 92.

[97] Davis, 'What About Justice?' p. 92.

structures. Racism, sexism, and economic oppression are an affront to God.[98]

The prayers of Jesus and the prayers of the first-century church were incessant. Pentecostal churches then, face the challenge to proclaim the Lordship of Christ, to seek the peace of the city (Jeremiah 29:7) and to pray always. Christians know that political engagement will not bring the Kingdom of God.[99] Yet, Pentecostals must discern specific areas in how to pray for His Kingdom to come (Luke11:2). The church must continue to be a 'house of prayer' in order to keep the presence of God in the community and in the world. Prayers must saturate the mission of the church to truly exhibit the Spirit of Christ to a world lost in sin and darkness.

Angelina Atyam of the Concerned Parents Association of Northern Uganda told a story about how her daughter had been kidnapped by the Lord's Resistance Army (LRA). One Sunday, as people in her church recited the Lord's Prayer, they realized they needed to forgive if they were to have hope and peace in the community. She addressed an audience at Eastern Mennonite University and said: 'Our gun is now prayer. It is a gun you can carry with confidence because it won't hurt anybody. We can take our gun with us even through the checkpoints because our gun is spiritual.'[100]

Conclusion

Latin America, including the Caribbean, is considered one of the most violent regions of the world. This region presents the highest rate of armed violence with 42 percent of global homicides occurring there. Gang and drug-related violence has emerged in Guatemala, El Salvador, and Honduras at an alarming rate. Young people are the most visible culprits and also the victims.[101] As churches become involved in prayer, they can become sensitive to unjust social structures and seek transformation of their social milieu.

---

[98] Davis, 'What About Justice?' p. 92.

[99] Villafañe, *Seek the Peace of the City*, p. 196.

[100] Davis, 'What About Justice?' p. 89.

[101] UNICEF, 'Fast Facts on Adolescents and Youth in Latin America and the Caribbean', www.unicef.org/media/files/Fast_facts__EN.doc (accessed December 14, 2015).

Although Latin America is deemed the heartland of the Christian world today, social exclusion and violence have created a very hostile environment for the majority of its citizens. Maras (gangs) have sprung up mostly in the poor barrios of major urban centers. Thousands of *mareros* (gang members) across Latin America employ violence to acquire justice, control, and economic benefits. The maras collect *impuesto de guerra* (war tax) from shop owners and, in some cases, from local residents. Refusal to comply has resulted in the assassination of innocent victims.

Paul Freston made an accurate observation on the presence of the church amidst the shantytowns of Latin America: 'The state is virtually absent. The Catholic Church is virtually absent. There are really only two things that function. One is organized crime. The other is the evangelical churches'.[102] A pastor in Tegucigalpa related how her church deals with gang members and addicts in the community of *Las Torres* (The Towers). Her church is producing an impact in a community that is very crime-ridden.[103] There are cases of families asking the church to celebrate funeral services for their sons who were gang members. Church members also drive their vehicles to pray around the vicinity of Las Torres. During special holidays, the church prepares meals and distributes them door-to-door. The church engages in weekly prayer meetings as they minister to people involved in illicit activities.

In Puerto Rico, Pastor Pedro Marrero is one of the organizers of a prayer movement in his city of Bayamón. The movement is called *Bayamón Postrado en Ayuno y Oración* (Bayamón Bows Down in Prayer and Fasting).[104] Pastors, church leaders, and church members meet from five to seven in the morning at the local stadium (Estadio Juan Ramón Loubriel). They plan prayer meetings for forty consecutive days and pray for different requests each day. The prayer topics include the church, the city, the government, families, education, social issues, and the economy. This prayer emphasis is also carried out in other cities throughout Puerto Rico.

---

[102] Paul Freston, 'Christianity and Conflict in Latin America', Pew Research Center, April 2006, http://www.pewforum.org/2006/04/06/christianity-and-conflict-in-latin-america/ (accessed December 14, 2015).

[103] Daisy Villatoro, interviewed by author, Tegucigalpa, Honduras, December 16, 2015.

[104] Pedro Marrero, interviewed by author, Bayamón, Puerto Rico, January 20, 2016.

Prayer holds the possibility for an increased involvement of churches in areas where violence predominates. Some churches remain isolated from ministering to those who suffer social injustice. However, praying churches yearn to see peace, justice, security, accountable leaders, and egalitarian governments.

6

IMMIGRATION

> 'My father was a wandering Aramean ...'
> —Deut. 26.5

An Overview of Immigration

Immigration is a hotly debated topic, especially with the growth of the nation's Hispanic or Latino population. Many people cross the Mexican border to escape conditions of extreme poverty caused by the forces of globalization and modernization in their nations. This chapter will discuss the meaning of immigration and the changing patterns of migration in the 20th century; the territorial expansion of the United States in the 19th century; and the significance and contributions of Hispanic Christians to the spiritual fabric of the American nation.

This first section discusses the meaning of immigration, the changing patterns of migration in the 20th century, the role of immigrants in the Bible, and the Christian diaspora in the United States.

Who are Hispanics or Latinos?

The growth of the Latino population in the U.S. has been the focus of much academic research from a sociological, economic, and political lens.[1] Controversies over immigration policy continue and comprehensive reform issues have prevailed among the presidential campaigns in the last twenty years. Latinos are recognized as a growing national minority of about fifty million people. Presidential candidates invest time in trying to capture the Latino vote. Undoubtedly, the global economic context has influenced the migration of laborers and professionals to the U.S.

It is necessary to clarify the terms Hispanic and Latino in order to understand various implications in reference to Latin Americans. The U.S. Census Bureau coined the term 'Hispanic' to describe people of Spanish-speaking origin living in the United States. It was first adopted during the Nixon administration, and it has been used in the U.S. Census since 1980.[2] The North American government uses the term Hispanic as an all-inclusive classification for the people of countries formerly ruled by Spain, who speak the Spanish language. Generally, Spanish speakers living outside the U.S. do not refer to themselves as Hispanics, but identify with their country of origin, for instance, *guatemalteco, hondureño, panameño, ecuatoriano*, etc.

In 2000, the US Census Bureau adopted the term Latino due to its growing usage. Latin Americans commonly refer to themselves as Latinoamericanos or *el pueblo Latino* [the Latin people]. Latinoamericanos share a common language and the same cultural heritage from the blending of the Amerindian dwellers and the Spanish settlers. Mexicans, Cubans, Puerto Ricans, Central Americans, and South Americans have been linked by language and the same colonial history since the 15th century.

In any case, to be Hispanic or Latino does not refer to a racial classification but to a cultural identity, heritage, language, and national

---

[1] Vanessa Cárdenas, Julie Ajinkya and Daniella Gibbs Léger, Center for American Progress, 'Progress 2050: New Ideas for a Diverse America', 2011, https://www.americanprogress.org/wp-content/uploads/issues/2011/10/pdf/progress_2050.pdf (accessed July 10, 2015).

[2] Edward Retta and Cynthia Brink, 'Latino or Hispanic: Which Term Should we Use?' 2007, http://www.crossculturecommunications.com/latino-hispanic.pdf (accessed August 10, 2015).

origin.[3] The *mestizaje* [mix, blend] of Latinos has three distinct strands in different degrees: the European, the Amerindian, and the African.[4] Latinoamericanos have a broad diversity in physical features, ranging from blonde, blue-eyed, to dark hair, and brown skin. Such mestizaje has produced a rich cultural heritage that Latinos have carried over into the U.S.[5] Due to the strong mestizaje, Hispanic/Latinos may each have their personal preferences on how to be addressed. The varying generations choose their identity as either Latino or Hispanic. These categories imply a social, political, geographical, and generational meaning.

For some the term Hispanic is a disrespectful term, of colonial usage. It was 'made in the USA' and thus imposed upon people of Spanish-speaking regions, without asking what they wanted to be called.[6] The use of the term Latino has grown in popularity through its use in magazines and social media, e.g., 'New Latino' (Fox News) and 'Latino Voices' (The Huffington Post). In Google search, the term Hispanic was more frequently used in New Mexico, District of Columbia, Florida, and Arizona. In Virginia, California, Texas, Florida, Arizona and New York, the term Latino was used more often.[7]

Jose Vasconcelos referred to Hispanics/Latinos as a *raza cósmica* [cosmic race], or a fully mixed race in which the best qualities of each race persist.[8] The National Council of la Raza (NCLR), an advocacy group, used the term Hispanic based on data generated by the government.[9] However, in recent years, they noticed the growing usage of the term Latino and now include both terms interchangeably.

The following section provides an explanation of immigration and the changing patterns of migration in the 20th century. Several

---

[3] Retta and Brink, 'Latino or Hispanic?'

[4] Eldin Villafañe, *The Liberating Spirit: Toward a Hispanic American Pentecostal Social Ethic* (Grand Rapids, MI: Williams B. Eerdmans, 1993), p. 3.

[5] Villafañe, *The Liberating Spirit*, p. 3.

[6] Juan Castillo, 'Latino? Hispanic? Chicano?' in Paul McCaffrey (ed.), *Hispanic Americans* (New York: H.W. Wilson Company, 2007), pp. 5-10.

[7] Cindy Rodriguez. CNN, 'Which Is It, Hispanic or Latino?' May 3, 2015, http://www.cnn.com/2014/05/03/living/hispanic-latino-identity/ (accessed July 10, 2015).

[8] See, Jose Vasconcelos. *La Raza Cósmica: Mision de la Raza Iberoamericana* (Barcelona: Espasa-Calpe, 1925).

[9] National Council of La Raza, 'Mission', http://www.nclr.org/index.php/about_us/ (accessed September 21, 2015).

immigrant experiences in the Bible are considered, as well as a new kind of Christian migration from the Global South.

Defining Immigration

Immigration is generally defined as the movement of people from one country to another. The word 'immigration' was used in the mid-17th century and is a term adapted from of the word 'migration', which comes from the Latin *migratus* (to move from place to place). The difference between migrants and immigrants is that immigrants tend to go through a process of legal requirements to be officially accepted into the new country. A topic of much debate since the 1950s is undocumented immigration, where people settle into a new country without the approval of the local or national governing authorities.[10]

A migrant is described as 'any person who lives temporarily or permanently in a country where he or she was not born, and has acquired some significant social ties to this country'.[11] The UN Convention on the Rights of Immigrants defines a migrant worker as a 'person who is to be engaged, is engaged, or has been engaged in a remunerated activity in a State of which he or she is not a national'.[12] Migrants make choices about moving even though these choices are at times somewhat limited. Among the categories of migrants there are refugees, displaced, or others who are forced to leave their homes. This is considered by some as involuntary migration.

Migration implies more than crossing a border. Instead, it is a life-long process that alters all aspects of the lives of individuals who settle in new regions. Receiving communities or nations are also affected by the transitioning of people in or out of their communities. The social structures of communities are transformed by new cultures, languages, and ethnic symbols. Many cities in the world have

---

[10] David J. Leonard and Carmen R. Lugo-Lugo (eds.), *Latino History and Culture: An Encyclopedia* (New York: Routledge, 2015), p. 250.

[11] UNESCO, 'International Migration and Multicultural Policies', http://www.unesco.org/most/migration/glossary_migrants.htm (accessed September 14, 2015).

[12] UNESCO, 'International Migration and Multicultural Policies'.

been and continue to be affected by the shifts in migration of different people.[13]

People migrate for economic reasons, family reunification, or as displaced persons. Migration can be authorized or undocumented. Immigration policies and categories may change from country to country. In 2013, UN global migration statistics indicated that 232 million international migrants were living abroad worldwide, equivalent to 3 percent of the world's population.[14] This makes international migration a key feature of globalization and it has become a vital issue in the U.S. and in many European nations.

Migration provides opportunities for the individuals and countries involved. For instance, migration represents access to employment, acquisition of skills and improvement of life conditions. Migration represents an impetus of growth and development for both the countries of origin and destination. At the same time, as a process it is also marked by tremendous inequalities and serious human rights abuses, for instance, forced repatriation or sexual abuse in detention centers. [15]

Immigration studies around the world have noted that family migration, defined as family reunification, has become the dominant form of migration in many countries. Family migrations are the direct result of the established labor migrants who are granted rights to sponsor their family members.[16] Some U.S. scholars have suggested that the large number of family migration has caused the explosive growth of migration in the last decades.[17]

Chain migration occurs when family members and relatives sponsor a series of family contacts. With the new waves of immigration affecting the economy, politics, culture, and demographics of Amer-

---

[13] David L. Brown and Kai A. Schafft, *Rural People and Communities in the 21ˢᵗ Century: Resilience and Transformation* (Cambridge: Polity Press, 2011), p. 139.

[14] Brown and Schafft, *Rural People and Communities*, p. 139.

[15] Human Rights Watch, 'Immigration', https://www.hrw.org/united-states/immigration (accessed August 10, 2015).

[16] Bin Yu, *Chain Migration Explained: The Power of the Immigration Multiplier* (New York; LFB Scholarly Publishing LLC, 2008), pp. 78-79.

[17] Yu, *Chain Migration Explained*, p. 78.

ican society, especially since the 1960s, there has been a surge of studies in the field of immigration studies.[18] As David Massey stated, 'Immigration tends to breed more immigration . . . and the current period of global immigration will continue'.[19]

Dynamics of the Immigration Process

Migration is more complex than a systematic process of moving people, as supposed by the push-pull economic models. Bin Yu refers to 'immigration multiplier' as an indicator that measures the direction of different ethnic groups and reproduction patterns of the migration process. Immigration studies trace the overall growth of the immigration population and ethnic groups in the United States.[20] Numerous findings have concluded that factors such as social networks, especially family units, have played a significant role in the international migration process.

Most immigrants transfer for economic reasons. People consider emigrating from places that have few job opportunities to places where jobs are most likely to be available. There are also involuntary factors that push people to move: war, famine, epidemics, natural disasters, unemployment, and a lack of economic opportunities. The greater the personal or regional danger, e.g. political persecution, the more likely the migrant will move. People are attracted to democratic countries that encourage individual choice in education, career, and place of residence.

---

[18] Yu, *Chain Migration Explained*, p. 6.
[19] David Massey, 'The Social and Economic Origins of Immigration', *The Social Contract*, 1994, http://www.thesocialcontract.com/pdf/four-three/massey.pdf, p. 185.
[20] Yu, *Chain Migration Explained*, pp. 1-5.

Figure 1
The World's Most Important Migration Routes in 2013.[21]

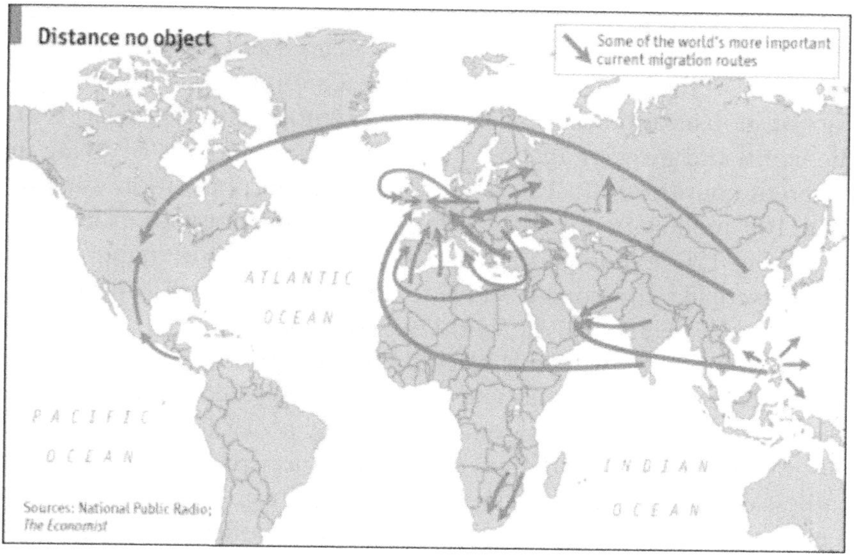

Globalization has impacted the economies of all nations, which in turn has changed the nature and volume of world migration. The flow of present-day migration occurs from the less developed to the more developed regions. There is a growing need among developed societies for manual labor and highly skilled workers. Many developed nations rely on migrant labor, partly due to declining fertility and population aging in their region.

Immigrant-receiving countries are confronted with issues such as the need to develop an immigration policy to attract immigrants with considerable human capital and to toughen security at their borders to restrict the entry of unskilled migrants and refugees. Nations from the Global South are also experiencing a loss of human capital or brain drain. 'The world community may be compelled to agree upon a universal framework under which, world migration could be regulated'.[22] International migration has become a key element of globalization and a main concern for developed countries. The process of migration is also marked by inequalities and discrimination.[23]

---

[21] Yu, *Chain Migration Explained*, p. 28.
[22] Peter S. John Li, 'World Migration in the Age of Globalization: Policy Implications and Challenges', *New Zealand Population Review* 34.1. (2008), pp. 1-22,
[23] Tanja Bastia, *Migration and Inequality* (New York: Routledge, 2013), p. 10.

Globalization has fostered the integration and interdependence of nations and increased the flow of goods, services, ideas, and people across national boundaries. Long before globalization, international migration also took place but the degree and density of world migration in the last four decades have been unprecedented. The impact of globalization causes an imbalance among different regions of the world and growing inequalities exist in the standards of living in different countries.[24] In 1980, the world migrant population was less than 100 million people. By 2005, the migrant population had increased to 190 million people. By 2013, 232 million international migrants were living abroad worldwide. Europe and North America account for 57 percent of the world migrant population.[25]

The flow of migration is affected by the spread of communication and ideas among family and friends who have already migrated.[26] Massey suggests that immigration has many social foundations, and the immigration networks allow the migration process to have an endless drive. In spite of sociopolitical factors, e.g., fluctuating wages, recession, and more restrictive immigration policies, immigration continues.[27]

After World War II, international migration emerged as a major demographic force and a global phenomenon throughout the world. In the meantime, European immigrants diminished in number.[28] On the other hand, the number of immigrants from Latin America, Africa, and Asia has steadily grown. Currently, the traditional destination countries for immigrants are Canada, the United States, the United Kingdom, France, Australia, and capital rich nations such as

---

[24] The Global Commission on International Migration, Report of the GCIM, 'Migration in an Interconnected World: New Directions for Action', 2005, https://www.unitar.org/ny/sites/unitar.org.ny/files/GCIM%20Report%20%20PDF%20of%20complete%20report.pdf (accessed February 16, 2016).

[25] United Nations Department of Economic and Social Affairs, 'Trends in International Migration', http://www.un.org/en/development/desa/population/publications/ pdf/policy/ InternationalMigrationPolicies2013/Report%20PDFs/g_Ch_1.pdf (accessed September 10, 2015).

[26] Alejandro Portes, 'Children of Immigrants: Segmented Assimilation and Its Determinants', in Alejandro Portes (ed.), *The Economic Sociology of Immigration* (New York: Russell Sage Foundation, 1995), pp. 248-280.

[27] Douglas Massey, *The Social and Economic Origins of Immigration*, http://www.thesocialcontract.com/pdf/four-three/massey.pdf (accessed August 3, 2015).

[28] Massey, *The Social and Economic Origins of Immigration*.

Saudi Arabia and United Arab Emirates. In general, countries are likely to receive immigrants from nations that are geographically close, key trading partners, political allies, or former colonies. The majority of immigrants to the United States come from Latin America, the Caribbean, or Asia. Immigrants from Africa and the Middle East have also increased.

Forced international migration has historically followed either slavery or political instability. For example, people were shipped from Africa as slaves from the 16th to the 19th centuries into the 'New World'. Wars have also pushed large-scale migration of ethnic groups in Europe and Africa. Many migrants have become refugees due to persecution, and they cannot return to their homelands. Political conditions can also operate as pull factors, especially the lure of freedom. For instance, during the Cold War (1945-1991), the Soviet government gained control of Eastern Europe, and many people in the region were drawn to the unrestricted nations in Western Europe or to North America.

In the case of Central Americans, dreadful economic conditions and increasing violence at home influence their decision to migrate north.[29] In spite of the risks involved and dangers along the way, they long for better living standards or to reunite with relatives already in the US. Hundreds of thousands of Central Americans have made the perilous journey through Mexico to reach the United States.

There are no passenger trains within Mexico, so the best option for Central Americans is to ride on cargo trains. It is the least costly, although the most inadequate, means of transportation to reach the US border. The network of Mexican train freights, known as *La Bestia* (The Beast) or *el tren de la muerte* (the Death Train) is the fastest route for migrants without visas. Migrants riding La Bestia are likely to be some of the most underprivileged in the region. Travelers get a ride on the cargo trains for a journey of 1450 miles. As they move along, they gain access to information networks or contacts in the United States who can connect them to smugglers or help fund their journey.

It is quite frequent in Hispanic churches to pray for family members who are making their journey north. There are hermanos in

---

[29] Rodrigo Dominguez Villegas, 'Central American Migrants and La Bestia: The Route, Dangers, and Government Responses', *Migration Policy Institute* (September 2014). http://www.migrationpolicy.org/article/central-american-migrants-and-la-bestia-route-dangers-and-government-responses (accessed August 3, 2015).

every congregation who can share their stories about how they crossed the border. These stories have elements of suffering and persecution. Newcomers undergo culture shock as they deal with new cultural roles and expectations. Immigrants face the dynamic of maintaining their cultural ties while still engaging in the acquisition of a new cultural identity. Many Hispanics come to get ahead in life and are willing to work sacrificially to do so.

On the long and perilous journey, Mexican families provide migrants with food, shelter, clothes, and medicine. In addition, government support groups, *Grupos Beta* (Beta Groups), help migrants as they wait several days for the next train.[30] They provide humanitarian assistance to the weary travelers along the train tracks and at the rest stops. Migrants are informed about the threats and risks they will face during the journey. Central Americans are vulnerable to attacks by *maras*, (gangs) that operate as cross-border crime systems. These networks contribute to the flourishing drug trade in the region. Robbers, kidnappers, sexual predators, and other forms of exploitation have increased within the Mexican frontiers.

Social dislocation is an important factor leading to migration. For example, capitalist economic development alters the organization of production. This causes an imbalance in working relationships and in communities. In Third World countries, where peasants engage in planting crops to provide for their subsistence, employers now hire a labor force and cut employment if it is not cost-efficient. The land that was used to produce for the local population is now dedicated to producing food and agricultural material for export to nearby growing cities or international markets. Machines take over manual labor. Farmworkers cannot compete with the more efficient commercial farmers. As agricultural production rises, manual workers are forced off their land. They migrate to the urban centers, which in Third World countries are chaotic and dangerous places.

Third World nations are plagued with urban slums, composed of marginalized people from both the rural and the urban economies.[31]

---

[30] Grupos Beta, 'Instituto Nacional de Migracion de Mexico', http://www.inm.gob.mx/index.php/page/Grupo_Beta (accessed September 9, 2015).

[31] Teresa Almeida, 'Globalization, Urbanization, and Slums', *Orange Ticker*, March 2013, https://orangeticker.wordpress.com/2013/03/03/globalization-urbanization-slums/ (accessed September 10, 2015).

Many people live in unsanitary and crowded conditions. Dwellings lack clean water, plumbing, or electricity. The masses have no legal rights to the land they occupy. 'The forces of globalization are one factor that explains the prevalence of such slum conditions in the developing world. Signs of great development such as skyscrapers exist alongside shantytowns'.[32] People are trapped into the informal networks, e.g., carrying bags at markets or airports, selling goods on the street. These labor patterns are the result of the dislocation of social life caused by economic growth, population growth, and capitalist penetration and commercialization.[33]

Latino immigrants come to the United States to get better jobs, to earn better wages, and to provide a better future for their children. Since the US remains one of the wealthiest countries in the world, it most certainly will continue to attract immigrants.[34]

Changes in Global Migration in the 20th Century

The decolonization after World War II generated an extensive migration to Europe. The European empires of Britain and France soon found that they had attained a substantial new population from their previous or remaining colonies as an unavoidable inheritance of their colonial past. Other European nations found a steady flow of people from troubled regions drawn into the labor market of their expanding economies. Germany coined the phrase 'guest worker' [*Gastarbeiter*] to describe the status of migrant laborers.[35]

Britain received migrants from Asia, Africa, and the Caribbean who mainly worked low-income jobs in hospitals, public transportation, and postal service.[36] France's migrant laborers contributed significantly to the rapid growth of the economy. In 1975, France experienced a large-scale immigration from its former colonies (Algeria, Morocco, and Tunisia) and also from southern Europe. Non-European immigrants were at the bottom of the labor market and worked

---

[32] Almeida, 'Globalization, Urbanization, and Slums'.

[33] John Isbister, *Immigration Debate: Remaking America* (West Hartford, CT: Kumarian Press, 1996), p. 101.

[34] Isbister, *Immigration Debate*, p. 92.

[35] Rita Chin, *The Guest Worker Question in Post War Germany* (Cambridge: Cambridge University Press, 2007), p. 52.

[36] Bulent Kaya, *The Changing Face of Europe: Population Flows in the 20th Century* (Strasbourg, France: Council of Europe Publishing, 2002), pp. 25, 28.

in conditions of exploitations.[37] Germany received a substantial migrant population from Turkey. About 300,000 migrants from Indonesia moved to the Netherlands. In addition, there were approximately 200,000 migrants from Suriname and 90,000 from the Dutch Antilles.[38]

Spain experienced an influx of Moroccan immigrants and later about one-half million migrants from Central and South America.[39] Italy employed non-European migrants mostly for housekeeping from the Philippines, South America, and the Cape Verdean Islands.[40] Europe also had a migration of refugees and asylum seekers from Angola, Afghanistan, Southern India, Sri Lanka, Somalia, China, Vietnam, Iraq, and Lebanon. It is estimated that the number of refugees in the world has increased from three to twelve million in the last four decades.[41]

The United States, which had been the main recipient of European migration, began to receive numbers of migrants of a new kind due to international obligations. Between World War II and the 1970s, migrants from Korea and Vietnam arrived. The U.S. has also maintained an inescapable relationship with the rest of the Americas. Central and South American workers arrived by the thousands. Interestingly, this new population did not follow the process of assimilation or 'melting pot'. The Latino immigrants did not let go of their cultural roots as the European migrants of earlier times had done.

Immigration from the Global South will continue to the Western world. Control of immigration has become an issue in European and North American politics in the last twenty years. Anti-immigration parties have developed in several European countries and immigration reform is on the agenda of U.S. presidential candidates. President Obama continually referred to the broken immigration system

---

[37] Stephen Castles, Hein de Haas, Mark Miller, *The Age of Migration: International Population Movements in the Modern World* (New York: Palgrave McMillan, 2014), p. 109.

[38] Castles, de Haas and Miller, *The Age of Migration*, p. 110.

[39] Kaya, *The Changing Face of Europe*, p. 28.

[40] Pieter C. Emmer and Leo Lucassen, 'Migration from the Colonies to Western Europe since 1800', *European History Online 2012*, eg-ego.eu/en/threads/europe-on-the-road/economic-migration/pieter-c-emmer-leo-lucassen-migration-from-the-colonies-to-western-europe-since-1800#NonEuropeanLabourImmigrants (accessed September 9, 2015).

[41] Emmer and Lucassen, 'Migration from the Colonies'.

that needs to be fixed. The developed world faces a paradox: it needs immigrants but does not want them.[42]

Migration and the Immigrant as a Biblical Motif

I was a stranger and you invited me in… (Mt. 25.35b)
In the book of Genesis, the first recorded migration is the displacement of Adam and Eve from Paradise. Migration has been a recurring reality in human history, and it has an impact on the lives of those who move to new territories. Cain also migrated (Gen. 4. 12-16) and an exodus of people followed the Babel event (Gen. 11.8-9). Abraham himself was called to leave his nation. Abraham's migration had a destiny and purpose for the people of God:
The Lord had said to Abram:

Go from your country, your people, and your father's household to the land I will show you. 'I will make you into a great nation, and I will bless you; I will make your name great, and you will be a blessing. I will bless those who bless you, and whoever curses you I will curse, and all people on earth will be blessed through you (Exod. 12.1-3).

Centuries later, when the Israelites prayed during their harvest offerings, they declared, 'My father was a wandering Aramean' (Deut. 26.5).

God initially revealed himself to the nomads, who were permanent migrants. God promised Abraham a land flowing with milk and honey, although Abraham did not get to dwell in it. Abraham became a symbol of a perennial immigrant. The New Testament refers to Abraham as a migrant. He is the archetypal believer who lives by faith (Rom. 4; Heb. 11). Believers are described as strangers in a foreign country (Heb. 11.9; 13), exiles (refugees), and foreigners (1 Pet. 1.1; 2.11).

When forced to migrate, Joseph assimilated into the Egyptian culture. The sons of Jacob later migrated to Egypt due to droughts and the need for survival. Abraham's grandson and great grandchildren were invited to live as immigrants in Egypt at a time when Joseph

---

[42] Andrew F. Walls, 'Mission and Migration: The Diaspora Factor in Christian Mission', in Chandler H. Im and Amos Yong, (eds.), *Global Diasporas and Missions* (Oxford: Regnum Books International, 2014), p. 34.

held an important position in Pharaoh's court. With time, a harsher administration reversed Egypt's stance toward the Israelites, and they were made slaves. Later, God used Moses to free the slaves. Moses became the leader of the massive departure of the twelve tribes of Israel to the Promised Land.

The Bible reveals examples of voluntary and involuntary migration. Once established as a nation, the people of Israel experienced several forced migrations to Assyria (2 Kgs. 17.5-23) and Babylon (2 Kings 25). Ezra and Nehemiah were able to lead a movement of reentry to Jerusalem. Isaiah refers to those in the Babylonian captivity as 'fugitives' (43.14). Cain, Jacob, and Moses were fugitives. Joseph was persecuted by his brothers, and he was transported as a slave. Joseph's brothers migrated to Egypt and became shepherds in the land of Goshen. Years later, they were forced into slavery. Ruth, the Moabite, was also a migrant worker in the fields of Boaz.

God gave the Israelites counsel on how to treat foreigners: When a foreigner resides among you in your land, do not mistreat them. The foreigner residing among you must be treated as your native-born. Love them as yourself, for you were foreigners in Egypt (Lev. 19.33-34).

The immigration standards that God instructed Israel to follow were one of compassion for the immigrant, based upon Israel's history that they too had been immigrants in Egypt.

The Bible points to the dual character of migration. For example, the 'Adamic' migration points to disaster, deprivation, and loss.[43] On the other hand, the 'Abrahamic' migration symbolizes an escape to a better future. Of course, the two models may intersect because in the divine plan, loss and disaster can have a redemptive purpose. Migrants bring their traditions and values from their homeland. They maintain their ethnic identity as they cope with new meanings and symbols in the host culture. In the Abrahamic migration, there is a promise of a better future while centered on the faithfulness to God. The New Testament conceives the migrant experience as the position of Christian believers in the world today: 'I urge you, [to live] as foreigners and exiles', (1 Pet. 2.11).

As a newborn, Jesus himself migrated with Mary and Joseph to Egypt (Mt 2.13). Joseph had a dream in which an angel told him to

---

[43] Walls, 'Mission and Migration', p. 21.

take Mary and Jesus and flee to Egypt because Herod was out to kill Jesus. Joseph fled to Egypt with the baby and his mother and lived in Egypt until the death of Herod, who died in 4 BCE. Jesus taught about the way to treat foreigners by recalling the words of Leviticus (19.34): 'I was a stranger and you invited me in...Truly I tell you, whatever you did for one of the least of these brothers and sisters of mine, you did for me' (Mt. 25.35-36; 45).

The spread of Christianity in the first century was deeply rooted in the Jewish migration out of the land of Palestine. After the martyrdom of Stephen, believers were persecuted, and as a result, cross-cultural missions took place (Acts 8.1-4). The people of Samaria were reached with the gospel message, and eventually so were the Greeks at Antioch. Escape from persecution and capture of prisoners played a role in the spread of the Gospel of Christ in the Roman Empire, e.g., the apostles (Acts 5.12-20); Peter (Acts 12.5); Paul and Silas (Acts 16.25).

Through the centuries, the Christian church traveled to the non-Western world. By the end of the twentieth century, Christians in Africa, Asia, and Latin America were significantly outnumbering the growth of the European and North American Christian adherents. Christianity was a European religion in 1500 but five hundred years later, it shifted into a non-western religion.[44] The collapse of the European imperial structures did not seem to have a declining influence on the movement. Instead, the Christianization of the New World accelerated after the European powers declined.

It is undeniable that Pentecostal and Charismatic churches constitute the fastest growing churches within Christianity today. Pentecostalism, which began about one hundred years ago, continues to grow in the twenty-first century. The Pentecostal experience has expanded in Asia, Africa, and Latin America. Believers from the Global South continue to promote a globalized Christianity that has not lost touch with its local context. According to Allan Anderson, the Christian church may be thankful for the expansion of Pentecostalism, for it out may mean the salvation of Christianity itself from decline and extinction in the next century.[45]

---

[44] Walls, 'Mission and Migration', p. 30.
[45] Anderson, *An Introduction to Pentecostalism*, p. 286.

The Christian Diaspora to the United States

Christianity is increasingly becoming associated with immigrants. Christian Evangelicals in North America are divided over the issue of undocumented immigrants.[46] Some Evangelicals believe immigrants do not belong in the American nation; however, the influx of immigrants, which may be God-ordained, have provided 'spiritual reinforcement' to a Christian community in the United States that had been in noticeable decline'.[47]

Generally, the Catholic Church has taken a stand that favors immigrants.[48] During his visit to the U.S., Pope Francis referred to his immigrant experience and encouraged a Latino audience in Philadelphia to keep a sense of pride and dignity of their traditions.[49] The Pope's statements about immigrants took place during a time when condescending remarks about Latino immigrants have pervaded the national dialogue. Generally, North American Evangelical and Pentecostal churches permit immigrants to use their church buildings for Spanish-speaking services although the Anglo constituency is politically conservative and generally favor tougher immigration laws.

Christianity is now mainly associated with the underprivileged and with some of the poorest nations of the world. People from the non-Western world are becoming the principal agents of Christian mission across the world. The churches that are growing in Europe are the African and the Afro-Caribbean churches. Such migrant churches are beginning to have an impact on the indigenous Western population. Immigrants from Africa, Asia or Latin America are evangelizing

---

[46] Soon-Chan Rah, *The Next Evangelicalism: Freeing the Church from Western Cultural Captivity* (Downers Grove, IL: Intervarsity Press, 2009), pp. 74-75.

[47] Rah, *The Next Evangelicalism*, 191.

[48] David A. Badillo, *Latinos and the New Immigrant Church* (Baltimore: Johns Hopkins University Press, 2006), p. 180; see also Paul Ehrlich and Anne Ehrlich, *One with Nineveh: Politics, Consumption, and the Human Future* (Washington DC: Island Press, 2004), p. 107.

[49] Manuel Roig-Franzia, Arelis Hernandez, and Pamela Constable, 'Pope Francis to Immigrants', *Washington Post*, September 26, 2015, https://www.washingtonpost.com/lifestyle/style/2015/09/26/8e1faa4c-6488-11e5-b38e-06883aacba64_story.html?utm_term=.e406e57568f1 (accessed October 19, 2015).

European residents who have been unreached by traditional Western Christianity.[50]

According to Andrew Pownall, it has been the immigrants through their church planting that slow down the process of secularization in Europe.[51] In Paris, 50 percent of the Protestant churches are immigrant churches.[52] In London, four out of the ten megachurches are African. Bart Pierce, a Pentecostal bishop in Maryland, stated, 'The African [immigrant] is the midwife for the next great move of God in America'.[53]

There is an international Christian diaspora migrating to the United States.[54] For instance, Hispanic, Asian and African congregations are proliferating in New York. The U.S.A., more than any other country in the world, is likely to remain the principal recipient of new migration, a new Christian diaspora of multicultural and multi-ethnic composition. The rich diversity of the diaspora, generally unfamiliar to the traditional, mono-cultural Anglo congregations, has the capacity to advance the Christian mission in both the Western and the non-Western worlds.

Brown-skinned missionaries continue to move across the globe. The Center for the Study of Global Christianity (CSGC) at Gordon-Conwell Theological Seminary estimated that approximately 400,000 international missionaries were sent out in 2010. At least five of the top missionary-sending countries are in the Global South, including Brazil, South Korea, India, South Africa, and the Philippines.[55] On October 24, 2015, the Asian Center for Missions (ACM) held a missionary conference with more than 900 in attendance. ACM has trained 1692 Filipino missionaries in the last twenty years. Other significant missionary senders include Mexico, China, Colombia, and

---

[50] Elena Vilaca, Enzo Pace Inger Furseth and Per Pettersson, *The Changing Soul of Europe: Religions and Migrations in Northern and Southern Europe* (Burlington, VT: Ashgate Publishing Company, 2014), p. 55.

[51] Andrew Pownall, 'The Church in a Multicultural Society', in Evert Van de Poll and Joanne Appleton (eds), *Church Planting in Europe* (Eugene, OR: Wipf and Stock, 2015), p. 158.

[52] Pownall, 'The Church in a Multicultural Society', p. 158.

[53] Pownall, 'The Church in a Multicultural Society', p. 161.

[54] Walls, 'Mission and Migration', p. 30.

[55] Melissa Steffan, 'The Surprising Countries Most Missionaries Are Sent from and Go to', July 25, 2013, http://www.christianitytoday.com/gleanings/2013/july/missionaries-countries-sent-received-csgc-gordon-conwell.html (accessed September 14, 2015).

Nigeria. Such a movement opens the possibility for the body of Christ to be built up as people of diverse ethnicities and cultures integrate Christian communities (Ephesians 4:12).

The new diaspora differs from the great European migration in considerable respects. In the old migration, ties with the original homeland faded and were often broken completely. The new diaspora seems to keep its ties with its places of origin. These growing congregations maintain international networks and plant new churches across the world. For example, Central Americans are involved in church planting in Spain, France, Italy, Alaska, and across the US.

Mission is being carried out not just by Western missionaries but by Christians from the Global South. Africans, Asians, and Latin Americans are advancing in the leadership of world missions. The context of the mission includes the legacies from the great European migration and the elements of the new Christian diaspora. Indigenous leadership in the Global South has variations with Western leadership. For example, the assertiveness of North American culture may clash with servant-oriented cultures.[56] Paul Borthwick asks, 'Are we ready to serve and let them lead?'[57] There may be paradigms shifts in which the North no longer tells the South how to do their mission, but instead those in the North listen and build relationships.

According to Allan Anderson, 'We must listen to the 'margins' by allowing ... the voiceless and often nameless to speak'.[58] This is a way to recognize the contribution of unsung Pentecostal workers in the majority world. The new blending can be a powerful means to evangelize and bring about social justice and reform in places of the world where it is most needed. For example, in the U.S.A., Latino Evangelicals are rising to make a stand in favor of immigration reform. Some of these Latinos are: Wilfredo de Jesus (Pastor New Life Covenant Church); Luis Cortés (CEO of Esperanza); Gabriel Salguero (National Latino Evangelical Coalition); and Samuel Rodriguez, President of the National Hispanic Christian Leadership Conference (NHCL);

---

[56] Paul Borthwick, *Western Christians in Global Missions* (Downers Grove, IL: Intervarsity Press, 2012), p. 120.

[57] Borthwick, *Western Christians*, p. 120.

[58] Anderson, *An Introduction to Pentecostalism*, p. 183.

The next chapter will review the history of the Spanish conquest of America and how North American expansionism gained Spanish and Mexican territory.

7

Territorial Expansionism of the United States During the 19th Century

> 'The victors of war always control the writing of history, forging and fixing exactly how events will be represented, remembered, and studied.'
>
> —Ramón Gutiérrez

Introduction

Hispanics are not strangers to the land known as the United States of America. They have lived in the U.S. longer than any other identifiable group except Native Americans. Many have long genealogies in this country. This is a significant element to consider among the average citizen and government officials in order for a more compassionate approach toward immigration. Many Mexican residents of the Southwest make their situation clear, 'We did not cross a border; the border crossed us'.[1] About three out of four Hispanics whose families have been here for centuries are English speakers, yet they also speak Spanish.[2] Other Hispanics migrated to the U.S. in the 20th century. Currently, the Latino population represents one of the youngest sectors of the nation with the average age of twenty-seven

---

[1] Josué David Cisneros, *Rhetorics of Borders, Citizenship, and Latino/a Identity* (Tuscaloosa: Alabama University Press, 2013), p. 12.

[2] Justo L. González and Carlos F. Cardoza-Orlandi, 'The Religious World of Latino/a-Hispanic Americans', in Jacob Neusner (ed.), *World Religions in America: An Introduction* (Knoxville, TN: Westminster John Knox Press, 2009), pp. 87-104.

for both males and females. 'Latinos are a force in the United States, both in the present and in the future'.[3]

The European settlers arrived in the Americas in two phases: (a) the Spanish Conquistadors dominated from the 16th through the 19th century; and (b) the English and the French arrived in the 17th century and occupied territories in the American continent. The Spaniards reached the Caribbean and occupied Cuba, Puerto Rico, and Hispaniola (present-day Haiti and Dominican Republic). These regions became their main centers of governance of the Spanish Royal Crown. Cuba remained one of Spain's most prosperous colonies. Several Spanish expeditions began in Cuba or Puerto Rico in order to explore and occupy additional territories in the Americas. For example, the Spaniard Juan Ponce de León, governor of Puerto Rico, was one of the first European settlers to arrive in Florida in 1513 (near present-day Daytona). He thought he had arrived at a large island and due to the vegetation that was in bloom; he named it *La Florida* (the flowery).[4] Hernando de Soto, governor of Cuba, landed near Tampa Bay in 1539 with 600 hundred soldiers, three Jesuit friars, and several civilians.

De Soto led several expeditions into the regions of modern-day Florida, Georgia, Alabama, and Arkansas. The Spaniards came in contact with and also engaged in confrontations with the neighboring Indian tribes.[5] Both Florida and Louisiana were closely tied to Cuba due to their geographical proximity. About 12 percent of Latinos in the U.S. trace their descent to the early settlements in Cuba and Puerto Rico.

In the 16th century, the Spanish explorers in Cuba heard of the gold mines in Mexico in the powerful Aztec empire. The Spaniards proceeded to conquer the Aztecs in 1521 and then continued to subdue the Mayas in Central America and the Incas in Peru in 1532. Mexico City was a center of Spanish governance. Mexico was connected to Europe through the Atlantic trade routes between Havana

---

[3] González and Cardoza-Orlandi, 'The Religious World', p. 90.
[4] Michael Burgan, *The Spanish Conquest of America* (New York: Infobase Publishing, 2007), p. 31.
[5] Burgan, *The Spanish Conquest*, p. 39.

and Veracruz. There were also Pacific routes between Mexico and Manila Bay in the Philippines.[6]

The Spanish Catholic Church also initiated a major effort to spread Christianity in the New World. Spanish friars established missions in the new American territories. The first mission established in the present state of Florida was St. Augustine in 1565, by Florida's first governor, Pedro Meléndez de Aviles.[7] Other missions were established near Tallahassee, Pensacola, and Southeastern Georgia.[8] There were other colonizing efforts by the French and the Portuguese.[9] Both the Spanish and French tolerated only Catholicism, and both implanted rigid systems of governing. Later on, the English settlements promoted greater religious freedom and economic opportunity.[10]

In *Las Californias*, Junipero Serra (1713-1784), baptized the indigenous dwellers and strengthened the first missions in California.[11] In Texas, Spanish Jesuits, Dominicans, and Franciscans established 26 missions. Between 1824 and 1830, the missions in Texas were officially secularized, except those in the El Paso district. The colonial buildings where missions were established are among the oldest structures and historic monuments in several states.

Sparks of Independence

By the end of the 18th century, there had been several uprisings in both Europe and the Americas. The French Revolution sparked struggles for independence in Saint Domingue, the most profitable colony in the Caribbean, which produced sugar and coffee based on

---

[6] Reilly Ridgell, *Pacific Nations and Territories* (Honolulu, HI: Bess Press, 1995), p. 39.

[7] Burgan, *The Spanish Conquest*, p. 49.

[8] Lee M. Panich and Tsim D. Schneider, 'Native Agency at the Margins of Empire', in Lee M. Panich and Tsim D. Schneider (eds.), *Indigenous Landscapes and Spanish Missions* (Tucson: University Press of Southern AZ, 2014), p. 10.

[9] James T. Fisher, *Communion of Immigrants: A History of Catholics in America* (Oxford: Oxford University Press, 2000), p. 16.

[10] *Infoplease*, s.v. 'European Exploration and Settlement', http://www.infoplease.com/encyclopedia/us/united-states-history.html (accessed October 2, 2015).

[11] Steven W. Hackel, *Junipero Serra: California's Founding Father* (New York: Hill and Wang, 2013), p. 96.

African slave labor. The ideals of the French Revolution emphasized equality, citizenship, and inalienable rights.

The inhabitants of the Spanish, English, and French colonies suffered heavy taxation, and the native inhabitants underwent abuse and discrimination. Unity between church and state prevailed. African slaves in Saint Domingue revolted, and many plantations on the island were destroyed. By 1794, France had abolished African slavery, an event that initiated slave revolts in the Spanish and English colonies. One region after another declared themselves independent states. Mexico and the Central and South American nations declared their independence in the early 19th century.

Religion in the New World was mixed with politics to create a hybrid system. With its aim of implanting the Catholic religion, Spain was also able to use the existing church governments for its own political purposes. Dominican, Franciscan, and Jesuit missionaries were often left in charge of large areas in what is now Texas, Arizona, New Mexico, and, later, California. Today, religion and politics continue to mix in Latin America.

The thirteen English colonies in North America declared their independence in 1776. By 1825, only Cuba, Puerto Rico and the Philippines remained under Spanish rule. It is interesting to note how the theme of independence was brought out in several national anthems in Latin America. For example, the Honduras anthem narrates the story of the Spanish conquest and refers to the three centuries of Spanish rule. The Honduran territory is described as a beautiful sleeping maiden discovered by the Spanish conquistador who became enchanted with her beauty. The land was filled with national resources, like wood, silver, and gold. The anthem states that the French revolution was an example to follow in seeking independence from Spain. France is referred to as 'la libre y la heróica' (the free and heroic). Honduras along with other Central American nations gained freedom from Spain in 1821.[12]

---

[12] 'Honduran National Anthem', http://lyricstranslate.com/en/honduran-national-anthem-himno-nacional-de-honduras-honduran-national-anthem.html (accessed September 10, 2015).

The Monroe Doctrine and Manifest Destiny

In the early 19th century, the U.S. consisted of sixteen states. In the course of the next one hundred years, the United States gained control over Louisiana, Texas, New Mexico, Arizona, California, Colorado, Utah, Nevada, Oregon, and Alaska. The U.S. also had overseas territories that included Cuba, Puerto Rico, the Philippines, Guam, and Hawaii.

In 1823, President James Monroe delivered his State of the Union Address in which he expressed his views regarding the intervention of European powers in the American continent.[13] It is important to consider the Monroe Doctrine expansionism to understand how the United States advanced to regions in the southwest previously occupied by Native Americans and Mexicans. Monroe's declaration was a defining moment in the foreign policy of the United States. President Monroe declared an end to European colonization in any U.S. territory and in Central and South America. In turn, Monroe indicated that the U.S. would not interfere with European territories or any conflicts among them.

The term 'Monroe Doctrine', coined in 1850, stated that further efforts by European nations to colonize or interfere with states in North or South America would be viewed as acts of aggression, requiring U.S. intervention. Monroe issued his statement at a time when nearly all Mexico, Central and South America, the traditional colonies of Spain and Portugal, were gaining independence from the Spanish and Portuguese empires. The United States, working in agreement with Great Britain, wanted to guarantee that no European power would move in.[14]

Several U.S. presidents would later invoke Monroe's declaration, for example, Ulysses S. Grant, Theodore Roosevelt, John F. Kennedy, Ronald Reagan and others.[15] Its alleged objective was to free the newly independent colonies of Latin America from European intervention and avoid situations, which could make the New World a battleground for the Old-World powers, so that the United States

---

[13] Yale Law School, 'Monroe Doctrine', http://avalon.law.yale.edu/19th_century/monroe.asp (accessed October 10, 2015).

[14] Magdalena Alagna, *The Monroe Doctrine: An End to European Colonies in America* (New York: Rosen Publishing Group, 2004), p. 18.

[15] George C. Herring, *From Colony to Superpower: U.S. Foreign Relations since 1776* (New York: Oxford University Press, 2008), pp. 4-8.

could exert its own influence undisturbed. The doctrine asserted that the New World and the Old World were to remain distinctly separate spheres of influence.[16]

Manifest Destiny

Manifest Destiny embodied a set of beliefs that the United States not only could but was destined to expand its control and bring civilization to the native dwellers, to eliminate monarchy, and implant democracy instead.[17] This attitude helped to encourage western settlement, Native American removal, and the war with Mexico. Manifest Destiny was fueled by the Protestant belief that the American nation was favored by God. This belief justified America's 'need for new lands, ports, and markets, for secure national borders, and most of all, for its God-ordained destiny to greatness'.[18]

Generally, American history overlooks the resistance and removal of native dwellers that were eradicated by the conquest. There were at least three major interventions that contributed to the expansion of U.S. territory. The U.S. acquired territories through the Louisiana Purchase, the War with Mexico, and the Spanish American War.

The Louisiana Purchase

In 1803, The U.S. paid France 15 million dollars for the Louisiana Territory belonging to France (828,000 square miles).[19] The area included New Orleans and portions of fifteen present U.S. states and two Canadian provinces. The territory consisted of segments in Arkansas, Missouri, Iowa, Oklahoma, Kansas, and Nebraska. In addition, part of Minnesota, a large portion of North Dakota and South

---

[16] Alagna, *The Monroe Doctrine*, 19.

[17] Jay Sexton, *The Monroe Doctrine: Empire and Nation in Nineteenth Century America* (New York: Hill and Wang, 2011), 98.

[18] Ramón A, Gutiérrez, 'The Latino Crucible: Its Origins in 19th Century Wars, Revolutions, and Empire', *American Latino Theme Study*, http://www.nps.gov/history/heritageinitiatives/latino/latinothemestudy/empireswars.htm (accessed September 5, 2015).

[19] The History Channel, 'Louisiana Purchase Completed', http://www.history.com/this-day-in-history/louisiana-purchase-concluded (accessed September 12, 2015).

Dakota, the northern portion of Texas, Montana, Wyoming, and Colorado. The region of Louisiana west of the Mississippi River and small portions of land within the present Canadian provinces of Alberta and Saskatchewan, were incorporated into U.S. territory.

The Louisiana Purchase occurred during the term of United States President Thomas Jefferson (1743-1826). Before the purchase was finalized, the decision faced domestic opposition as some argued that it was unconstitutional for President Jefferson to acquire the territory.[20] Jefferson agreed that the U.S. Constitution did not contain provisions for acquiring territory, but decided to proceed with the acquisition, being advised that within the strictest understanding of the Constitution, the President was allowed to negotiate treaties. The purchase included an agreement to remove the presence of France in the territory and to protect U.S. trade access to the port of New Orleans and the Mississippi River. The original thirteen colonies of the United States expanded westward and eventually extended into fifty states.

The Mexican-American War or Guerra de Estados Unidos a Mexico: 1846-1848

In 1845, James Polk made the annexation of Texas, Oregon, and California his main promise during the presidential campaign.[21] Polk used the Monroe Doctrine to legitimize America's westward expansion and enter into a territorial war with Mexico (1846-1848). The war against Mexico was fought on four fronts.[22] The Pacific Squadron seized the ports of northern California by July 1846. The Army of the West seized Santa Fe on August 1846. Part of the company proceeded to southern California and occupied Chihuahua in February 1847.

President Polk dispatched an armada to occupy Veracruz in March 1847. American troops advanced to Mexico City which they occupied

---

[20] Herring, *From Colony to Superpower*, pp. 89-90.

[21] Amy S. Greenberg, *A Wicked War: Polk, Clay, Lincoln, and the 1846 U.S. Invasion of Mexico* (New York: Vintage Books, 2012), p. 34.

[22] David G. Gutiérrez, 'An Historic Overview of Latino Migration and the Demographic Transformation of the United States', http://www.nps.gov/history/heritageinitiatives/latino/ latinothemestudy/immigration.htm (accessed October 12, 2015).

on September 15, 1847.[23] Mexican President Santa Anna and his troops fought bravely but they could not match the skilled American army.

The U.S. Peace Commissioner, Nicholas P. Trist, arrived in Mexico City to negotiate the war's end.[24] The Mexican government was devastated and not ready to negotiate the unfavorable terms of the treaty presented by Trist. On February 2, 1848, in the town of Guadalupe Hidalgo, a treaty was signed between U.S. and Mexico under extreme coercion.[25] It became known as the Treaty of Guadalupe Hidalgo. Mexico was asked to surrender more than half of its national territory which included New Mexico, Colorado, Arizona, Utah, and California. Mexico received $15 million for indemnification.

The Spanish-American War of 1898.

The territorial gains of the Spanish American War were Cuba, Puerto Rico, the Philippines, Guam, and the Wake Islands. Most of Spain's colonies in Latin America were independent by 1825. In 1805, Thomas Jefferson sent delegates to Cuba with offers to purchase the island from Spain. Cuba's proximity and strategic location appealed to the U.S. Spain attempted to diminish the Cuban independence movement on January 1, 1898. On April 11, 1898, President McKinley declared war on Spain. Simultaneously, U.S. naval forces took over Manila Bay in the Philippines and blockaded the major ports of Cuba.

On December 10, 1898, Spain and the U.S. signed the Treaty of Paris, thus ending the war. Cuba was allowed to declare its own independence in 1902. American forces occupied Puerto Rico on July 26, 1898. From October 1898 to May 1900, Puerto Rico was administered by the U.S. as a colony. Puerto Rico was declared an unincorporated territory through the Foraker Act of 1901, later replaced by the Jones Act of March 2, 1917.

---

[23] Greenberg, *A Wicked War*, p. 210.

[24] Greenberg, *A Wicked War*, p. 175.

[25] Gutiérrez, 'An Historic Overview of Latino Migration'.

Hispanic Immigration to the United States in the 20th Century

Immigration from Mexico and other parts of Latin America to the United States was slight during the early 20th century. The 1924 immigration act did not impose quotas on Western Hemisphere countries, and for years the border was unpatrolled. People would cross the river in Lower Rio Grande Valley to work in the Texan fields during the day and then return to their homes in Mexico at night, or they might reside in Texas. The United States was much more affluent than Mexico or other Latin American countries and its culture and language so different that the possibility of migrating was regarded as impractical to many Latin Americans, except in times of severe political instability.[26]

Despite their geographic proximity, the differences between the United States and Latin America have been intense. Latin America has traces of the colonial past and the customs of the early native dwellers. Spanish rule was established at least one hundred years before the founding of the British colonies in North America. In addition, elements of pre-Colombian societies remain beneath the layers of the Spanish language and the Catholic religion. Native Amerindian languages are still spoken today not only in small communities of Latin America but also among large populations in Mexico, Guatemala, Panama, Ecuador, Brazil, Peru, Bolivia, and Paraguay. Indian folkways remain in mountainous areas and in cities where residents have migrated.

Mexico and the rest of Latin America, have a culture of mestizaje (mixedness), a blend of European and indigenous people. Although the conquest destroyed the indigenous world and built a different one, there is a hidden worldview of continuity between the Amerindian societies and the contemporary Latino cultures. The Catholic Church took on much of the characteristics of indigenous religions. The *Cristos negros* [Black Christs], dark brown wooden statues of Christ on the cross, are found in village churches where candles and

---

[26] L.H. Gann and Peter J. Duignan, *The Hispanics in the United States* (Boulder, CO: Westview Press, 1986), p. 3.

flowers are brought as offerings, for example in Esquipulas, Guatemala and in Yoro, Honduras.[27]

The customs and food of religious holidays inherited from the natives are still maintained and have become a part of the Latino cultural heritage. The village dwellers pray to local saints and celebrate fiestas (holidays) that have their roots in pre-Columbian times.[28] Some traditions also include African music and dance originating from African migrants who were shipwrecked or escaped the slave trade, e.g., the *Garífunas* (Black Caribs) in the Caribbean coast of Guatemala, Belize, Honduras, and Nicaragua.

The Spanish Crown ruled in Latin America from the 16th century until the struggles for independence in the early 19th century. During the 1580s, Phillip II read his reports from viceroys in Mexico City and Lima and sent detailed directives to the Spanish colonies. In the case of Latin America, the king's orders would arrive almost a year later, but they were to be strictly followed. Such remote, authoritarian control was unproductive. The centralist imperial form of government continued even after most Latin American nations became independent in the early 1820s. The exceptions to independence were Cuba and Puerto Rico, ruled by Spain until 1898.

Dictatorial or arbitrary leadership has often been the reality in Latin American governance. Upon gaining independence, most Latin American countries declared themselves republics, modeled after the United States. Yet the history of Latin America reveals most nations have had political systems in which those in power have manipulated power and often fixed elections. Democracy and social equality have been almost nonexistent in Latin America. Nations face the challenge of consolidating democracy and gaining economic reforms to alleviate poverty and social exclusion.

Dictatorships and coups d'état have been common. For example, the Mexican government under the Party of the Institutional Revolution (PRI) from 1929 to 2000 was in many respects authoritarian. Business interests were usually entangled with government. Voluntary associations were few and labor unions had little independence. Trust in institutions, and indeed trust in anyone outside the family,

---

[27] Jesús Muñoz Tábora, *Folklor y turismo* (Tegucigalpa, Honduras: Editorial Guaymuras, 2002), p. 61.
[28] Michael Barone, *The New Americans* (Washington, DC: Regnery Publishing, 2001), p. 152.

has typically been very low. Since 1929, Mexico has been officially an anti-clerical nation.[29]

Attempts to seek democratic participation in some Latin American nations occurred through revolutionary experiences—for example, Fidel Castro in Cuba (1960s), the Sandinista revolution in Nicaragua (1980s), and Hugo Chávez and the Bolivarian revolution in Venezuela (2000). These movements featured the prominent role of one or a few charismatic individual leaders. It is not accidental that they arose in the Latin American region that has a long experience of colonial rule. These nations have been the 'backyard' of US hegemony.[30] However, these revolutions have not alleviated poverty nor improved the economy of the cited nations. The poverty of Cuba, Nicaragua, and Venezuela contradict the principles of freedom for the popular classes. The revolutionary leaders mentioned amassed great wealth while *el pueblo* (the people) suffered hunger and inequalities continue.

Currently, the economic and political instability continue in most of the Latin American nations. This may very well be the main factor for Latin migration.[31] Latino migration to the U.S. has expanded from a population of about five million in the 1950s to more than fifty million in 2012.[32]

About fifty percent of Latino immigrants to the United States are Mexican. Other Latino immigrants include Cubans, Dominicans, Salvadorians, Guatemalans, Hondurans, Colombians, Peruvians, Ecuadorians, Argentinians, and Brazilians. The explosive growth of Latinos is the result of several national, regional, and global economic factors. The history of U.S. military and foreign policy in Latin America, the inconsistent history of border enforcement, and the aspirations of Latino migrants exert an interplay of factors in the history of migration. The following section will explore the three main Hispanic populations of migrants: Mexican, Puerto Rican, and Cuban.

---

[29] Barone, *The New Americans*, p. 153.

[30] Diana Raby, 'Democracy and Revolution: Latin America and Socialism Today', Venezuelanasys.com, http://venezuelanalysis.com/analysis/2005 (accessed September 14, 2012).

[31] Ed Jackiewicz, *Placing Latin America: Contemporary Themes in Human Geography* (Lanham, MD: Rowman and Littlefield, 2012), p. 216.

[32] Gutiérrez, 'An Historic Overview of Latino Migration'.

Los Mexicanos: The Mexican Population Movement

'The U.S.–Mexican border *is una herida abierta* (it's an open wound) where the Third World grates against the First and bleeds. And before a scab forms, it hemorrhages again, the lifeblood of two worlds merging to form a third country—a border culture.'[33]

Latino migration to the U.S. is rooted in the North American territorial and economic expansion. The U.S. appropriated a large extension of land from Mexico, including the current states of California, Nevada, Utah, Arizona, New Mexico, Colorado, Texas, and parts of other states under the terms of the Treaty of Guadalupe-Hidalgo that ended the Mexican-American War (1846-1848).[34] This war helped to consolidate the position of the United States as a rising global power.[35] The war resulted in the acquisition of more than 500,000 square miles of Mexican territory by the United States extending west from the Rio Grande to the Pacific Ocean. The treaty included the naturalization granted to an estimated 100,000 former citizens of Mexico who chose to remain north of the new border at the end of the War.

Generally, migration from Mexico was hardly significant during the 19th century with an average of three thousand to five thousand people annually from 1840 to 1890. During the Gold Rush, about ten thousand Mexican miners entered California (1848-1855).[36] By the 1900s, the American West had a boost in its economic development mainly due to the expansion of the rail system in the 1870s and 1880s. Employers from the U S. began to look to Mexico for manual labor in industries such as agriculture, mining, construction, and railroad construction.[37] By 1900, about 100,000 Mexicans had migrated to the U.S. basically along the border region mainly enabled by the connection of the American and Mexican rail systems.

---

[33] Gloria E. Anzaldúa, *Borderlands/La Frontera: The New Mestiza* (San Francisco: Aunt Lute Books, 1987), p. 25.

[34] Burgan, p. 97.

[35] Cisneros, *Rhetorics of Borders*, p. 20.

[36] Ronald H. Limbaugh and Willard P. Limbaugh, *Calaveras Gold: The Impact of Mining on a Mother Lode County* (Reno: University of Nevada Press, 2004), pp. 111-112.

[37] David G. Gutiérrez, *Walls and Mirrors: Mexican Americans, Mexican Immigrants, and the Politics of Ethnicity* (Berkeley, CA: University of California Press, 1995), p. 45.

Figure 2
Territory ceded to the U.S. during the Mexican-American War (1846-1848)

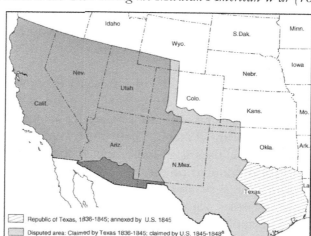

The eruption of the Mexican Revolution (1910) contributed to the influx of migration across the U.S. border and the movement continued into the 1930s.[38]

At the beginning of the Great Depression (1930s), there were at least 639,000 Mexicans and in combination with the descendants of the former citizens of Mexico living in the Southwest, the total population of Mexican heritage was 1.5 million.[39] The largest Mexican populations were concentrated in several states: Texas, California, and Arizona. A smaller number worked in industrial jobs in the metropolitan areas of Chicago and Detroit.

It was during the Great Depression that an approximate half a million Mexicans were forced to leave due to a repatriation campaign imposed by the U.S. government.[40] However, due to a labor shortage after the Second World War, lobbyist employers convinced the Federal Government to implement a bilateral labor agreement with Mexico. Mexican government officials were unwilling to enter into such

---

[38] Gann and Duignan, pp. 33-47.
[39] David G. Gutiérrez, *The Columbia History of Latinos in the United States Since 1960* (New York: Columbia University Press, 2004), p. 45.
[40] Gann and Duignan, *The Hispanics in the United States*, pp. 48-49.

a program due to the degradation inflicted upon the Mexican population during the repatriation of the 1930s. But U.S. officials guaranteed that the Mexican manual laborers would receive fair wages, decent housing, transportation to and from Mexico, and basic human rights protections. The U.S. and Mexico signed the Emergency Farm Labor Agreement in 1942.[41]

The agreement was soon called the Bracero Program, from the Spanish word *brazos* (arms), referring to labor done by people 'who work using their arms'. The selection procedures took place at Mexican and U.S. processing centers.[42] Men underwent interviews and hand inspection for calluses as an indication of their farming experience. Braceros also endured physical exams in order to assess their physical aptitude for agricultural labor. Prospective braceros were sprayed while undressed with insecticide or DDT at the U.S. reception centers. The applicants lined up and were questioned by labor contractors.[43]

During the years between 1955 and 1960, more than 400,000 Mexican laborers were employed in the U.S. By 1964, almost 5 million contracts had been issued. A smaller number of Jamaicans, Bahamians, and Hondurans were employed by the U.S. as well. For example, in the port city of New Orleans, Louisiana, Honduran migrants began to arrive and settled there during the early 1960s. New Orleans imported bananas from Central America to distribute across the U.S. and two New Orleans firms, particularly, the Standard Fruit Company and the United Fruit Company, developed close ties with Honduras. The banana companies owned plantations in the northern coast of Honduras and were able to influence the local government politics.[44] Many Honduran natives arrived through these connections and worked as dockyard laborers, while other upper-class Hondurans sent their children to study at Catholic schools.

Because of the guest worker program between U.S. and Mexico, there was also an increase in unauthorized migration across the border. Thousands of working-age male Mexicans crossed the border

---

[41] Gutiérrez, *Walls and Mirrors*, p. 134.

[42] Cisneros, *Rhetorics of Borders*, p. 57.

[43] Deborah Cohen, *Braceros: Migrant Citizens and Transnational Subjects in the Postwar United States and Mexico* (Chapel Hill, NC: University of North Carolina Press, 2011), p. 99.

[44] Anita Ganeri and Nicola Barber, *Central America* (London: Franklin Watts, 2004), p. 24.

seeking better economic opportunities. There was also a rise in the number of apprehensions of undocumented immigrants. Between 1950 and 1960 about 800,000 undocumented Mexican workers were apprehended.[45] The Bracero Program eventually reinforced the image of the Mexican as migrant stoop laborer.[46]

The increase of undocumented workers benefitted employers who sought to avoid the official regulations and high costs associated with the labor program. The number of undocumented workers, approximately 5 million, equaled the number of those issued by official contracts.[47] Potential braceros who were unable to secure contracts through formal means also sought a way to remain in the U.S. The mutual economic benefits for undocumented entries, strengthened by financially lucrative smuggling, document forging systems, and improved means of communication, greatly increased during the twenty-year period of the bracero program. The Mexican migration during the Bracero Program inevitably contributed to a steady increase in the permanent residency of the Mexican population.[48]

The Bracero Program, which brought millions of Mexican guest workers to the United States, lasted two decades (1942-1964). Scholars have begun to document this historic chapter of Mexican migration. Recent studies have proceeded to an examination of the images, stories, documents, and artifacts of the Bracero Program. Such endeavors will contribute to the understanding of the lives of migrant workers in Mexico and the United States. It will enhance awareness of immigration, agriculture, labor practices, race relations, the family, and citizenship.

Migration from the Caribbean: A Consequence of U.S. Expansion

This section will review historical events that led to migration to the mainland U.S.A. from the islands of Puerto Rico and Cuba. It is nec-

---

[45] Armando Navarro, *The Immigration Crisis: Nativism, Armed Vigilantism, and the Rise of a Countervailing Movement* (Lanham, MD: Altamira Press, 1980), p. 80.

[46] Cisneros, *Rhetorics of Borders*, p. 57.

[47] Philip Martin, *There is Nothing More Permanent than Temporary Foreign Workers* (Washington, DC: Center for Immigration Studies, 2001).

[48] Bracero, *History Archive*, http://braceroarchive.org.

essary to understand that the United States began a westward expansion in order to establish a stronger U.S. presence in several areas of the world. Mainly driven by economic reasons, the U.S. began a naval expansion that eventually led to crucial consequences for U.S. foreign policy. In order to establish diplomatic relations and commercial trade with China, the U.S. set up several ports in the Pacific region.

In 1853, the United States established relations with Japan. In addition, the U.S. The government opened consulates in several of these Pacific Islands: Fiji in 1844, Samoa in 1856, and the Marshall Islands in 1881. Hawaii became a substantial base of operations in the Pacific in order to support U.S. interests in China. Eventually, the U.S. annexed the Hawaiian territory in 1898 due to its key location as a base of operation.

The North American expansion movement sought the island of Cuba and eventually Puerto Rico. The Spanish-American War (April 25, 1898–August 12, 1898) was a conflict between Spain and the United States because of the intervention of the United States in the Cuban struggle for independence from Spain. Revolts against Spanish rule occurred in Cuba during a period called the Ten Years War (1868-1878).

President William McKinley declared war on Spain. Initially Spain sought a compromise, but finally Madrid formally declared war.[49] Although the main issue was Cuban independence, the ten-week war was fought in both the Caribbean and the Pacific. The United States naval power proved decisive as forces disembarked in Cuba against a weak Spanish garrison and epidemics of yellow fever. The U.S. along with Cuban and Filipino forces gained the surrender of Santiago de Cuba and Manila. After two obsolete Spanish squadrons sank in Santiago de Cuba and Manila Bay, Spain sought peace.

Spain surrendered its colony of the Philippines to the United States through the Treaty of Paris. Spain also surrendered control of Cuba, ceding Puerto Rico, parts of the Spanish West Indies, and the island of Guam to the United States. The Treaty of Paris signaled the defeat and collapse of the Spanish Empire in the Americas. It was

---

[49] Megan M. Gunderson, *William McKinley* (Edina, MN: ABDO Publishing Company, 2009), p. 22.

signed on December 10, 1898, and put an end to the Spanish–American War.[50]

Los Puertorriqueños

After the Spanish-American War, Puerto Rico became an 'unincorporated territory' of the United States. Puerto Ricans were governed under the Foraker Act of 1900, which established the island as a self-governing territory of the U.S. The civil government of Puerto Rico consisted of a governor appointed by the U.S., an executive council comprised of six Americans and five Puerto Ricans, and an integrated court system.

There was a growing independence movement and the U.S. responded by passing the Puerto Rican Federal Relations Act signed by President Woodrow Wilson on March 2, 1917. This act granted U.S. citizenship to the people of Puerto Rico. In addition, it created the Senate of Puerto Rico, recognized a bill of rights, and approved the election of a *Comisionado Electo de Puerto Rico* (Resident Commissioner), previously appointed by the U.S. President.[51]

The Jones Act of Puerto Rico (1917) opened the door to migration from the island to the mainland U.S. In the case of Balzac v. Porto Rico (1922), the Supreme Court ruled that although Puerto Ricans on the island did not have the same constitutional standing as ordinary U.S. citizens, it also ruled that the granting of citizenship allowed Puerto Ricans to migrate anywhere within U.S. jurisdiction. Furthermore, the Court ruled that once in U.S. territory, Puerto Ricans were by law 'to enjoy every right of any other citizen of the U.S., civic, social, and political'.[52]

After the Balzac ruling, but more so after the Great Depression (1929-1941), increasing numbers of Puerto Ricans began to migrate, mainly to New York City. The economic conditions on the island did not provide sufficient employment for the growing population. The

---

[50] U.S. Department of State, Office of the Historian, 'United States Maritime Expansion across the Pacific During the 19th Century: 1830-1860', https://history.state.gov/milestones/1830-1860/pacific-expansion (accessed July 28, 2015).

[51] James Climent and John Radzillowski, *American Immigration: An Encyclopedia of Political, Social, and Cultural Change* (New York: Routledge, 2015), p. 229.

[52] Gutiérrez, *The Columbia History of Latinos,* p. 14.

Puerto Rican economy depended heavily on sugar cane plantations, but the sugar industry demanded intensive labor only for six months.

With high unemployment, the first wave of Puerto Rican migrants left the island searching for jobs or recruitment in the agricultural industry. Between 1930 and 1940, the Puerto Rican population in mainland U.S.A. grew from 53,000 to 70,000.[53] About 90 percent of the Puerto Rican migrants settled in New York City and worked in low–paying jobs, such as clothing manufacturing and service sectors. Puerto Rican entrepreneurship began to service the needs of the region's rapidly expanding population.

After World War II, Puerto Rican migration accelerated due to chronic unemployment on the island. The Puerto Rican population in the U.S.A. escalated from 70,000 in 1940 to more than 300,000 in 1950. By 1960, the Puerto Rican population had reached 888,000. Generally, the large communities of puertorriqueños have lived in marginalized or ghettoized areas in large cities due to language, culture, and race.

The U.S. government began Operation Bootstrap (*Manos a la Obra*, meaning 'Hands that Labor') which invested millions of dollars into the Puerto Rican economy.[54] Predicting that the Puerto Rican economy could not subsist on an agrarian economy, the government encouraged the establishment of factories. The U.S. government appealed to North American companies to invest in Puerto Rico by providing lower labor costs than those on the mainland. It also eliminated import duties and allowed profits that could transfer to the mainland free from federal taxes.

As a result, Puerto Rico's economy shifted from an agricultural one to manufacturing and tourism. The manufacturing of tobacco, leather, and clothing changed to industries such as, pharmaceuticals, chemicals, machinery, and electronics. However, by 1960, the growing unemployment hindered Operation Bootstrap. Chronic unemployment and the economically driven migration have been the harsh reality in the lives of many Puerto Ricans.[55]

---

[53] John Lipski, *Varieties of Spanish in the United States* (Washington, DC: Georgetown University Press, 2008), p. 121.

[54] Lipski, *Varieties of Spanish in the United States*, p. 119.

[55] Center for Puerto Rican Studies, 'Manos a la Obra: The Story of Operation Bootstrap', Hunter College, The City University of New York, http://centropr.hunter.cuny.edu/library/film-and-video-list/manos-la-obra-story-operation-bootstrap (accessed July 28, 2015).

The Puerto Rican population is currently over 5 million in the U.S., and they represent 1.5 percent of the total population. Puerto Ricans compose 9 percent of the Latino population and are the second largest Hispanic group in the nation. New York City continues to be home to the largest Puerto Rican community, and Philadelphia has the second largest one. The majority of Puerto Ricans reside in the northeastern states and in Florida. There are also a significant number of Puerto Ricans in Chicago.

The Puerto Rican community has organized itself to represent its interests in stateside political institutions. In New York City, Puerto Ricans first began running for public office in the 1920s.[56] In 1937, they elected their first government representative, Oscar Garcia Rivera, to the New York State Assembly. In Massachusetts, Nelson Merced became the first Hispanic elected to the Massachusetts House of representatives.[57]

There are four Puerto Rican members of the House of Representatives: Luis Gutierrez of Illinois (Democrat), Jose Enrique Serrano of New York (Democrat), Nydia Velasquez of New York (Democrat), and Raul Labrador of Idaho (Republican). Puerto Ricans have been elected as mayors in three major cities: Miami, Hartford, and Camden. Luis A. Quintana was the first Latino mayor of Newark, New Jersey, in 2013. Puerto Ricans in the U.S. have exercised their influence through protests, campaign contributions, lobbying, and voting. Puerto Ricans have had relative success in electing their own to significant public offices throughout the United States.

Los Cubanos

In 1959, Fidel Castro and Ernesto 'Che' Guevara led an insurgency in Cuba to overthrow the regime of the dictator Fulgencio Batista (1952-1959). Although Castro's political intentions remained unclear in the first months of his rule, by 1960 the revolutionary junta made it clear that Cuba would be ruled by Marxist principles. Soon after, a

---

[56] James Jennings and Monte Rivera, *Puerto Rican Politics in Urban America* (Westport, CT: Greenwood Press, 1984), p. 18.

[57] Susan Diesenhouse, 'From Migrant to State House in Massachusetts', *The New York Times*, November 27, 1988, http://www.nytimes.com/1988/11/27/us/from-migrant-to-state-house-in-massachusetts.html (accessed September 23, 2015).

series of political purges and trials began. Expropriations and the nationalization of key industries occurred. The unsuccessful attempt by Cuban exiles at the Bay of Pigs in 1961 led to a mass emigration of disappointed Cubans to the U.S. This first wave of Cuban immigration was known as the golden exile due to the level of education, wealth, and positive reception.[58]

A second wave of Cuban immigration occurred in 1965 when the Castro regime allowed Cubans who wanted to reunite with family members to leave for the U.S. Initially caught by surprise by the Cuban's government decision, U.S. immigration officials provided a mechanism for the orderly entry of nearly 300,000 additional Cuban refugees. As a result, the Cuban population of the U.S. reached 665,043 by 1977.[59] During the 1980s a third wave of immigration from Cuba occurred. Referred to as the Mariel boatlift (April to October 1980), there were 125,000 Cubans who arrived in Florida. Fidel Castro permitted any person who wanted to leave Cuba free access to depart from the port of Mariel. Hundreds of small craft departed Miami and sailed to Mariel, where they loaded up with refugees, in most cases more passengers than the craft was designed to carry safely. Such an event was a major operation for the U.S. Coast Guard that provided search and rescue assistance to vessels bound for the United States. By 2004, the total population of Cuban immigrants in the U.S. reached 1.5 million.[60]

These three major waves after 1960 provided the foundations for the modern Cuban-American population, which currently stands at nearly 1.8 million or 3.5 percent of the Latino population of the United States.[61] The majority of Cubans, nearly seventy percent, have tended to settle in South Florida but over time, Cuban Americans have become more geographically dispersed. Although the different

[58] Rebecca M. Callahan and Patricia Gándara, *The Bilingual Advantage: Language, Literacy and the US Labor Market* (Bristol, UK: Multilingual Matters, 2014), p. 55.

[59] Maria Cristina Garcia, 'Exiles, Immigrants, and Transnationals: The Cuban Communities of the United States', in David Gregory Gutierrez (ed), *The Columbian History of Latinos in the United States Since 1960* (New York: Columbia University Press, 2004), pp. 146-86.

[60] Pew Hispanic Center, 'Cubans in the United States, 2006', http://www.pewhispanic.org/files/factsheets/23.pdf (accessed September 23, 2015).

[61] Ted Hanken and Dimas Castellanos, 'Migration and Diaspora', in Ted Hanken, Miriam Celaya, and Dimas Castellanos (eds.), *Cuba*, (Santa Barbara, CA: ABC-Clio, 2013), pp. 242-259.

socioeconomic profiles of the three distinct waves of Cuban migration created a heterogeneous population, overall, the Cuban American population has the highest level of socioeconomic attainment of the three major Latino subpopulations in the United States that is, Mexicans, Puerto Ricans, and Salvadorians.[62]

In 2008, twenty-five percent of Cubans over age twenty-five had obtained at least a college degree compared to 12.9 percent of the overall Latino population in the U.S. The median income per persons over 16 was $26,478 compared to $21,488 for all Latinos. About 13 percent of Cubans live below the poverty line, compared to 21 percent of the Latino population and 13 percent of the general U.S. population.[63]

Los Centro Americanos

The political turmoil in Central America during the 1970s and 1980s, contributed to significant migration to the U.S. from the countries of El Salvador, Guatemala, Honduras, Nicaragua, Costa Rica, and Panama. About 10% of Central American immigrants have been approved for temporary residence as refugees.[64] During the 1960s, migrants of these countries had established small communities in the U.S. However, civil wars and national disasters caused thousands of Central Americans to flee the violence of their homelands. In January 1976, Guatemala experienced a devastating earthquake. Besides the deepening debt crisis, a damaging earthquake occurred in Mexico in 1985. Hurricane Mitch ravaged Honduras in 1998.

Central Americans faced political events such as civil wars and pro-communist revolutions in the 70s and 80s.[65] The Sandinista Na-

---

[62] Mark Hugo Lopez and Daniel Dockterman, Pew Research Center, 'U.S. Hispanic Population by Country of Origin', May 26, 2011, http://www.pewhispanic.org/2011/05/26/us-hispanic-country-of-origin-counts-for-nation-top-30-metropolitan-areas/ (accessed July 28, 2015).

[63] Mark Hugo Lopes, Ana Gonzalez-Barrera and Danielle Cuddington, Pew Research Center, 'Diverse Origins: The Nation's 14 largest Hispanic-Origin Groups', June 19, 2013, http://www.pewhispanic.org/2013/06/19/diverse-origins-the-nations-14-largest-hispanic-origin-groups/ (accessed July 28, 2015).

[64] Callahan and Gándara, *The Bilingual Advantage*, p. 58.

[65] Marc Becker, 'Dictatorship in Latin America', http://science.jrank.org/pages/7630/Dictatorship-in-Latin-America.html (accessed September 3, 2015).

tional Liberation Front overthrew the government of Anastasio Somoza in Nicaragua (1979). Clashes between a military government in El Salvador and the Faribundo Marti Liberation Front (left-wing militias), caused a bloody civil war for about two decades (1970 to 1990). In Guatemala a civil war raged since the 1970s and ended in 1996 by the signing of a peace treaty between the Guatemalan government and the weakened guerilla forces.

In order to enhance military security in the region, a North American military base, Palmerola, was established in the central region of Honduras in 1982.[66] Roberto Suazo Cordova, the President of Honduras (1980-1984) referred to Honduras as an 'oasis of peace'. Honduras became a key base for the Reagan administration's response to the crisis in Central America. The nation hosted bases for the Nicaraguan Contras along the Nicaraguan border. U.S. troops held large military exercises in Honduras during the 1980s, and trained thousands of Salvadorians. In addition, the military established the Battalion 3-16 (1984-1986) in order to prevent the spread of civil wars from the neighboring countries. There were operations that involved the disappearances of leftists.

Latin America became a battlefield of the Cold War in the late 20th century. Military dictatorships in the 1960s and 1970s overthrew some of the democratically elected governments in Argentina, Brazil, Chile, Uruguay, and Paraguay.[67] To curtail opposition, these governments detained thousands of political prisoners, many of whom were tortured or killed. Throughout the 1980s and 1990s, Peru faced a guerilla insurgence of the *Sendero Luminoso* (Shining Path). Argentina and Britain fought a territorial dispute over the Falkland Islands in 1982. Colombia endured internal conflicts, which started in 1964 with the creation of Marxist guerilla groups, *Fuerzas Armadas Revolucionarias de Colombia* (Revolutionary Armed Forces of Colombia).[68] In order to fund their operations, powerful drug lords made use of these leftist groups to smuggle narcotics out of Colombia. The nation witnessed kidnapping, bombings, land mines, and assassinations against both government officials and citizens.

---

[66] Military Bases, 'Soto Cano Air Base', http://www.militarybases.us/airforce/soto-cano-air-base (accessed October 19, 2015).

[67] Jennifer Browdy de Hernandez, *Women Writing Resistance* (Cambridge, MA: South End Press, 2005), p. 3.

[68] Gus Martin, *Understanding Terrorism* (Thousand Oaks, CA: Sage, 2016), p. 182.

South America has experienced the election of several leftist and center-left administrations in most countries of the area, except Colombia. The political and economic restructuring of South America after the Bolivarian Revolution headed by Hugo Chávez (1998-2013), led to a situation in which highly educated and highly skilled individuals from Venezuela, Argentina, Chile, Colombia, Peru, Ecuador, and Brazil migrated to the U.S. seeking economic opportunities not available to them in their countries.[69]

Caught between authoritarian regimes (often overtly or covertly supported by elements of the U.S. government) and left-wing insurgencies, Central American migrants became a significant part of the U.S. Latino population. By 1990, they reached a population of more than one million. Central Americans have clustered in different areas with Salvadorians prominent in Los Angeles, Houston, San Francisco, New York, and Washington, D.C. Guatemalans settled in California, Texas, New Jersey, and New York. Hondurans relocated to New Orleans, Miami, and Houston. Nicaraguans established themselves in Miami. In the last ten years, there has been a growing population of Central Americans in the southern states: Georgia, North and South Carolina, Tennessee, and Virginia.[70]

Although most of the Central American nations have had democratic presidential elections since the 1980s, the grim economic conditions and civil unrest have contributed to the continuing growth of this population.[71] Practically any political turmoil in Latin America produced a wave of immigrants to the Hispanic milieu of South Florida.[72] Central America has been ravaged by extended civil-and guerilla wars, the maras (violent gangs), and drug trafficking in the region. The sociopolitical conditions of Latin American nations have stimulated the explosive growth of the Latino population and the rise of undocumented workers.

---

[69] Ida Zerpa, *Silent Invasion of the U.S.A.* (Buenos Aires, Argentina: Libros en Red, 2006), pp. 70-71.

[70] Jamie Winders, 'Re-Placing Southern Geographies: The Role of Latino Migration Transforming the South, Its Identities, and Its Study', *Southeastern Geographer* 5.2 (2011), pp. 342-358.

[71] Norma Stoltz Chinchilla and Nora Hamilton, 'Central American Immigrants: Diverse Populations, Changing Communities', in David G. Gutierrez (ed.), *The Columbia History of Latinos Since 1960* (New York: Columbia University Press, 2004), pp. 186-228.

[72] Joan Moore and Henry Pachon, *Hispanics in the United States* (Englewood Cliffs, NJ: Prentice Hall, 1985), p. 36.

Deportations and enforced departures of undocumented immigrants have risen sharply in the U.S. Heightened security measures and the recession have contributed to the decline of unauthorized migration in recent years. During President Obama's administration, about two million immigrants were deported, more than in any other previous administration.

In 2005, the total Hispanic population was 42 million or 14 percent of the total U.S. population. Since the flow of Latinos has diminished since 2008, it is estimated that by 2020, the growth in the Hispanic population in the U.S.A. will reach 20 percent; by 2030, it will reach 22 percent; and by 2040, it will reach 24 percent of the population; although the Pew Research Center predicts that by 2050, Latinos will be 128 million or 29 percent of the population.[73]

Issues of Immigration: From Conquistadors to Transnational Capital

Migration is a growing dilemma and an inevitable consequence of globalization. The public discourse of several political figures dehumanizes immigrants. Lawmakers and church leaders must remember that immigrants are created in the image of God. Brown-skin immigrants suffer the struggles of cultural adaptation while they are susceptible to intimidation by the media. They are 'constantly scrutinized by the demeaning gaze of the many native citizens'.[74] Every political campaign, especially after September 11, has been saturated by violent discourse that dehumanizes immigrants. Immigrants are perceived as sources of 'cultural contaminations'.[75]

Sadly, I have never heard the Anglo-Saxon churches offer prayers for the well-being of immigrants or for changes in immigration laws. Yes, churches offer their spaces, but public affirmation of immigrants is never heard. In the month of November 2015, two buses were burned at a Hispanic church in Norfolk, Virginia, and a pastor in Monticello, New York, received threats that his building would be

---

[73] Jeffrey Passel and D'Vera Cohn, Pew Research Center, 'US Population Projections: 2005-2050', February 2008, http://www.pewhispanic.org/2008/02/11/us-population-projections-2005-2050/ (accessed September 3, 2015).

[74] Luis Rivera-Pagán, 'Xenophilia or Xenophobia: Toward a Theology of Migration', in Elaine Padilla and Peter Phan (eds.), *Contemporary Issues of Migration and Theology* (New York: Palgrave MacMillan, 2013), pp. 31-52.

[75] Rivera-Pagán, 'Xenophilia or Xenophobia', p. 43.

set on fire. Violent discourse has instilled fear and aggressive behavior among the Anglo population.

In our era of globalization, God has allowed waves of migrants to reach the U.S. with a beneficial purpose. Exchanges with people of different cultural heritages can be a source of revitalization and an expansion of cultural understanding and appreciation. Hispanic roots were planted in U.S. soil before the English settlers arrived. Lack of knowledge makes people misunderstand and be critical of other human beings.

Compassion, hospitality, and care for the vulnerable should begin among Christian churches. More prayers and affirmations of immigrants should be expressed in Christian public meetings. Migration will continue to be a growing international crisis. The powerful American nation has made use of cheap labor, and Latin American nations have been consumers of their capitalist industries.

'Globalization implies not only the transfer of financial resources, products, and trade, but also the worldwide relocation of people, the transnational migration of labor, the movement of human beings'.[76] Globalization will continue to make daily subsistence more difficult for people in Latin America. Industrial agriculture seizes land from subsistence farmers and indigenous people. Trade agreements shatter local economies, and 'manufacturing migrates around the world in search of the most exploitable workforces'.[77]

---

[76] Rivera-Pagán, 'Xenophilia or Xenophobia', p. 43.

[77] Clifton Ross and Marcy Rein, 'Introduction', in Clifton Ross and Marcy Rein (eds.), *Until the Rulers Obey: Voices from Latin American Social Movements* (Oakland, CA: PM Press, 2014), p. xxvi.

8

LATINO CONTRIBUTIONS TO THE SPIRITUAL FABRIC OF AMERICA

'How can we sing the songs of the Lord while in a foreign land?'
—Psalm 137.4

Today's immigrants from Latin America ... keep parishes open and even thriving.

—John Castleberry
President, Northwest University

Immigrant Hispanic Religiosity

Undoubtedly, churches and other faith-based organizations have been safe havens for Hispanic immigrants. They continue to play a critical role in the adaptation and assimilation for Hispanics into North American society. In addition, some schools have also played a positive role to support students by providing academic and emotional support to immigrant students. In the years 2012 to 2014, the number of deported parents reached 205,000.[1] Children who have experienced a separation from their parents need counseling. Immigrant community organizations and leaders have provided a network to address concerns that affect the community and to recommend

---

[1] 'The Great Expulsion', *The Economist,* February 2014, http://www.economist.com/news/briefing/21595892-barack-obama-has-presided-over-one-largest-peacetime-outflows-people-americas (accessed October 10, 2015).

plans in case of need.[2] In Hispanic church gatherings, it is common to pray for families that have been separated due to deportation.

The Latino migration has brought a new element into the way that religion is practiced in the United States. Hispanics compose about one third of the membership in the Catholic Church and the church has responded by making sure that new priests are bilingual. Nevertheless, despite these efforts, many Hispanics have joined Evangelical, Pentecostal, or other Protestant denominations.[3] Protestant, Evangelical, and Pentecostal churches in North America are learning 'to speak Spanish' and to cross over into the Latino culture.[4] These churches offer an appealing message to immigrant communities that are *luchando* (struggling) to get ahead in their new spaces.

Latino Pentecostals and Evangelicals are significantly reshaping religion in America through their religious zeal. Pastor Wilfredo de Jesus, at the New Life Covenant in Chicago, believes Latinos are changing America in Christ's name. He concludes that Latinos 'are saving American Christianity ... No doubt, every denomination would have decreased in membership if it had not been for Hispanic growth'.[5]

In regard to religious affiliation, Mexicans are more likely to be Catholic; Central Americans are most likely to be former Catholics; and Hispanics of Caribbean are most likely to have never been Catholic. Hispanic immigrants are uncomfortable with what they perceive as the impersonality of North American churches in comparison to the churches in their home countries. Hispanics indicated that they sense a lack of community and a lack of emotion during the liturgy in the Anglo congregations.[6]

---

[2] Sylvia Romero and Melissa Romero Williams, 'The Impact of Immigration Legislation on Latino Families', *Advances in Social Work* 14.1 (2013), p. 239.

[3] AARP, 'Keeping the Faith: Spirituality and Religion among Hispanics Age 40+', http://assets.aarp.org/rgcenter/general/hispanic_spirituality_1.pdf (accessed August 20, 2015).

[4] Eduardo Porter, 'Protestant Faiths Are Learning to Speak Languages of Latinos', *Wall Street Journal*, July 2, 2002, www.wsj.com/articles/SB102555851 1670173280 (accessed September 8, 2015).

[5] Tony Castro, 'How Hispanics are Changing Religion in the US', *Latino Voices*, April 18, 2015, http://www.huffingtonpost.com/2014/04/18/hispanics-changing-religion-_n_5173258.html (accessed September 30, 2015).

[6] Castro, 'How Hispanics are Changing Religion'.

About fifty percent of Catholics who leave the Church join an Evangelical or Pentecostal church. There was a time when being Hispanic meant being Roman Catholic, but that reality has changed. A survey by the Pew Charitable Trusts found that 74 percent of Latino immigrants are Catholic, but by the third generation, the number drops to 59 percent.[7] The Catholic Church has a clerical shortage with one Spanish-speaking priest for every 10,000 Catholics. Furthermore, the training of a priest can be as long as twelve years. On the other hand, Protestant or Pentecostal churches have shorter training periods for their pastors.

People are attracted to Evangelical/Pentecostal churches because their environment satisfies their spiritual, emotional, social, cultural, and in some cases, their financial needs. The reasons for being involved in a Pentecostal church include emphasis on the Bible, greater spiritual fulfillment, inspiring or enthusiastic sermons, genuine emotion in worship services, and a sense of being welcomed and recognized as an individual. Evangelical converts find new avenues in their personal growth, knowledge from reading the Bible, and a sense of community. The sense of belonging to a community is important to Hispanics and the church plays a strong role in cultivating community.[8]

Hispanics have brought their culture and their religious beliefs to America.[9] According to Hernandez founder of the U.S.-México Studies at the University of Texas, immigrants seek the church for words of encouragement, a warm embrace, and a place to continue seeking God.[10] Newly arrived Hispanics look for churches where they can find social acceptance and assistance in their new places of residence. Hispanic churches are characterized by a demonstrative style of worship and sometimes longer services. In comparison, the Catholic rituals may exhibit a cold and impersonal approach to God. Immigrants find a nurturing environment that offers guidance and refuge. Although Hispanics have slight cultural variations, language is a bond that unites them all.

---

[7] Castro, 'How Hispanics are Changing Religion'.
[8] AARP, 'Keeping the Faith'.
[9] Richard Hoffman, 'A Wave of Spirituality: How our Faith is Transforming America'. *Hispanic* 18.2 (January 2006), pp. 44-45.
[10] Hoffman, 'A Wave of Spirituality', p. 45.

Jesse Miranda, leader of the National Evangelical Hispanic Association, indicated that 'Latinos bring a more practical, experiential faith with them, less doctrinal and intellectual, moving away from the European Christian emphasis on private religiosity towards a more public and communal expression of faith'.[11] Hispanics bring their moral and social values to America that leads eventually to a wave of spirituality in the nation. In the same manner, David Lizarraga, President of the East Los Angeles Community Union, believes that Latinos have a deep sense of faith and belief in God: 'a strong sense that we are here in this world to make a difference. The pioneering spirit and sense of faith is why people go north'.[12]

Pentecostal churches are generally perceived as churches of the poor or marginalized. In many cities, there are storefront churches that are sometimes close in proximity to one another. Pentecostals know how to take the church to the people and earn the love and respect of struggling immigrants. The message in Pentecostal churches is that God is alive and that he is everywhere. Spiritual gifts are manifested freely, and people genuinely commit themselves to spreading the gospel. Some churches distribute food and clothing. Pastors or church leaders take people to medical examinations or to lawyers and serve as interpreters for them.

The Latino community has been in the shadows, hidden from the eyes of mainstream society. Most North Americans have a blurred image of Latinos, and they are uncertain about what to call them.[13] Latinos? Hispanos? Chicanos? Boricuas? However, Latino Pentecostals do not fit into a traditional racial, cultural, or political category. For liberals, Latino Pentecostals must be progressive since non-white urban poor people attend their churches. On the other hand, since Latinos are pro-family and anti-abortion, conservatives assume they embrace traditional political views.

For Gallegos, Latino Pentecostals are not quite as passive as some people may assume.[14] They challenge assumptions and blur the lines between liberal and conservative. For example, they may support tougher laws to combat gangs in their neighborhoods but welcome

---

[11] Hoffman, 'A Wave of Spirituality', p. 46.
[12] Hoffman, 'A Wave of Spirituality', p. 51.
[13] Aaron Gallegos McCarroll, 'Where the Spirit Leads', *Sojourners Magazine* 37.4 (April 2008), pp. 12-15.
[14] Gallegos, 'Where the Spirit Leads', p. 14.

gang members into their churches without denigrating them. They are redefining the political, theological, and social categories of previous generations by striving for justice in the Holy Spirit and the liberation of the oppressed.

Latinos gave George Bush 64 percent support in the 2004 elections. However, Latinos have experienced a lack of support in the immigration debate, even by the Obama administration. The Republican and Democratic presidential candidates are aware that Latinos are closely watching those who will act on an honorable plan for immigration reform.

For Gabriel Salguero, the Latino Evangelical church ought to be a major contributor in affecting public opinion on the issues of immigration in the US. The church has a pastoral and prophetic role to play regarding values and principles of national identity. Faith leaders should promote immigration policies that allow an earned path to citizenship.[15]

Latin American immigration and the status of millions of undocumented Latino immigrants in the U.S. will certainly continue to be one of the most complicated and difficult issues in the American political landscape. On one hand, growing international market competition makes it likely that the U.S. economy will continue to depend heavily on the labor of foreigners. It is almost certain that Latin American immigrants of all statuses will continue to play a major role in the economic development of the nation.

According to Juana Bordas, Latinos will be the majority population entering the workforce in 2017.[16] In 1980, immigrants made up 7 percent of the workforce.[17] There was an increase to 12 percent in 1990, and 16 percent in 2000.[18] Immigrants work in construction as roofers, painters, and plasters. Immigrants are employed as packaging workers, housekeepers, cooks, dishwashers, laundry workers, and textile workers. They are also involved in traditional farming and in the

---

[15] Gabriel Salguero, 'Immigration, Integration, and National Identity: Making the Case for a Hispanic Evangelical Contribution', *The Review of Faith and International Affairs* 9.1 (2011).

[16] Juana Bordas, *The Power of Latino Leadership* (San Francisco: Berrett-Koehler, 2013), p. 1.

[17] William A.V. Clark, *Immigrants and the American Dream* (New York: The Guilford Press, 2003), p. 99.

[18] Clark, *Immigrants and the American Dream*, p. 89.

meat and fish processing industry. Indeed, the Latino workforce is undeniable.

Violent Opposition to Hispanic Immigrants

President John F. Kennedy observed, 'Everywhere immigrants have enriched and strengthened the fabric of American life'. However, Republican congressman from Texas, Blake Farenthold, lamented, 'I am troubled by the demonization of immigrants, legal or illegal, in our party. We've got a country that was built on immigrants and immigration, and we've kind of lost sight of that.'

The increasing presence of the Latino population has fanned the flames of dissent and nationalism among those who are angry about the expansion of undocumented population. Fears about the aging of the 'white' citizen population and the rapid growth of a comparably youthful non-white Latino population have tended to increase resentment against the foreign-born Hispanics and their children. In 2012, the median age of non-Hispanic white person was 37, compared to a median age of 27 for Latinos.[19] There is a widespread perception that the federal government and lawmakers in both political parties have not seriously enforced the existing immigration laws which adds to the frustration of people who hold an anti-immigrant stance.

The immigration debate was clearly altered after the terrorist attacks of September 11, 2001.[20] George W. Bush had defined immigration reform as one of his national priorities while still a presidential candidate in 1999. He aimed for the Latino vote in California, New Mexico, Arizona, Texas, Florida, and New York. On January 25, 2001, George W. Bush announced that his first trip out of the country would be to Mexico to meet with the Mexican President, Vicente Fox, to discuss issues of immigration of documented and undocumented Mexican workers into the United States. However, the September 11 attacks on the World Trade Center in New York City and

---

[19] Pew Research Center, 'Median Age for Hispanics', http://www.pewresearch.org/daily-number/median-age-for-hispanics-is-lower-than-median-age-for-total-u-s-population/ (accessed September 25, 2015).

[20] Edilberto Roman, *Those Dammed Immigrants: America's Hysteria over Undocumented Immigrants* (New York: New York University Press, 2013), p. 123.

the Pentagon in Washington, D.C. immediately altered the immigration reform debate in the United States.

Border security became the principal issue for the Bush administration and for the American public. Latinos or brown-skin immigrants became the scapegoat of 9/11.[21] In the months that followed, a number of measures were implemented to conduct background checks on foreign students and scientists working in defense industries. Immigrants with little probable cause were detained and deported.

Before the terrorist attack, there were expectations of a comprehensive immigration reform. However, immigrant laws focused on harsher enforcement measures. John McCain co-sponsored a reform bill with Ted Kennedy in 2005 that incorporated legalization, guest worker programs, and border enforcement mechanisms. The Secure America and Orderly Immigration Act (McCain-Kennedy Bill) was never voted on in the Senate. The top priority became the fight against terrorism and the government focused on protecting the nation's borders as a counter-offense against terrorists.[22]

In 2002, Congress passed the Homeland Security Act, legislation created to keep U.S. territory safe from future terrorist attacks. Federal funding for the Department of Homeland Security cost the U.S. $589 billion in one decade (2001-2011). Immigration enforcement was intensified, and deportations rose from 200,000 people in 2001 to almost 400,000 in 2011. States, towns, and cities enacted a range of measures designed to pressure undocumented persons to leave their jurisdictions. For example, in 2007, Mayor Lou Barletta of Hazleton, Pennsylvania, vowed to make the city 'one of the toughest places in the United States' for illegal immigrants.[23]

Other local initiatives were modeled on Hazleton's ordinances; however, these were never put in effect because of the legal challenges. In Escondido, California, the local authorities passed laws such as banning the hiring of undocumented workers. These

---

[21] José Torres-Tama, *Immigrant Dreams and Alien Nightmares* (New Orleans, LA: Dialogos Books, 2014), p. 21.

[22] ABC News, Ted Hasson, 'Five ways Immigration System Changed After 9/11', Sept 11, 2012, http://abcnews.go.com/ABC_Univision/News/ways-immigration-system-changed-911/story?id=17231590 (accessed July 29, 2015).

[23] Julia Preston, 'Judge Voids Ordinance on Illegal Immigrants', *New York Times*, July 27, 2007, http://www.nytimes.com/2007/07/27/us/27hazelton.html?_r=1& (accessed, July 29, 2015).

measures made it illegal to rent to undocumented residents. The city could suspend business licenses of firms who employed immigrant workers and criminalize the public use of languages other than English.[24]

In 2010, states passed more than 300 similar laws, including measures requiring local law enforcement officials, teachers, social workers, health care providers, private sector employers, and others to verify the citizenship of any individual they encountered in their official duties or businesses and make it a crime for non-citizens not to have documents verifying their legal status.[25] Some have gone so far as to propose that states should not recognize the U.S. citizenships of infants born of unauthorized residents, regardless of the birthright citizenship provision of the Fourteenth Amendment to the U.S.

Hispanics expected immigration reform during the presidency of Barack Obama. However, deportations under the Obama administration almost reached two million.[26] President Obama announced that measures were needed to fix the immigration system. He pledged to enact legislation to favor undocumented immigrants. But there was no immigration reform during the Obama administration. An immigration enforcement program called Secure Communities was in effect from 2008 to 2014.

Anti-immigrant measures increased, including deportation efforts and information sharing between Immigration and Customs Enforcement (ICE) and state level enforcement. The administration's Secure Communities deportation program targeted 'dangerous' and 'criminal' immigrants. A police officer could arrest someone for a traffic violation and threaten the undocumented arrestee with deportation. Amidst the expulsion of immigrants, many who had been working in America for decades were deported. Others charged with

---

24 David Gutierrez, 'An Historic Overview of Latino Immigration and the Demographic Transformation of the United States', National Park Service: American Latino Theme Study, http://www.nps.gov/history/heritageinitiatives/latino/latinothemestudy/immigration.htm (accessed August 2, 2015).

25 Gutierrez, 'An Historic Overview of Latino Immigration'.

26 Walter E. Ewing, 'The Growth of the U.S. Deportation Machine', *American Immigration Council*, April 9, 2014, http://www.immigrationpolicy.org/justfacts/growth-us-deportation-machine (accessed October 10, 2015).

minor offenses without conviction were expatriated and families were torn apart.[27]

The president highlighted his good intentions as a border enforcer by publicly stating that he had deported more undocumented immigrants than his predecessor. On the other hand, in 2012 the administration issued a number of memos explaining the intent of immigration officials to exercise 'prosecutorial discretion'. For example, ICE could assist an immigrant by asking a judge to close his or her case. The administration also enacted a 'deferred action' plan to benefit youth qualified for the DREAM (Development, Relief, and Education for Alien Minors) Act. The Deferred Action for Childhood Arrivals (DACA) plan would allow a halt to deportation procedures against undocumented youth or allow undocumented youth to seek permission to remain in the United States for two years and apply for employment authorization.

In 2015, the Secure Communities program was replaced by Priority Enforcement Program (PEP), which arrests individuals with a criminal violation since many individuals were arrested and deported even for a minor traffic violation. PEP deports individuals if they have been convicted of an offense listed under the Department of Homeland Security (DHS). Their biometric data is sent to ICE in order to determine whether an individual is a priority for removal. There are enforcement priorities, that is, those who have intentionally participated in an organized criminal gang, or pose a danger to national security, are deported.[28] PEP wants to ensure that individuals who are integrated members of community will not be arrested and detained.

On June 15, 2012, President Obama announced that the U.S. The Department of Homeland Security (DHS) would not deport certain undocumented youth who came to the United States as children. These children would be granted a type of temporary permission, or 'deferred action' to stay in the United States. Unaccompanied chil-

---

[27] 'The Great Expulsion', *The Economist,* Feb 2014, http://www.economist.com/news/briefing/21595892-barack-obama-has-presided-over-one-largest-peacetime-outflows-people-americas (accessed October 10, 2015).

[28] Homeland Security, 'Priority Enforcement Program—How DHS is Focusing on Deporting Felons', July 30, 2015, http://www.dhs.gov/blog/2015/07/30/priority-enforcement-program-%E2%80%93-how-dhs-focusing-deporting-felons (accessed October 10, 2015).

dren usually traveled through Mexico by bus or van on journeys arranged by coyotes. In 2013, an unexpected surge in unaccompanied child migration from El Salvador, Guatemala, and Honduras occurred, with more than 50,000 Central American minors intercepted at the U.S.-Mexico border. Some children traveled to be reunited with their parents, and others were sent by their parents, hoping for a better future for their children.

On November 20, 2014, President Obama announced an expansion of the DACA program. However, on February 16, 2015, a federal district court in Texas issued an order that placed the expanded DACA program on hold temporarily. Currently, DACA no longer receives applications.[29] Congressional gridlock has prevented any substantial consideration of immigration reform.[30]

Figure 3
Number of Children Entering the U.S.A. Between 2012 and 2014.[31]

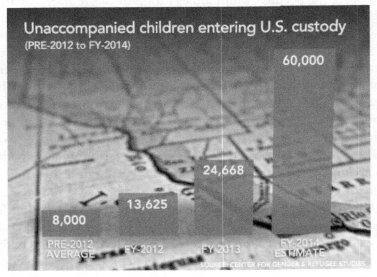

---

[29] National Immigration Law Center, 'The Obama's Administration Deferred Action for Childhood Arrivals (DACA)', August 14, 2015, https://www.nilc.org/FAQdeferredactionyouth.html (accessed September 23, 2015).

[30] Josue David Cisneros, *The Border Crossed Us: Rhetorics of Borders, Citizenship, and Latina/o Identity* (Tuscaloosa: University of Alabama Press, 2011), p. 139.

[31] P.J. Jobia, 'No Country for Lost Kids', Public Broadcasting Service, June 20, 2014, http://www.pbs.org/newshour/updates/country-lost-kids/ (accessed July10, 2015).

Undoubtedly, a hostile climate for Latinos and non-citizens has increased within the U.S. During the summer of 2015, Donald Trump, Republican presidential candidate, made incendiary remarks mainly targeting Hispanics. His anti-immigrant discourse has saturated the media. He continues to aim hostile rhetoric toward undocumented immigrants. Trump proposes to triple the number of ICE officers, end birthright citizenship, and make Mexico pay for a permanent wall along its northern border.[32]

Arizona leads the nation in the anti-immigrant movement with an increasing number of restrictive laws.[33] The Jim Crow type of legislation legalizes racial profiling, discrimination, and the unnecessary harassment of Latinos whether immigrants or U.S. citizens. For Cleary, 'racial profiling occurs when a law enforcement officer uses race or ethnicity as one of several factors to stop, question, arrest, and/or search someone'.[34] Besides Arizona, Utah, Alabama, Georgia, and South Carolina have enacted such laws. Alabama's HB-56 legislation passed in 2011, called the harshest state immigration law in the nation, its regulations placed emotional and mental anguish on parents and their children, since schools were required to check on the immigration status of children. However, two years later, HB 56 was halted. Its foundations proved to be 'unconstitutional, unworkable, or politically unsustainable'.[35] Elected officials, social workers, clergy, human rights activists, and residents recognized the tension in their communities finally ended.

It is likely that the historical debate over border enforcement, the continuing growth of the Latin American population, and the status of unauthorized persons will persist into the near future. The current presidential candidates are all speaking up on issues of immigration

---

[32] Donald Trump, 'Immigration That Will Make America Great Again', 2015, https://www.donaldjtrump.com/images/uploads/Immigration-Reform-Trump.pdf (accessed August 30, 2015).

[33] Romero and Romero Williams, 'The Impact of Immigration Legislation', p. 230.

[34] Jim Cleary, Information Brief, 'Racial Profiling Studies in Law Enforcement: Issues and Methodology', (St. Paul, MN: Minnesota House of Representatives, 2000), www.house.leg.state.mn.us/hrd/pubs/raceprof.pdf (accessed August 30, 2015).

[35] Benjy Sarlin, 'How America's Harshest Immigration Law Failed', MSNBC, December 16, 2013, http://www.msnbc.com/msnbc/undocumented-workers-immigration-alabama (accessed September 1, 2015).

reform. Both Republicans and Democrats understand that Hispanic voters could be the deciders in the next presidential elections.

Dolores Huerta, a civil rights activist, who has been a forerunner of the Latino and immigrant rights movement, believes Latinos in the U.S. will play a larger role in the electorate as occurred in the 2008 and 2012 elections.[36] In 2008, George Bush won 44 percent of the Hispanic vote. In 2012, 71 percent Latinos voted for Barack Obama over 27 percent to Republican Mitt Romney. It is estimated that Latinos will make up 10.4 percent of the electorate.[37]

Latino immigrants are transforming local landscapes and social terrains across America. They are establishing roots, as they buy houses, enroll children in schools, pay taxes, and contribute to the economy. Houses and businesses change hands, new flags go up, and schools look and sound different. There are new meanings, new boundaries, and variations in the physical forms of home, communities, and neighborhoods.[38]

America, a nation of immigrants, must come to the realization that it needs to create a lawful way for foreigners to enter its borders and support the economy. There must be a reasonable and humanitarian way to deal with undocumented immigrants. The case for immigrants is complicated, but it must be resolved in a way that treats immigrants with dignity. The presence of the Hispanic/Latino population has contributed to the economy through their labor and work ethic. In addition, the Hispanic/Latino community has contributed to the cultural enrichment of the American nation and to the spiritual fabric of the nation through their religious and family values.

Undocumented immigrants continued to be under attack during Donald Trump's administration. The US has benefited from immigration and trade. Yet, Latino immigrants are angrily signaled out as criminals to justify the construction of a wall to keep out 'illegals'.

---

[36] Aaron Morrison, '2016 Presidential Elections: Hispanic Voters Could Be the Deciders', *International Business Times,* June 9, 2015, http://www.ibtimes.com/2016-presidential-election-immigration-reform-activist-dolores-huerta-says-hispanic-1958382 (accessed September 1, 2015).

[37] Griselda Nevarez, NBC News, 'GOP 2016 Win Will Need More Than 40 Percent of Latino Vote, Says Study', July 17, 2015, http://www.nbcnews.com/news/latino/gop-2016-win-will-need-more-40-percent-latino-vote-n394006 (accessed September 1, 2015).

[38] Winders, 'Replacing Southern Geographies', p. 344.

'The true essence of 'American' identity is ultimately anchored on such universal values as freedom, democracy, justice, and equality, rather than on a presumption of monolithic language and cultural traditions'.[39]

[39] Miguel Carranza and Lourdes Gouveia, 'The Integration of the Hispanic/Latino Immigration Workforce', May 31, 2002, report, University of Nebraska, http://www.unomaha.edu/ollas/pdf/HLIWSREPORTfinal.pdf (accessed October 3, 2015).

9

New Blood: Portraits of Latino Immigrants

This chapter includes a few stories that capture the lives and experiences of undocumented immigrants. Latinos are a highly mobile population due to job opportunities or because they move to live in proximity to family members. The southern states have not usually been the site for Hispanics. But in the last ten years, Central Americans have become more geographically dispersed and have settled in Georgia, North and South Carolina, Tennessee, and Virginia.[1]

The individuals interviewed in these narratives have lived in the U.S. anywhere between ten and twenty years and attend Hispanic congregations. They were born between 1975 and 1985. All of them have children born in this country who are U.S. citizens, under the age of eighteen. The adults interviewed noted the risk they took coming to the U.S. to escape conditions of poverty. Most of them work in the housekeeping, construction, and manufacturing industries. Their lives reflect resiliency and faith in God. They verbalized their expectations to work hard in order to get ahead. The stories reflect their love for prayer, family, and a longing for a pathway to citizenship. Pseudonyms have been used in order to protect confidentiality. Each individual signed a consent form for human subject research. The interviews were video-recorded and transcribed.

---

[1] Winders, 'Re-Placing Southern Geographies', p. 345.

Adriana: Mentored with Love

Adriana was born in Mexico and arrived in the US at the age of five. Her mother was working in the United States and petitioned her children for resident status because she perceived America as a land of opportunities where her children could prosper. Adriana came with *papeles* (papers, legal documents) or residency. She is now forty years old, married, and a mother of three children. Adriana is a high school graduate and has served in her church for ten years under three different pastors. She preaches occasionally and is respected for her dedicated and consistent service to others. She is fluent in English. Her husband does construction work, and he operates the sound system at church. Adriana is petite, vivacious, and always eager to learn. She was very enthusiastic about the opportunity to be interviewed about her life.

We met with Adriana at the church fellowship hall. She recalls how confused she felt when she arrived in the U.S., mainly during her first two years in elementary school:

> I was very depressed for the first two years. You think little kids will get used to it, but it's not that easy. I remember being very small and very young, and I got depressed. I would go to school, but my mind was somewhere else. It was very hard not knowing the language, not knowing the people around me, not knowing what they were saying, not being part of the other kids. I didn't learn any [sic] English whatsoever in the first two years.

Fortunately, Adriana and her family lived in Texas, which contributed to their adaptation since there was strong Hispanic support in language, customs, and Mexican food. Adriana recalls a very caring principal who was really concerned about immigrant children. He assigned Adriana a one-to-one mentoring opportunity with an English teacher. Within a year, Adriana was already speaking and writing English. Adriana continued to do well in school, and she is still grateful for that opportunity.

It was at the age of nineteen that Adriana faced difficult circumstances in her life. One day, she walked by a small Pentecostal church and decided to enter. She responded to an altar call, and when the preacher prayed for her, she began to cry and feel the presence of God. She recalls, 'I wanted to stop crying, but I just couldn't. And he said to me something that no one had known about me...I remember from that day on, I was a different person'.

Adriana's family remained strong Catholics, and they would make fun of her new faith. From that time on, prayer became extremely important in her life. She explained:

I would pray a lot. I was in my room, always reading the Bible, singing, and praying. And they couldn't understand why at a young age, I was praying, reading the Bible, and that's all I wanted to do. And I was always talking about God. You know, they just couldn't understand those things.

Her mother, who visited from Texas recently, told her, 'Adriana, you're different. You do things very differently than what I used to do, you know. And I just feel peace at your house'. Other relatives have stayed at her house while they find stable jobs, and Adriana wondered:

God, why are you bringing them or sending them to my house? But I know God has given them a purpose. They get to know God. We bring them to church, and right now I have a cousin at my house...and he came for the same reason. He's there and we're bringing him to church, so they get to hear the Word. We talk about God in the house.

Before Adriana and her family moved to Virginia Beach, her family prayed, and they waited for God's confirmation for their relocation. The church in Texas gave her prophetic words about her future:

I just did not move like that. I prayed and waited, got an answer, and moved...and it's been prayer that has kept me going...They told me I was going to be like a co-pastor. And you know, that was the title they gave me [now] at my church, and...I had already forgotten about that. And then I thought, This is going to happen like in many, many years, you know, but it happened.

Adriana underwent culture shock when moving to Virginia, where she had no relatives, and the Hispanic community was hardly noticeable. Although fluent in English, the transition into a predominantly Anglo culture was not easy. Eventually, her family found a family atmosphere in a Hispanic congregation. She acknowledged that the church contributed to her cultural adjustment. She reflected on the church's fellowship and prayer as a source of strength:

> So that's the time that we have fellowship, and you know, it feels good, especially when you don't have any family here. Really, it's two things. My intimacy with God is through prayer and through the word. There's nothing else I can do to give credit for that. You know, even if it's my husband, and my kids and the congregation, but that's after my intimacy with God.

As immigrants, Adriana and her family have faced hardships and discrimination. For example, in spite of being a legal resident, her husband did not receive pay on several occasions. At times, Hispanics working in construction do not get paid or get only half of the wages. The American managers explained that they themselves had not received earnings. Immigrants are willing to work hard, even though they are often subject to unfair treatment. Adriana pointed out that Hispanics focus on their work. Sometimes they miss out on Sunday services because their goal is to work and make money. It is not so much that they only care about money; they are trying to improve themselves and their standard of living. Most immigrants are determined to get ahead for their families, and they work long hours.

Latino families sacrifice themselves in order to make life better for their children. Several families live in one house and share rent expenses, even though their privacy is restricted. Mothers stay home to look after their children since daycare costs exceed the family budget. In relation to Adriana's family future, they see themselves remaining in the U.S., especially due to the education of their children. One thing that Adriana longs for is to see her children have closer ties with relatives who live far away. She remarked:

> One of the things I want, and I think that we need as a family, is that my children get to know my family because they are growing up with no family whatsoever. And that's one of my prayers. I want them to have a relationship with their grandparents, their cousins, and their uncles.

For this reason, Adriana would like to move back to Texas one day. Family life is everything for Hispanic immigrants. They try to live or stay in close contact with one another. Decisions are made within the family circle. Love and respect for parents and the extended family are cultivated. Hispanics feel at home in churches that emphasize community and their cultural traditions.

Mariella: A Voice from the Shadows

Mariella is a petite redhead from Honduras who is thirty-two years old. She is a single mom who was able to bring her 12-year-old daughter, Carla, to the U.S. in 2013. Her daughter entered during the Central American children's immigration crisis. Although she was detained after crossing the border, Carla was allowed to stay under the Obama administration's Deferred Action for Childhood Arrivals (DACA). Mariella is very soft-spoken and bashful. She wanted to make sure to remain in the dark while filming. Mariella revealed her gladness that her daughter is now living with her:

> My daughter was two years old when I came to the US. I wasn't thinking that I would bring her here. I thought I would return. I missed her. My mother took care of her. Some time ago, I suddenly felt anxiety about wanting to bring her here. Thank God she arrived well. It has been God who has guided all this process. The lawyer and the judge have helped too.

As with most immigrants, Mariella longs for a better future to help her family. At first, it was very difficult for Mariella to make the adjustment to living in the States, especially not speaking English. It was not easy to feel like a stranger in a new place. Upon her arrival, she contacted family members in North Carolina but remained there for only two months. For the past ten years, she has done construction work in Virginia. She currently lives in a small house with two cousins and her daughter. Like most immigrants, Mariella sends money to her mother back home.

Mariella was living under stressful conditions before knowing Jesus Christ as her Lord and Savior. She admits the church and prayer have helped her adapt to an Anglo-Saxon culture. Mariella suffered anxiety attacks that paralyzed her, although she never received a medical diagnosis for her condition. She visited a church where she accepted Jesus as her Lord and Savior. She recalls the day she received complete healing in a *tienda* (shop):

Well, as I was going out of the hospital [at that time] when I used to get those sudden attacks. I went to look for a newspaper [at the tienda] so I could find a neurologist. And then, in that place there, well, I asked if they knew a neurologist, and they told me, sir, that it was Jesus. Soon after, an evangelist came by church, and he prayed for me, and I was healed.

Mariella is a worship leader and believes that knowing God is the best thing that has happened to her while in the U.S. She has peace in her heart and recognizes that prayer has made a big difference in her life. Since knowing Jesus as her Savior, Mariella spends more time seeking God, which facilitates her everyday struggles. In spite of her English language limitations, Mariella is now more at ease in the Anglo culture and has adapted well to construction jobs. She commented about her work:

Americans say we work better. Well, I apply prayer at each moment. When I'm at work I'm praying in my mind. I'm thanking God each moment. I can't be without talking to Him. I miss talking to Him. I remember Him at each moment.

In spite of her life improvements Mariella longs to be reunited with her family one day:

Well… in my heart, I've always thinking… that I want to return to Honduras. I don't know what the reason is. I always say He might be preparing me here to later return to my country…to go and evangelize. I think God is preparing me for the future. I feel he's working in a special way…I would not like to live here anymore…when I get older.

Mariella stated that she would not recommend that someone come to the U.S. because they will face times of loneliness and distress without their family. Mariella calls home up to three times a week. Her family in Honduras has not yet converted to Jesus Christ. But they are happy that Mariella is serving the Lord. Mariella is waiting on the Lord to know when she'll go back to Honduras. She is aware that crime and delinquency are on the rise in Honduras but looks forward to an improvement in the social conditions.

In relation to her adaptation, people in general have treated her well. She is fortunate because employers have appreciated her work skills. For her, North Americans are 'a bit different than us, but certain people are just like us, and they treat us in a good way'.

Mae: An Intercultural Missionary

Mae arrived with her family from the Philippines in California in 1997. Her father waited twenty years for resident papers for his wife and daughters. Mae recalls the strenuous changes of those early years:

> We were told just to bring one suitcase. So, packing your eighteen years of life into one suitcase is difficult. Everyone thinks Mickey Mouse is running around the street and that money grows on trees. But it wasn't like that at all. I lived a not-so-rich life, but we were more of the middle class in the Philippines. I was a pre-med student in the Philippines, and I was eager to start school. But I had to wait because the affordability of tuition was a big issue.

The change in lifestyle was hard for Mae and her family. They no longer had a car and could only afford items from thrift stores. Due mainly to language problems, Mae's parents were not able to find jobs in their field. It was Mae who first found a job, which helped pay the rent for their apartment. She cried when she realized that she had to work hard to have a roof over her head and that her parents now depended on her. She was eighteen years old when she got her first job as a receptionist in a doctor's office. Later, she worked as a restaurant manager for a Chinese food chain. Her parents eventually got jobs.

Her mother worked as an accounting clerk in San Diego County, and her father worked as a parking lot attendant. Mae recalls the painful experience of watching her father demoted from a large company as a mechanical engineer back home to sitting in a white booth in a hotel parking lot:

> It was heart-wrenching to see my father. But also, to see at the same time, that he had paid the price to see his family in America. His dream was to bring us here, and he did, all of us. All five of us came at the same time. The family was together.

Mae came to fully embrace the Christian faith in July 1999. A young Salvadorian man, who later became her husband, invited her to a church service in East San Diego. The environment in the Spanish-speaking church, *Alcance Victoria* (Victory Outreach) was a totally new experience for Mae. Mae responded to the altar call and accepted Jesus as her savior.

> I see everybody dancing, shouting, and having a whole lot of fun. I didn't understand every word that they were saying 'cause it was in Spanish. Spanish was not my first language… a young man testified…that he was an ex-gang member and how God transformed his life. At that very moment, every word that came out of his mouth, I understood in Spanish! From that very moment on, Spanish became something very special to me… I was able to understand the preaching; songs were different to me now. I was reading the Bible in Spanish. I was studying in Spanish and translating in English. And it was just something very beautiful that had happened. Spanish just became a natural to me. There was just something about the place and something about the presence there. And I believe God sent me out here in July of 99. I am in a very privileged position. I'm a Filipina who received salvation and came to know Christ in a Spanish congregation.

Mae and her husband moved to Virginia in the year 2000. They attended a Hispanic church for about ten years and now pastor a bilingual congregation. Mae and her family are involved in an urban mission outreach. They feed over one hundred homeless people every Friday (Not By Bread Alone) and distribute Hope bags (socks, toiletries, snacks). People are welcome to sit inside the ministry bus and participate in a Bible study. Mae concluded, 'I think we're going to be a church with no borders, no roofs, and our congregation is going to be of people of whoever is on the street'.
Mae is often mistaken as a Latina. She explained:

> They can't figure me out, my own Filipino people don't even think that I'm Filipino. We kind of mesh everywhere we go, I guess. They think I'm Samoan, they think I'm Hawaiian. The last thing on their minds would be Filipino. And my husband is the same way. Some think my husband looks more Filipino than me. The appearance, I think, gives us an advantage.

Mae understands that Latinos have a strong sense of family, faith, and brotherhood in the church. For immigrants, church is not just a place of worship but a place of refuge where they are treated with dignity. Mae indicated that the church gives Latino immigrants security that the time will come when they too will have *papeles* (legal documents). Mae added, 'But I think there's one thing that Latinos don't realize-- that they are actually missionaries here'.

Prayer is a vital part of what Mae and her family do with the homeless. They are aware of the spiritual struggles people face. Mae responded:

> Prayer is very important. Are there moments when I slack off? Yes. But it is very important because it's very intimate for me. Now, some people might spend four hours in prayer. But doing four to six hours of prayer is something I've never done. But I pray to God as I speak to God all throughout the day. That is something that's very important to me. Before making a decision, before my children go to bed, or before anything that we do as husband and wife, we pray for each other. Before he goes to work, we pray and bless each other.

Mae and her family cross borders for missions in Guatemala, El Salvador, and Honduras. They have fallen in love with the city of Quetzaltenango, Guatemala, and even think of the possibility of moving there one day. Mae made the following observations about prayer among churches in Central America:

> One thing that I really salute in the churches is the dedication to the prayer service. They really have a prayer service. And the number of people that show up for their prayer service is the same as the number of people that show up for the Sunday service. And there was power. Children and adults of different ages were there, and it was like a Sunday morning service. It was an amazing service for me.

Mae has become a transcultural missionary, touching the lives of Hispanic immigrants and homeless people in Virginia Beach. She understands that Jesus died for all people. Her family ministers to Anglos, Latinos, and Filipinos in the area. Dealing with three cultures has its challenges, but Mae believes they are involved much more than just in a local church. She called it a 'kingdom culture'. They desire to serve wherever there are open doors, not just among Americans or

Hispanics. She explained, 'I am thankful for that, because we are pursuing a kingdom culture'.

Santiago: A Street Preacher

Santiago is a forty-year-old Salvadorian who arrived in the U.S. at the age of nineteen. He recalled:

> In my country, there was no work. When I finished high school, I had to face the reality that there was no work. So it really was a desperate situation. It was a shocking situation. I don't know how to describe it.

Santiago served in his church as a youth leader. He resigned from his ministry and did not inform the church about his decision to migrate.

> When I decided to leave, it was a very difficult decision. And I just decided to leave everything behind. My goal was never to return to my country until I could return with legal documents. I left everything behind—father, mother, brothers, and sisters—with the hope of a better world.

Santiago recalls how prayers kept him safe during his journey to the U.S. As he traveled through Mexico to approach the border, Santiago said he knew people were praying for him, and he felt God's protection along the way. Very difficult things happened during that perilous route. He realized that God had strengthened and protected him all the way to his destination. His mother would tell him, 'We're praying for you'. He knew that brothers and sisters who saw him grow up in the church were praying for him too.

Santiago rode on the train called *La Bestia* (the beast) which for him was very difficult and traumatic. Migrants ride atop the moving trains, and they risk their lives if they fall asleep and fall over. People on *La Bestia* are mostly from Mexico, Central America, and South America, but some Africans and Asians also make this journey. Along the way, people show kindness to the travelers by giving them food like cookies and tortillas. Santiago remembers:

> They tell you, 'Have some; you better eat'. Because they know that we don't have anything to eat. They also let you know how much more you have left to reach the border, and in each town, they explain the [details of the trip] to you.

Santiago hitchhiked all along the Mexican border from Texas to California, where his relatives lived. He made it to Tijuana and to the fence at the border, which is under heavy surveillance. According to Santiago, you just need to jump the fence to be in the U.S. However, Santiago and his friend waited several days for the best time to cross. They could see immigration officers moving along the border. Finally, one foggy winter day at five in the morning, Santiago and his friend walked across the fence. They did not have to run because no one was following them. They followed the footprints left behind by other sojourners, and finally they were inside U.S. territory. Santiago's sister paid the *coyote* (smuggler) a sum, which he eventually paid back in small amounts.

Santiago's sister placed him in an ESL learning center, and he enjoyed the books and the courses. He was not able to get a job for at least a year and eventually participated in manual labor. He was twenty-one when he began to make friends among his co-workers, although he eventually drifted away from his Christian principles. Santiago recalled:

> The world began to embrace me. Pride gets to you, you know; you get your own car, you have brand-name clothes, and you have your own job. You even have two jobs, and you're making good money. These were all things that really ensnared me...when I had recently arrived in *Los Angeles* (the U.S).

Santiago believes the prayers of his loved ones led him once again to God. He responded to the preaching of the gospel by a Cuban street preacher in San Diego. Santiago resisted God's calling, but eventually he attended church with the Cuban preacher. He felt the Lord speak to his heart about ministry, and he began to participate in street evangelism.

Santiago's life changed dramatically in San Diego. He described his service to the Lord:

> The Spirit of God brought that part of me back to life. And everything happened really fast because the Spirit began working in me, and I began to preach in the streets of San Diego. And to preach in the streets, you need the Spirit of God! You know, without the spirit of God and prayer, you can't do these things. I remember preaching on the streets of San Diego. And I would

climb on a box to preach there. And the same brother who shared the gospel with me would get together to preach on the streets.

Santiago recognizes the need for prayer in ministry. He compares prayer to the water that nourishes a plant. In ministry, people need to be continually in prayer. For Santiago, people in ministry need to be connected with God. They need to listen to God because God will speak to them, and they will hear from God. He believes this can only happen through prayer.

I asked Santiago if Latinos make positive contributions to this nation. He answered:

> Yes, we do contribute to this nation. There are more of us now, and we do play an important part in this nation. There's a lot of contributions that we make to the U.S. Well, companies require that you have some kind of document, so if you work, you have to pay taxes. I think it's a lie to say that Latinos don't pay taxes. When I did not have legal documents, I used to pay taxes here. Taxes are deducted from your paycheck. So that always takes place, and we do contribute as taxpayers.

Most importantly, Santiago believes Latinos are bringing a spiritual impact to the U.S. He added that Latinos and Anglos are joining together. In the church, Latinos bring a sense of joy and happiness. Santiago sees a special sense of fellowship when they minister on the streets. He added, 'People on the streets don't see our skin color but they are just glad when we minister to them'.

Santiago is stirring people's lives in the church and on the streets: Anglos, Latinos, Blacks, and Filipinos. For now, he is focused on ministry, his family, and his children. As for future plans, he walks in obedience to God each day that goes by and wants to serve God with all of his strength.

José: Crossing the Desert

José is 37 years old and a man of few words, rather shy and introverted. He has been a construction worker for the past ten years. His decision to come to the U.S. was a hasty one. His wife really got excited when her brother said he could help José get to the U.S. Several of his friends were already living in the States.

José had a job in Honduras, and he was not really eager to travel to *Los Estados Unidos*. His wife also worked, but she really longed to get ahead in life by working in the U.S. and taking their family along. José left his village in 2005 not knowing his destination. His wife and two children stayed behind, thinking it was best for him to get to the U.S. first. He traveled by bus across Guatemala and made friends along the way. He rode on *La Bestia* until he reached the Mexican border. Whenever the train stopped, the migrants would get down and ask the local people for food. People always helped them when they asked. José did not pay anyone to get to the border. The trip from his village to the Mexican border took sixteen days.

According to José, crossing the Mexican border is very difficult. He had to swim across the river. He and some friends walked for about six hours, and they reached a hill in a place near El Paso. They saw a train and got on it, but immigration officers caught them at two in the morning. One officer got on the train, and the one that stayed behind grabbed José by his shirt collar. He led José to the patrol car, but while opening the car door, he let go of José. At that very moment, José started to run as fast as he could. His friend got caught, but no one captured José.

When José realized he was no longer in danger, he waited until dawn the following morning and began to walk along the railroad tracks. Four hours went by, and a man stopped to give him a ride. He dropped José off at a furniture store, and he told José in Spanish that he could do nothing more for him. José did not know what to do. He kept walking until he reached an auto shop, where he worked for about one month. José was treated well, and people gave him food and clothes. Soon he told his employer he would be moving to Virginia with his brother-in-law. His employer offered to drive him to Virginia and just asked José for gas money.

José's wife arrived in the U.S. about three months later, in 2005, but their two sons stayed behind. Their two boys, ages four and six, arrived ten years later. The boys were accompanied during the trip, so there was a fee paid to the *coyote* (smuggler). Unfortunately, immigration officers caught them in Texas. José received a call, and the boys were released. They were given permission to stay, and a lawyer is working on their immigration documents. Their arrival took place during the crisis of unaccompanied Central American children at the border (2013).

José attended church in Honduras, and he currently attends a Hispanic church. He admits:

> I have grown more in the Lord while I've been here than in Honduras...Prayer helps me a lot. It helps me to be strong. When I left Honduras, I had faith that God would protect me and guide my way. But I've gotten closer to God here in the U.S. because I stopped going to church and slipped back...The church has helped me a lot. Because when you arrive in this country, you really feel lonely. My family and I felt all alone. By coming to church, we're happier and motivated to keep going...Prayer is really important. There are times when you can get depressed, and prayer helps me and my family.

For José, language has been the most challenging obstacle in his adaptation to the U.S. At work, he speaks Spanish with the other Latino workers. José has always worked with American supervisors, and he considers that his bosses are satisfied with his work. José believes Latino immigrants contribute significantly through their hard work. When immigrants come here, they have the mentality to work sacrificially because they want their family to get ahead.

As for the future, José sometimes considers that he may return to his hometown once his children are independent. He and his wife think about their parents, who still live in Honduras. On the other hand, José reflects that it is very difficult for immigrants to come here. He would advise them to stay home 'because the situation is really difficult, and there are a lot of *aflicciónes* (afflictions) here'.

Alicia: A Desperate Mother

Alicia is a 37-year-old Honduran female who lived in a condition of poverty and had a lot of family problems. She thought about the welfare of her two children and their education. She was determined to come to the U.S., knowing it would involve some risks. She convinced her husband to make the journey, which she would follow. She left her hometown in 2005 with her brother-in-law. One of the trains in Mexico had derailed, so they waited two weeks for the next train. They slept on the sidewalks, covered with pieces of plastic as blankets. Once they got on the train, they traveled for several days without food or water. There were hundreds of people on the train from Mexico, Guatemala, El Salvador, and Honduras. Once they reached the town of Aguas Calientes, police officers began to chase after the migrants. She and others threw themselves off the train, and her leg was scraped severely.

Alicia was pregnant with her third child. She and her brother-in-law were able to get back on the train a few days later. They finally reached the border, and they were told they would have to walk across the desert. At the Arizona border, immigration officers began to chase after them with dogs. Alicia began to run fast and ended up separated from her brother-in-law and the other ten people who were traveling together. She hid herself in a deep hole and waited until dawn to begin her journey. Alicia was all alone and completely lost, not knowing which direction to take. She kept walking and tried to follow in the direction where she heard sounds.

Eventually, she saw some houses and heard cars as they drove by. As she got closer, Alicia said to herself, 'My God, this is it!' She saw a low fence, crossed over the fence, and walked down the street. An American lady who spoke Spanish really well saw her, and she said to her, '*Muchacha*, (Girl) what are you doing?' Alicia's clothes were dirty, and her lips were blistered from not drinking water. She had no strength to walk, and she felt like she was going to faint. It was around noon, and the lady told her to be careful because she could get caught. The lady told her there was a construction site ahead. Alicia arrived at the construction site and greeted the people in Spanish. She was surprised because several Americans there spoke Spanish.

One of them said, 'What are you doing here, lady? Look at you. Come in because they [immigration officers] pass by here and they can catch you'. Alicia prayed in her heart, 'My Lord, help me, protect me because I don't know these people'. They treated her well and gave her a McDonald's meal which she ate hungrily. Afterwards, she called her husband to give him the address of the construction site. Alicia then realized she was in Phoenix, Arizona.

About a week later, a man took her to Los Angeles, where she met with her brother-in-law, and he drove her to Virginia. Alicia became distressed with all the changes in her new place. She recalls:

> Well, it wasn't easy at first. You know, there's a lot of racism and it was difficult because I couldn't speak English. People asked me a lot of questions, so it was very hard at the beginning. He [my husband] worked, and I didn't drive. And I needed someone to

take me to doctor's appointments. I began to see a doctor for pre-natal care three months after I arrived. At the clinic, they would go tell me, 'You have to speak English. We speak English here, not Spanish'. So, I really felt intimidated. Because if someone is pregnant, they should be taken care of regardless. But at the beginning, it was hard. And I felt frustrated and sad thinking [about all of this] because I said, 'Look how they treat you, when you come to this country'.

Amidst the initial hardships, Alicia began to smile and said to herself, 'Things are going to get better'. When labor pains began, her husband was working, and a friend drove her to the hospital. It was a difficult labor because the baby weighed ten pounds. But in spite of all the difficulties, everything went well, and the hospital staff brought her gifts. There were some hospital charges due to the C-section. Alicia arranged a payment plan and finished paying the hospital bill in small amounts.

But most importantly, Alicia began to live for Jesus since she had abandoned her Christian lifestyle while in Honduras. Alicia asked God to keep her away from anything that could harm her in any way. Her friends used to invite her to go out to parties and drink. She avoided those friends, and they asked her, 'What's wrong with you?' But she told them that nothing was wrong and that she was a Christian. Alicia concluded:

> I have really tried to get closer to God, and sometimes my work doesn't allow me to go to church as often. But I asked God to bless me. And every night I pray and ask God to forgive me in case I have offended someone with words or with my actions. And I ask God to continue to bless my home.

Alicia is content now and grateful to God because her two older children recently arrived in the U.S. She explains that her four children are getting along better now that the family has been separated for ten years. Alicia expressed that God has blessed her because all of her children are now close to her. She believes God brought her with a purpose, and up to this day, God has protected her:

> He has not abandoned me. There are moments that I have been weak with things that happen, but I feel God has blessed me in

thousands of ways. God has never abandoned us. I know God has a purpose for my life, and one day he will reveal it.

Prayer has also become more important in Alicia's family. Alicia stated:

I think that prayer is the best remedy for anything that can happen. I go to sleep like at midnight, and my mind keeps thinking of things like bills I have to pay, that I don't have enough money, and other things. So, I tell God, 'I know You are the only one who will provide for us and for all that we need'. I know they are material things, but in this country they are necessary things. Prayer has helped me a lot, a lot. Prayer has really made a difference in my life.

When Alicia calls home, her mother tells her, 'Continue in God's ways. If we don't see each other in this world, we'll see each other in the next'. Alicia is aware her mother has helped her through her advice and prayers. She hopes to see her again one day, either in Honduras or by bringing her mom to visit them. Alicia is grateful because only God made it possible for her family to be where they are today. They are together, and she does not want to see her home fall apart.

Carmen: Abandoned by Her Husband

Carmen was born in Mexico and arrived in the U.S. in the year 2000. Her husband was a U.S. resident who worked in construction. He sent for Carmen and their five-year-old daughter, Sandra. Carmen worked as a nurse in Mexico. She came to America with a tourist visa and joined her husband in Virginia. Carmen underwent culture shock most of all because of the language barrier, the food, the lack of warmth in dealing with others, and the fact that neighbors did not interact with each other. Carmen is *amicable* (friendly) to people and exhibits a pleasant and respectful demeanor.

Carmen was a Roman Catholic, but her ex-husband was not a churchgoer, so they stayed away from church for a long time. On Christmas or on special feasts, they went to the Spanish Mass at a nearby Catholic church. One day, Carmen's world turned upside down when her daughter was diagnosed with cancer at the age of six. Her baby boy was seven months old. Carmen and her husband were undergoing marital difficulties, and their marriage disintegrated. Carmen felt all alone as her daughter's health grew worse.

A friend had talked to Carmen about salvation in Jesus Christ, and she persisted in inviting Carmen to church. One night, Carmen cried out desperately to God. Her heart was filled with anguish.

> I made a promise to God. It was then that I could see his hand. Well, I was alone with my daughter, without a husband who had promised to help us. It was there that I made a covenant with God. It was then that I started going to church.

Tears filled her eyes as she remembered her loneliness and sense of hopelessness. It was after this experience that prayer became very important in Carmen's life. At first, it was her friend who prayed since Carmen was not used to *orar a dios* in the Catholic Church. For Carmen, prayer was reciting the *Padre Nuestro* and the *Ave Maria*. But she eventually learned to *hablar con Dios* (talk to God) in the hospital. Carmen smiles as she remembers that she grew in her faith while in the hospital. People would come by and pray for her daughter. During those twenty-nine days at the hospital, she prayed to God every day. She noticed a new direction in her life.

Carmen made a promise to God: 'If you heal her, I will serve you'. Carmen's daughter is now fifteen years old and participates in the youth group at church. Carmen believes the Lord brought this miracle so she would grow in faith and get closer to God. Carmen continues to faithfully serve at church, along with her three children:

> With my family, my children, we have prayer time on Fridays since they don't have homework on weekends. So we have a family service, and everyone chooses a Bible verse, and everyone shares what God tells them through the word. My son, Christian, who is only four, is the one who reminds us. He's like the motor to make sure everyone has their Bible. And he chooses Bible verses, and he says, 'Mom, read this one'. And it's amazing because the word has a message for what I'm going through at that moment. He's always praying, and dancing, and if I'm feeling sick, he prays for me. If my older son has a headache, he takes a pill, but he [Christian] prays. He always carries his Bible, everywhere he goes. He's the one who reminds us that we have to pray.

Carmen points out that life as an immigrant in the U.S. is not easy. There are moments of loneliness in the lives of immigrants. People leave everything behind, and they might think that material things are important, but that is not so. Hispanics work hard, and they carry out the roughest jobs that Americans do not want to do. One employer said he preferred to hire Hispanics over Americans.

For Carmen, family is more important than material possessions. Her children also miss an extended family life because they ask Carmen, 'Why don't we have grandparents or cousins?' Carmen cries when she shares what her children long for. Unfortunately, Carmen has lost contact with relatives back home, and they cannot visit them. Her father no longer recognizes her because he has Alzheimer's.

The church has played a vital role in Carmen's life. The church helped her get a job. Her children have friends at church. Carmen desires to see her children love God and remain faithful Christians. Through prayer and church fellowship, Carmen *Sigue Luchando cares* for her three children. She observed, 'No matter how many friends you make, even at church…and at the end we end up alone with God. He is the only one who remains with us'. Carmen's source of strength is her faith and trust in God.

Pedro: *Luchar por la Vida* (To Struggle for Life)

Pedro is a thirty-year-old Mexican from a small village bordering Guatemala. He speaks an indigenous language and also speaks Spanish. He has six brothers at home and one brother lives in the U.S. In his own words, Pedro stated:

> I came to *luchar la vida* (struggle for life) …I wanted my own house, my own things, and my own money. That's what I thought about coming here. My mother and father cried a lot because they did not want to let me go. My father said, 'Even though we only eat beans and tortilla here, I don't want you to go'. But I came against my mother's and father's wishes. I came from Mexico, and I was thirteen years old.

Pedro and four other men walked through the desert for five days, including a *coyote* (smuggler). His father had told him, 'I don't want you to die there'. It was truly a difficult experience, but they finally reached Phoenix, Arizona. About four days later, another man picked them up and drove them to North Carolina to meet with their relatives. In spite of living with his brother, Pedro often cried when feeling overwhelmed with loneliness and culture shock. He began to work immediately, getting up early to harvest potatoes, cabbages, tomatoes, and peanuts. Pedro recalled how he missed his family, and his parents asked him to return. His brother also offered to pay for his trip back to Mexico. But Pedro told his family, 'I'm going to *aguantar* (endure)'. He still calls his family in Mexico every week.

Pedro comes from a Christian home. He said, 'When I was in Mexico, we worshiped the Almighty God. We lived in a *colonia* (subdivision), and we'd go to another one and meet at a ranch to worship God. We held services at home and had *campañas* (crusades)'. Pedro's father has slipped back to his old lifestyle. His dad drinks, and only his mom goes occasionally to church. Pedro tells them *echen ganas para el Señor* (give your best to serve the Lord). His father has started to attend church occasionally. Pedro still sends money to his parents.

Pedro has a modest and respectful demeanor, and he has been fortunate to work with American employers in landscaping and gardening. His bosses appreciate his hard work and loyalty. Pedro observed:

> I get along well with Americans, by the grace of God. I make myself understood. My boss gives me a list of what I have to do every day, and I get there and tell people what my boss has sent me to do. I carry out assignments well, by the grace of God.

Pedro has adapted to life in America and does not want to go back like he did in his teenage years. Life conditions have changed in his hometown. When he was there, people could appropriate a piece of land to build their house. But now, people have to buy it. Pedro realizes that life in America means hard work. Some people may think things are easy here, but it requires hard work. He shares about his Christian faith at work, and he gets along well with his boss and other workers. Some people have been criticized him for working in the U.S. Pedro explained:

> One time, they disapproved of my employment here. They asked me if I had *papeles* (documents) to come here. I said no, and they said I was here to take away other people's jobs. I responded by saying, 'I don't think so. I came to work and not to steal'. For me, I'm helping them, even though they told me I'm taking people's

jobs. Well…I came to work to contribute and to pay taxes. And I told them, You know I also need to make money.

Pedro has an American wife and a three-year-old daughter. He has a hectic schedule and would like to participate more in church activities.

Yet he remains faithful to his Christian walk. Pedro admits, 'At work, it's easy to share about the Lord. We talk about the Lord at work. And we talk with our boss; he's a Christian too'. Pedro is grateful for his job and his Mexican companions at work. He concluded, 'This [work] has been given to us by His grace. We do this job all year round. Sometimes it decreases, like in winter. And sometimes work increases'. Pedro believes God has a purpose for him and his family. He believes God protects him and will be with him until the end of the world. He senses God's great love for him and his family.

Patty: An Entrepreneur

Patty is a Salvadorian female who arrived in the U.S. in 1999. She is the single mom of a sixteen-year-old girl. Currently, she's involved in women's ministries at her local church. Her demeanor is outgoing and cheerful. Patty and her siblings lived with their father in El Salvador while their mother worked in California. Patty was the first one in her family to complete high school. Her siblings had to quit studying in order to work. One day, Patty made the decision to join her partner in the U.S. Her mother advised her to stay in El Salvador. But Patty responded, 'Even if you agree or disagree with me, I'm going anyway'. Patty thinks it was a good decision and the Lord allowed her to make the trip to the U.S.

Patty rode several buses across Mexico until she reached the border. By that time, she had joined a group of eight people. They walked across the desert for a whole night and swam across the Rio Grande in *neumáticos* (tires). Back then, they never encountered immigration officers or thieves, and it was not as dangerous as it is today. They stayed in a house in Texas for a few days. She had planned to meet with her partner, but first she traveled to Los Angeles, where she remained for six months with her mother. Her mom passed away one year later, and Patty was grateful she got to spend time with her. Patty then traveled to Virginia to meet her partner, who was a U.S.

resident. The city where he lived had a very small Hispanic population, which made Patty's transition difficult.

After six months, Patty became pregnant with their daughter. She looked for medical assistance, but her limited language skills were a barrier to finding resources. She was denied Medicaid because she lacked a Social Security number. Patty recalls that she felt like Mary was looking for a place where Jesus could be born. She ended up having medical checkups out of state. Her first checkup was during her fifth month of pregnancy. She gave birth to a baby girl in North Carolina.

Patty began to work in 2000, when her daughter was ten months old. She applied for Temporary Protected Status (TPS). She was grateful that this allowed her to remain in the USA. Her first stable job was in a boat factory in North Carolina.

When her daughter turned three, Patty moved to Virginia, where she began to work in construction since no other jobs were available. She and her sister poured concrete, and it was *bien pesado* (very exhausting). Although Patty and her sister received ten dollars an hour, they left this job because it was physically demanding for their small frames. Soon after, she worked at an oyster factory, where she remained for twelve years. She became a supervisor at the packing factory and left in 2015 because the company closed down. The Hispanics who worked there were very responsible and trustworthy.

Patty's working experience has built entrepreneurship skills into her life. Her bosses liked how she worked. She supervised a team of seventeen people. The team members were always very committed and responsible in their jobs. Patty described how Hispanics gave of themselves sacrificially. If twenty-four hours are needed to work without stopping, Hispanics *sacan fuerzas* (are resilient) and they fulfill their responsibilities. She recalls that during a power outage, they all stayed until two in the morning to comply with the work orders. Patty never heard any of them complain.

Patty recently began her own housecleaning business. So far, she has several houses to clean, and her customers are people she previously worked for in the factory. Patty explained, 'They really like me a lot and they helped me to start this business'. Patty's conversion occurred in 2007. She began to have conflicts with her partner. Patty recalls:

My partner treated me badly, and the Lord said that I was a pearl. So, I began to compare—that is, I began to compare everything in my home to the Word. And I also began to know about the enemy. While I prayed and the Lord ministered to me, I saw things, and I began to realize how the enemy works.

Patty no longer wanted to live a life away from God. She realized she lived in sin before the Lord. Patty began to pray. She prayed and fasted. Eventually, she sensed that the Lord responded to her prayers. She told the Lord, 'I've made mistakes, but I really want for you to restore this'. She realized she wanted to leave her situation behind. Her partner was a man whom she met when she was seventeen years old. He had told her he was single, but he had a wife in the U.S. Patty was heartbroken.

I began to go to church in 2005, but it wasn't regularly. I would still stumble. It was like I didn't want to leave my way of being, of living in sin, because I loved my daughter's dad. But I made a clear-cut decision in 2006. And in 2007, I gave myself completely to the Lord.

Patty continues to serve in her church, and her prayer is essential. She says prayer has sustained her life. She is proud of her daughter, who also serves in the youth group at church. Patty tries to live a solid Christian life as an example for her daughter. In her new business, Patty takes time to pray each day. She explained:

I took time to pray when I went to clean my first house. Imagine a house that I had not been to before, belonging to an *Americano*. I always pray, 'Lord, give me grace and favor'. Because I know that he will give it if we ask. And I pray and get ready. And up to this time, even until today, I've always seen God's grace and favor in everything I do.

Patty is optimistic about her future and is well-adapted to life in the U.S. She knows God has led her to this point and that He has promised to prosper her business. She confides, 'I know it's him, these are His plans ... I am an administrator of the Lord because the Lord has plans for this ... I feel happy in what I do'. Patty will certainly inspire other Latinas to get ahead in life.

CONCLUSION

Pentecostals read the Word and pray believing they will experience the power of God. They are aware God can move in their midst. Prayer is a way to enter into the presence of God and receive the saving work of God in Christ through the Spirit. [1] Pentecostals affirm the life of the Spirit, whose 'wind blows wherever it pleases. You hear the sound of it, but you cannot tell where it comes from or where it is going' (Jn 3.8).

For Pentecostals, the Holy Spirit is present and moves amidst the life of believers. In a Latino Pentecostal service, the manifestations of the Holy Spirit are perceived in spontaneous prayers, joyful singing, speaking in tongues, and improvised changes in the service. Otto Maduro explains that Pentecostalism 'is a reconstruction of Christianity in a simplified way—a way that is seen as more faithful to the spirit of early Christianity'. [2]

The Latino culture allows a more open expression of emotions in comparison to the Anglo-American culture. For immigrants undergoing culture shock and feelings of disorientation, the church becomes a community of acceptance and consolation where they can cry, laugh, and express vociferous worship. Believers share their life stories, joys, and struggles, knowing others care and pray for them.

> There are all of these raw emotions that come to the surface when one is in this very fragile, insecure situation of being an immigrant in a new land with a different language, with racism and so on. All of these emotions can be loudly, physically, explicitly expressed over

---

[1] Yong, Amos, 'Reading Scripture and Nature: Pentecostal Hermeneutics and Their Implications for the Contemporary Evangelical Theology and Science Conversation', *Perspectives on Science and Christian Faith*, 63.1 (March 2011), pp. 3-15.

[2] Wallace, Bruce. 'The Latino Pentecostals', Drew Magazine, Fall 2008 ww.drew.edu/news/2016/04/13/the-latino-Pentecostals

and over again in Pentecostal services without anybody looking down on you. [3]

The modern Pentecostal movement has interpreted Luke–Acts as a basis for the power and tangible manifestations of the Holy Spirit that occurred in several parts of the world around the beginning of the twentieth-century. This persistence is in alignment with Luke's intention both in his gospel and in the Book of Acts. Luke–Acts reveals the redemptive-historical acts of God occurring in a context of prayer. The Holy Spirit in Luke–Acts was a power 'enabling believers to see, speak words they would otherwise be unable to speak, and perform mighty deeds that would otherwise lay beyond their abilities'.[4] Luke made accurate descriptions of supernatural manifestations as evidence of the active presence of the Holy Spirit amidst the community of believers.

The emphasis on prayer is also traced in the current Pentecostal movement and among Hispanic and Latino churches. Intense prayers are characteristic of Pentecostals and more so among immigrants who flee hunger, poverty, and violence. The stories of Latino immigrants reflect suffering and how they value prayer in their lives. While interviewing Latino immigrants, some interesting themes surfaced. For example, they recount the hardships they encountered in their journeys and how prayer helped them cope with grief and even depression. The role of women in the sustenance of the immigrant family is amazing. The resilience of immigrant families enables them to survive in adverse circumstances and under the pressure of blatant discrimination.

If people understood why Latinos leave their countries, many would feel less threatened by their ethnic and cultural differences. Immigrants work sacrificially to give their children a better future. They have a strong sense of family and introduce a sense of community and togetherness wherever they go. Latino communities are steeped in family values, respect for elders, and hospitality. Their vibrancy can enrich the fiber of American society. This is a time to celebrate the many cultures God has allowed to come to the United States. Their accents are not a sign of inferiority or less intelligence.

---

[3] Wallace, 'The Latino Pentecostals.

[4] J.R. Michaels. 'Luke Acts', in Stanley M. Burgess and Gay B. McGee V. (eds.), *Dictionary of Pentecostal and Charismatic Movements* (Grand Rapids, MI: Zondervan Publishing House), p. 560.

Hispanic churches continue to be a powerful source of meaning, identity, and community to immigrants. Latinos are significantly reshaping religion in America through their religious zeal. A wave of Pentecostals and Evangelicals is molding spirituality in the country. For some religious leaders, Hispanics 'are saving American Christianity...No doubt, every denomination would have decreased in membership if it had not been for Hispanic growth'.[5]

It is important for the American nation to understand that Hispanics are not strangers to the land known as the United States of America. It would seem that historical meta-narratives overlook the reality of the Spanish conquest before America was established as a British colony. Hispanics have lived in the U.S. longer than any other identifiable group except Native Americans. Many have long genealogies in this country. This is a significant element to consider for the average citizen and government officials so that a more compassionate approach toward immigration can be envisioned. Countless Mexican residents of the Southwest make their situation clear, 'We did not cross a border; the border crossed us'.[6] About three out of four Hispanics whose families have been here for centuries are English speakers, yet they also speak Spanish.[7]

International migration is a key feature of globalization, and it has become a vital issue in the U.S. and in many European nations. In the same manner, Christianity has been crossing cultural boundaries from its start on the day of Pentecost up to the present.[8] Chandler Im refers to the scattering of people around the world as one of God's mission strategies or 'divine conspiracy' to bring renewal to churches in many nations.[9] It is inevitable that global diaspora churches will continue to

---

[5] Tony Castro, 'How Hispanics are Changing Religion in the US', *Latino Voices,* April 18, 2015, accessed September 30, 2015, http://www.huffingtonpost.com/2014/04/18/hispanics-changing-religion-_n_5173258.html

[6] Josué David Cisneros, *The Border Crossed Us: Rhetorics of Borders, Citizenship, and Latino/a Identity* (Tuscaloosa, AL: Alabama University Press, 2013), p. 12.

[7] Justo L. González and Carlos F. Cardoza-Orlandi, 'The Religious World of Latino/a-Hispanic Americans', in Jacob Neusner (ed.), *World Religions in America: An Introduction* (Louisville, KY: Westminster/John Knox Press, 1994), pp. 87-104

[8] Bradley P. Holt, *Thirsty for God: A Brief History of Christian Spirituality* (Minneapolis: Fortress Press, 2005), p. 17.

[9] Chandler H. Im, 'Epilogue', in Chandler H. Im and Amos Yong (eds.), *Global Diasporas and Mission* (Oxford: Regnum Books International, 2014), pp. 263-65.

play significant tasks in the mobilization of churches including evangelism, church planting, discipleship, social services, justice and human rights issues, etc.[10]

Latinos represent a diaspora in the United States. Groups of impoverished Latinos risk their lives to obtain better conditions of life for themselves and their families. They cling to God in prayer out of their stress and discomfort. Pentecostal churches offer closeness and solidarity, and church leaders generally deal with problems that affect the hermanos (brothers and sisters).

While immigration issues continue to affect the political scene of North America it would seem America cannot perceive the visitation of God through Latino immigrants. Many people cannot see or hear that the Spirit of God 'has been dispersing and gathering the nations for his missional plans and purposes through the means of the global diasporas'.[11] From this perspective, diaspora is a God-orchestrated mission strategy for reaching the lost and fostering spiritual vitality among the nations. Diaspora churches in the U.S.A. 'hold a key to what happens in the resurgence of American Christianity and new global Christian movements'.[12]

Thus, through prayer, Pentecostal and Latino immigrants are bringing a fresh presence of the Spirit of God to the American nation. Latinos are remaking religion in America in growing numbers, especially in Pentecostal churches. The growth of the Latino population and a surge of Pentecostal worship are shaping the Hispanic spiritual fabric of the American nation. It is critical that Hispanic and Latino churches keep prayer alive to preserve their vitality and to bring renewal and transformation to the Hispanic community and to the American nation. From visiting Hispanic churches in many states, I can see how Latinos contribute to the revival of the evangelical Christian movement in the United States through the many ways their communities depend on prayer. Latinos will keep Christianity vibrant and alive in America in the years to come.

---

[10] Im, 'Epilogue', p. 263.
[11] Im, 'Epilogue', p. 264.
[12] Im, 'Epilogue', p. 264.

BIBLIOGRAPHY

Alagna, Magdalena, *The Monroe Doctrine: An End to European Colonies in America* (New York: Rosen Publishing Group, 2004).

Albrecht, Daniel E., 'Pentecostal Spirituality: Ecumenical Potential and Challenge'., *Cyberjournal for Pentecostal-Charismatic* Journal 2 (1997). http://www. pctii.org/cyberj/cyberj2/albrecht.html. Accessed May 7, 2014.

Albrecht, Daniel E., *Rites in the Spirit: A Ritual Approach to Pentecostal/Charismatic Spirituality* (Sheffield, UK: Sheffield Academic Press, 1999).

Alexander, Estrelda. 'Introduction', in Estrelda Alexander and Amos Yong (eds.), *Philip's Daughters: Women in Pentecostal- Charismatic Leadership* (Eugene, OR: Wipf and Stock, 2009).

Alvarez, Miguel, 'A Century of Pentecostalism in Latin America', in Vinson Synan, Amos Yong and Miguel Alvarez (eds.), *World Renewal Chritianity* (Lake Mary, FL: Charisma House, 2015).

Anderson, Allan, *An Introduction to Pentecostalism: Global Charismatic Christianity* (Cambridge: Cambridge University Press, 2014).

Andruske, Cynthia Lee, 'Self-Directed Learning Projects of Women on Welfare as Political Acts', *Adult Learning* 14 (2003).

Anzaldúa, Gloria E., *Borderlands/La Frontera: The New Mestiza* (San Francisco: Aunt Lute Books, 1987).

Archer, Kenneth, *A Pentecostal Hermeneutics for the Twenty-First Century: Spirit, Scripture, and Community* (London: T & T Clark International, 2004).

Armstrong, Karen, *The Battle for God* (New York: Random House, 2000).

Arrington, French, *The Spirit-Anointed Jesus: A Study of the Gospel of Luke* (Cleveland, TN: Pathway Press, 2008).

Asian Development Bank. 'Women and Labour Markets in Asia: Rebalancing for Gender Equality'. *Geneva: International Labor Organization*, 2011. http://www.ilo.org/wcmsp5/groups/public/---asia/---ro-bangkok/documents/publication/wcms_154846.pdf. Accessed January 2015.

Badillo, David A., *Latinos and the New Immigrant Church* (Baltimore: Johns Hopkins University Press, 2006).

Baker, Coleman A., *Identity, Memory, and Narrative in Early Christianity* (Eugene, OR: Wipf and Stock, 2011).

Barone, Michael, *The New Americans* (Washington, DC: Regnery Publishing, 2001).

Becker, Marc, 'Dictatorship in Latin America'. http://science.jrank.org/pages/7630/Dictatorship-in-Latin-America.html. Accessed September 3, 2015.

Beta Grupos. 'Instituto Nacional de Migracion de Mexico', http://www.
inm.gob. mx/index.php/page/Grupo_Beta. Accessed September 9, 2015.

Bordas, Juana, *The Power of Latino Leadership* (San Francisco: Berrett-Koehler,
2013).

Borthwick, Paul, *Western Christians in Global Missions* (Downers Grove, IL: InterVarsity Press, 2012).

Bounds, E.M., *The Complete Works of E.M.* Bounds (Radford, VA: Sublime
Books, 2014).

Brown, David L., and Kai A. Schafft, *Rural People and Communities in the 21st
Century: Resilience and Transformation.* Cambridge (Polity Press, 2011).

Brusco, Elizabeth, *The Reformation of Machismo: Evangelical Conversion and Gender
in Colombia* (Austin: University of Texas Press, 1995).

Buckingham, Jamie, *Daughter of Destiny: Kathryn Kuhlman* (Plainfield, NJ: Logos
International, 1976).

Burgan, Michael, *The Spanish Conquest of America* (New York: InfoBase Publishing, 2007).

Cadbury, Henry J., *The Making of Luke–Acts* (London: Methuen, 1927).

Callahan, Rebecca M., and Patricia Gándara, *The Bilingual Advantage: Language,
Literacy, and the US Labor Market* (Bristol, UK: Multilingual Matters, 2014).

Campos, Bernardo, 'In the Power of the Spirit: Pentecostalism, Theology and
Social Ethics', in Benjamin F. Gutierrez and Dennis A. Smith (eds), in *The
Power of the Spirit: The Pentecostal Challenge to Historic Churches in Latin America*
(Louisville, KY: Presbyterian Church U.S.A. Worldwide Ministries Divi-
sion, 1996), pp. 41-50

Cárdenas, Vanessa, Julie Ajinkya, and Daniella Gibbs Léger, 'Progress 2050:
New Ideas for a Diverse America', Center for American Progress, 2011,
https://www.americanprogress.org/wp-content/uploads/is-
sues/2011/10/pdf/progress_2050.pdf. Accessed July 10, 2015.

Carr, Anne E., *Transforming Grace* (San Francisco: Harper and Row, 1988).

Carranza, Miguel, and Lourdes Gouveia, 'The Integration of the His-
panic/Latino Immigration Workforce' (Report, University of Nebraska,
May 31, 2002). http://www.unomaha.edu/ollas/pdf/HLIWSREPORT-
final.pdf. Accessed October 3, 2015.

Carson, D.A. (ed.), *Teach Us to Pray: Prayer in the Bible and the World* (London:
Baker Book House, 1990).

Casper, Jayson, 'How Libya's Martyrs are Witnessing to Egypt', *Christianity
Today*, February 23, 2015. http://www.christianitytoday.com/ct/2015/
february-web-/how-libyas-martyrs-are-evangelizing-egypt.html. Accessed
April 21, 2015.

Castillo, Juan, 'Latino? Hispanic? Chicano?' In *Hispanic Americans* (ed. Paul
McCaffrey; New York: H.W. Wilson Company, 2007), 5-10.

Castles Stephen, Hein de Haas, and Mark Miller, *Age of Migration: International Population Movements in the Modern World*, 5th ed. (New York: Palgrave McMillan, 2014).

Chaves, Mark, *Ordaining Women: Culture and Conflict in Religious Organizations* (Cambridge, MA: Harvard University Press, 1997).

Chin, Rita, *The Guest Worker Question in Post-War Germany* (Cambridge: Cambridge University Press, 2007).

Cisneros, Josue David, *The Border Crossed Us: Rhetorics of Borders, Citizenship, and Latina/o Identity* (Tuscaloosa: The University of Alabama Press, 2011).

———, *Rhetorics of Borders, Citizenship, and Latino/a Identity* (Tuscaloosa, AL: Alabama University Press, 2013).

Clark, William, *'A.V. Immigrants and the American Dream'* (New York: The Guilford Press, 2003).

Cleary, Edward L., and Juan Sepúlveda. 'Chilean Pentecostalism: Coming of Age', in Edward L. Cleary and Hannah W. Stewart-Gambino (eds.), *Power, Politics and Pentecostals in Latin America* (Boulder, CO: Westview, 1998), pp. 98-113.

Cleary, Jim, 'Racial Profiling Studies in Law Enforcement: Issues and Methodology' (St. Paul, MN: Minnesota House of Representatives, 2000). www.house.leg.state.mn.us/hrd/pubs/raceprof.pdf. Accessed August 30, 2015.

Climent, James, and John Radzillowski, *American Immigration: An Encyclopedia of Political, Social, and Cultural Change* (New York: Routledge, 2015).

Cohen, Deborah, *Braceros: Migrant Citizens and Transnational Subjects in the Postwar United States and Mexico* (Chapel Hill: University of North Carolina Press, 2011).

Collings, Patricia Hill, *Black Feminist Thought: Knowledge, Consciousness, and the Politics of Empowerment* (New York: Routledge, 2000).

Conn, Charles W., *Pillars of Pentecost* (Cleveland, TN: Church of God Publishing House, 1956).

Conzelmann, Hans, *The Theology of St. Luke* (trans. Geoffrey Buswell; New York: Harper and Row, 1961).

Cox, Harvey, *Fire from Heaven: The Rise of Pentecostal Spirituality and the Reshaping of Religion in the Twenty-First Century* (Cambridge, MA: De Capo Press, 1995).

Crump, David, *Jesus the Intercessor: Prayer and Christology in Luke–Acts* (Grand Rapids, MI: Baker Book House, 1992).

Cullman, Oscar, *Baptism in the New Testament* (Naperville, IL: Alec R. Anderson, 1950).

———, *Prayer in the New Testament* (Minneapolis: Fortress Press, 1995).

Davis, Robert, 'What About Justice?' *Transformation: An International Journal of Holistic Mission Studies* 26.2 (April 2009).

Deere, Jack, *Surprised by the Power of the Spirit* (Grand Rapids, MI: Zondervan, 1993).

Dempster, Murray, and Klaus, Byron D., *The Globalization of Pentecostalism: A Religion Made to Travel* (Eugene, OR: Wipf and Stock, 1999).

Dugdale, Kate, 'Understanding the Lord's Prayer as a Paradigm for Prayer', *The New Zealand Journal of Christian Thought and Practice* 19.3 (September 2012).

Dunn, James D.G., 'Prayer', in Joel B. Green, Scot McKnight, and I. Howard Marshall (eds.), *Dictionary of Jesus and the Gospels* (Downers Grove, IL: IVP, 1992).

Ehrlich, Paul, and Anne Ehrlichm, *One with Nineveh: Politics, Consumption, and the Human Future* (Washington DC: Island Press, 2004).

Emmer, Pieter C., and Leo Lucassen, 'Migration from the Colonies to Western Europe since 1800', *European History Online*. ieg-ego.eu/en/threads/europe-on-the-road/economic-migration/pieter-c-emmer-leo-lucassen-migration-from-the-colonies-to-western-europe-since-1800#NonEuropeanLabourImmigrants. Accessed September 9, 2015.

Espinosa, Gaston, 'Third-class Soldiers: A History of Hispanic Pentecostal Clergywomen, in Estrelda Alexander and Amos Yong (eds.), *Philip's Daughters: Women in Pentecostal-Charismatic Leadership* (Eugene, OR: Wipf & Stock, 2009), pp. 95-111.

Ewing, Walter E., 'The Growth of the U.S. Deportation Machine', *American Immigration Council*, April 9, 2014. http://www.immigrationpolicy.org/just-facts/growth-us-deportation-machine. Accessed October 10, 2015.

Fisher, James T., *Communion of Immigrants: A History of Catholics in America* (Oxford: Oxford University Press, 2000).

Fitzmyer, Joseph A., *The Acts of the Apostles: A New Translation with Introduction and Commentary* (New York: Doubleday, 1998).

Freston, Paul, 'Christianity and Conflict in Latin America', Pew Research Center, April 2006. http://www.pewforum.org/2006/04/06/christianity-and-conflict-in-latin-america. Accessed December 14, 2015.

Ganeri, Anita, and Nicola Barber, *Central America* (London: Franklin Watts, 2004).

Gangi, Kelly, *Mother Teresa: The Essential Wisdom* (New York: Fall River Press, 2006).

Gann, L.H., and Peter J. Duignan, *The Hispanics in the United States* (Boulder, CO: Westview Press, 1986).

Garcia, Maria Cristina, 'Exiles, Immigrants, and Transnationals: The Cuban Communities of the United States', in David Gregory Gutierrez (ed.), *The Columbian History of Latinos in the United States Since 1960* (New York: Columbia University Press, 2004), pp. 146-186.

Gaylor, Annie Laurie, *Woe to Women: The Bible Tells Me So* (Madison, WI: Freedom for Religion Foundation), 1981.

Gilligan, Carol, *In a Different Voice: Psychological Theory and Women's Development*. (Cambridge, MA: Harvard University Press), 1982.

Global Commission on International Migration. 'Migration in an Interconnected World: New Directions for Action', Geneva: Global Commission on International Migration, October 2005. https://www.iom.int/jahia/webdav/site/myjahiasite/shared/shared/mainsite/policy_and_research/gcim/GCIM_Report_Complete.pdf

González, Justo L., and Carlos F. Cardoza-Orlandi, 'The Religious World of Latino/a-Hispanic Americans', in Jacob Neusner (ed.), *World Religions in America: An Introduction* (Nashville, TN: Westminster John Knox Press, 2009), 87-104.

Gooren, Henri, 'The Pentecostalization of Religion and Society in Latin America', *Exchange* 39 (2010), pp. 355-362. doi:10.1163/157254310X537025. Accessed March 23, 2015.

Green, Michael. *Evangelism in the Early Church* (Grand Rapids, MI: William B. Eerdmans, 1970).

Greenberg, Amy S., *A Wicked War: Polk, Clay, Lincoln, and the 1846 U.S. Invasion of Mexico* (New York: Vintage Books, 2012).

Grenz, Stanley, *A Primer on Postmodernism* (Grand Rapids, MI: Eerdmans, 1996).

Gunderson, Megan M., *William McKinley* (Edina, MN: ABDO Publishing Company, 2009).

Guthrie, Donald, *New Testament Introduction* (Downers Grove, IL: InterVarsity Press, 1970).

Gutiérrez, David G., *Walls and Mirrors: Mexican Americans, Mexican Immigrants, and the Politics of Ethnicity* (Berkeley: University of California Press, 1995).

———, *The Columbia History of Latinos in the United States Since 1960* (New York: Columbia University Press, 2004).

———, 'An Historic Overview of Latino Immigration and the Demographic Transformation of the United States', National Park Service: American Latino Theme Study. http://www.nps.gov/history/heritageinitiatives/latino/latinothemestudy/immigration.htm. Accessed August 2, 2015.

Gutiérrez, Ramón A., 'The Latino Crucible: Its Origins in 19th Century Wars, Revolutions, and Empire', National Park Service: American Latino Theme Study. http://www.nps.gov/history/heritageinitiatives/latino/latinothemestudy/empireswars.htm. Accessed September 5, 2015.

Haan, Cornell, *The Lighthouse Movement* (Sisters, OR: Multnomah Publishers, 1999).

Haavik, Charles Elias, *Joyful in My House: Introducing Postmoderns to the Life of Prayer*, D.Min. diss., Assemblies of God Theological Seminary, 2006.

Hackel, Steven W. , *Junipero Serra: California's Founding Father* (New York: Hill and Wang, 2013).

Haddad, Mimi, 'Egalitarian Pioneers: Betty Friedan or Catherine Booth?' *Priscilla Journal Papers* 20.4 (Autumn 2006).

Han, Kyu Sam, 'Theology of Prayer in the Gospel of Luke', *Journal of the Evangelical Theological Society* 43.4 (December 2000) pp. 675-693. Academic Search Complete, EBSCO host. Accessed February 14, 2015.

Hardesty, Nancy, *Women Called to Witness* (Knoxville, TN: University of Tennessee Press, 1999).

Harris, Lindell O., 'Prayer in Luke–Acts: A Study in the Theology of Luke', PhD dissertation, Vanderbilt University, 1966.

———, 'Prayer in the Gospel of Luke', Southwestern Journal of Theology 10.1 (1967), pp. 59-69.

Henry, Astrid, *Not My Mother's Sister: Generational Conflict and Third-Wave Feminism* (Bloomington: Indiana University Press, 2004).

Hernandez, Jennifer Browdy, *Women Writing Resistance* (Cambridge, MA: South End Press, 2005).

Herring, George C., *From Colony to Superpower: U.S. Foreign Relations since 1776* (New York: Oxford University Press, 2008).

Hoffman, Richard, 'A Wave of Spirituality: How our Faith is Transforming America', *Hispanic* 18. 2 (January, 2006).

Holt, Bradley P., *Thirsty for God: A Brief History of Christian Spirituality* (Minneapolis: Fortress Press, 2005).

Hurley, Joanna, *Mother Teresa: 1910-1997 A Pictorial Biography* (Philadelphia: Running Press, 1997).

Ireland, Rowan, *Kingdoms Come: Religion in Brazil* (Pittsburgh, PA: University of Pittsburgh Press, 1991).

Isbister, John, *Immigration Debate: Remaking America* (West Hartford, CT: Kumarian Press, 1996).

Jennings, James, and Monte Rivera, *Puerto Rican Politics in Urban America* (Westport, CT: Greenwood Press, 1984).

Jeremias, Joachim, *The Prayers of Jesus* (Philadelphia: Fortress, 1977).

Johns, Cheryl Bridges, *Pentecostal Formation: A Pedagogy Among the Oppressed* (Sheffield, UK: Sheffield Academic Press, 1993).

Kaya, Bulent, *The Changing face of Europe: Population Flows in the 20th Century* (Strasbourg, France: Council of Europe Publishing, 2002).

Kinn, James W., *The Spirit of Jesus in Scripture and Prayer* (Oxford: Sheed and Ward, 2004).

Kraft, Charles, *Christianity with Power: Your Worldview and Your Experience of the Supernatural* (Ann Arbor, MI: Servant Books, 1989).

Land, Steven J., *Pentecostal Spirituality: A Passion for the Kingdom* (Cleveland, TN: CPT Press, 2010).

Lawless, Elaine, *Handmaidens of the Lord: Pentecostal Women Preachers and Traditional Religion* (Philadelphia: University of Pennsylvania Press, 1988).

Leonard, David J., and Carmen R. Lugo-Lugo, (eds.), *Latino History and Culture: An Encyclopedia* (New York: Routledge, 2015).

Li, Peter S., 'World Migration in the Age of Globalization: Policy Implications and Challenges', *New Zealand Population Review* 1 (2008), pp.33-34. http://www.population.org.nz/wp-content/uploads/2010/01/nzpr-vol-33-and-34_peter-s-li.pdf. Accessed September 13, 2015.

Limbaugh, Ronald H., and Willard P. Limbaugh, *Calaveras Gold: The Impact of Mining on a Mother Lode County* (Reno: University of Nevada Press, 2004).

Lipski, John, *Varieties of Spanish in the United States* (Washington DC: Georgetown University Press, 2008).

López, Dario, *La Fiesta del Espíritu: Espiritualidad y Celebración Pentecostal* (Lima, Perú: Ediciones Puma, 2006).

Lopez, Mark Hugo, Ana Gonzalez-Barrera, and Danielle Cuddington, 'Diverse Origins: The Nation's 14 Largest Hispanic-Origin Groups', Pew Research Center, June 19, 2013. http://www.pewhispanic.org/ 2013/06/ 19/diverse-origins-the-nations-14-largest-hispanic-origin-groups. Accessed July 28, 2015.

Lopez, Mark Hugo, and Daniel Dockterman, 'U.S. Hispanic Population by Country of Origin', Pew Research Center, May 26, 2011. http://www.pewhispanic.org/2011/05/26/us-hispanic-country-of-origin-counts-for-nation-top-30-metropolitan-areas. Accessed July 28, 2015.

Lynne Bundesen, *The Feminine Spirit: Recapturing the Heart of Scripture* (San Francisco: Jossey-Bass, 2007).

Ma, Julie, 'Pentecostal Evangelism, Church Planting, and Church Growth', in Wonsuk Ma, Veli-Matti Kärkkäinen, and J. Kwabena Asamoah-Gyadu (eds.), *Pentecostal Mission and Global Christianity* (Eugene, OR: Wipf and Stock, 2014) pp. 87-106.

Malone, Mary, *Women and Christianity: The First Thousand Years* (Maryknoll, NY: Orbis, 2000).

Marshall, I. Howard, *The Gospel of Luke: A Commentary on the Greek Text* (Grand Rapids, MI: Eerdmans, 1978).

———, *The Acts of the Apostles*. Sheffield, UK: Sheffield Academic Press, 1992.

Martin, David, *Tongues of Fire: The Explosion of Protestantism in Latin America* (Oxford: Blackwell, 1990).

Martin, Gus, *Understanding Terrorism* (Thousand Oaks, CA: Sage, 2016).

McCarroll, Aaron Gallegos, 'Where the Spirit Leads', *Sojourners* 37.4 (April 2008).

McClung, Grant, *Azusa Street and Beyond: Pentecostal Missions and Church Growth in the Twentieth Century* (South Plainfield, NJ: Bridge Publishing, 1986).

———, 'Waiting on the Gift': An Insider Looks Back on One Hundred Years of Pentecostal Witness', *International Bulletin of Missionary Research* 30.2 (April 2006).

Medina, Néstor, and Sammy Alfaro, *Pentecostals and Charismatics in Latin America and Latino Communities* (London: Palgrave McMillan, 2015).

Metzger, Bruce M., *The New Testament: Its Background, Growth, and Content* (Nashville, TN: Abingdon Press, 2003).

Michaels J.R. 'Luke Acts', in Stanley M. Burgess and Gary B. McGee (eds.), *Dictionary of Pentecostal and Charismatic Movements* (Grand Rapids, MI: Zondervan, 1988), pp. 544-61.

Miller, Donald, and Tetsunao Yamamori, *Global Pentecostalism: The New Face of Christian Social Engagement* (Los Angeles: University of California Press 2007).

Moore, Joan, and Henry Pachon, *Hispanics in the United States* (Englewood Cliffs, NJ: Prentice Hall, 1985).

Mullaly, Sarah, 'More Women Leaders Will Help to Counteract Macho Culture', *Nursing Standard* 23.13 (December 2008).

National Council of La Raza, 'Mission', http://www.nclr.org/index.php/about_us. Accessed September 21, 2015.

National Immigration Law Center, 'The Obama's Administration Deferred Action for Childhood Arrivals (DACA)', August 14, 2015, https://www.nilc.org/FAQdeferredactionyouth.html. Accessed September 23, 2015.

Navarro, Armando, *The Immigration Crisis: Nativism, Armed Vigilantism, and the Rise of a Countervailing Movement* (Lanham, MD: Altamira Press, 1980).

Offutt, Stephen, 'The Transnational Locations of Two Leading Evangelical Churches in the Global South', Pneuma 32 (2010).

Olthius, James H., 'On Worldviews', *Christian Scholar's Review* 14 (1985). http://www.freewebs.com/jamesolthuis/OnWorldviews.pdf. Accessed March 20, 2014.

Panich, Lee M., and Tsim D. Schneider, 'Native Agency at the Margins of Empire', in Lee M. Panich and Tsim D. Schneider, *Indigenous Landscapes and Spanish* Missions (Tucson: University Press of Southern Arizona, 2014), pp. 5-20.

Passel, Jeffrey, and D'Vera Cohn, 'US Population Projections: 2005-2050', Pew Research Center, February 2008. http://www.pewhispanic.org/2008/02/11/us-population-projections-2005-2050. Accessed September 3, 2015.

Penney, John Michael, *The Missionary Emphasis of Lukan Pneumatology* (Sheffield, UK: Sheffield Academic Press, 1997).

Pew Hispanic Center, 'Cubans in the United States', Pew Hispanic Center, 2006. http://www.pewhispanic.org/files/factsheets/23.pdf. Accessed September 23, 2015.

———, 'Changing Faiths: Latinos and the Transformation of American Religion', Pew Forum on Religion and Public Life, 2007. http://www.pewforum.org/files/2007/04/hispanics-religion-07-final-mar08.pdf.

———, 'Median Age for Hispanics', http://www.pewresearch.org/daily-number/median-age-for-hispanics-is-lower-than-median-age-for-total-u-s-population. Accessed September 25, 2015.

Plymale, Steven F., *The Prayer Texts of Luke–Acts* (New York: Lang, 1991).

Portes, Alejandro, 'Children of Immigrants: Segmented Assimilation and Its Determinants', in Alejandro Portes (ed.), *The Economic Sociology of Immigration* (New York: Russell Sage Foundation, 1995), pp. 248-280.

Powell, Mark Allan, *What Are They Saying About Luke?* (Mahwah, NJ: Paulist Press, 1989).

Pownall, Andrew, 'The Church in a Multicultural Society', in Evert Van de Poll and Joanne Appleton (eds.), *Church Planting in Europe* (Eugene, OR: Wipf and Stock, 2015) pp. 148-162.

Raby, Diana, 'Democracy and Revolution: Latin America and Socialism Today', Venezuelan Analysis. http://venezuelanalysis.com/analysis/2005. Accessed September 14, 2012.

Rah, Soon-Chan, *The Next Evangelicalism: Freeing the Church from Western Cultural Captivity* (Downers Grove, IL: InterVarsity Press, 2009).

Reardon, Patrick Henry, 'Most Excellent Theophilus', *Touchstone*, December 2002. http://www.touchstonemag.com/archives/article.php?id=15-10-026-c#ixzz3DEMaBPMS Accessed September 13, 2014.

Reimer, Ivoni Richter, *Women in the Acts of the Apostles: A Feminist Liberation Perspective* (Minneapolis, MN: Fortress Press, 1995).

Retta, Edward, and Cynthia Brink, 'Latino or Hispanic: Which Term Should we Use?' *Cross Culture Communications*, 2007 http://www.crossculturecommunications.com/latino-hispanic.pdf. Accessed August 10, 2015.

Rivera-Pagán, Luis, 'Xenophilia or Xenophobia: Toward a Theology of Migration', in Elaine Padilla and Peter Phan (eds.), *Contemporary Issues of Migration and Theology* (New York: Palgrave MacMillan, 2013), pp. 31-52.

Rodriguez, Samuel, 'How God is Exploding Among Latinos', *Charisma*, 2012. http://www.charismamag.com/spirit/revival/15089-gods-latino-explosion.

Roebuck, David, *Limiting Liberty: The Church of God and Women Ministers 1986-1996*, PhD diss., Vanderbilt University, 1997.

Roman, Edilberto, *Those Dammed Immigrants: America's Hysteria over Undocumented Immigrants* (New York: New York University Press, 2013).

Romero, Sylvia, and Melissa Romero Williams, 'The Impact of Immigration Legislation on Latino Families', *Advances in Social Work* 14.1 (Spring 2013), pp. 229-246.

Ross, Clifton, and Marcy Rein, *Until the Rulers Obey: Voices from Latin American Social Movements* (Oakland, CA: PM Press, 2014).

Roth, S. John, 'Jesus the Pray-er', *Currents in Theology and Missions* 33.6 (December 2006).

Salguero, Gabriel, 'Immigration, Integration, and National Identity: Making the Case for a Hispanic Evangelical Contribution', *Review of Faith and International Affairs* 9.1 (2011).

Sample, Kristen, 'No Hay Mujeres: Latin American Women and Gender Equality', *Open Democracy*, February 2009. https://www.opendemocracy.net/article/idea/no-hay-mujeres-latin-america-women-and-gender-equality. Accessed December 14, 2014.

Sanchez, Maria, *Acerquemonos al Nuevo Testamento* (Tegucigalpa, Honduras: CCI Publicaciones, 2013).

Sánchez-Walsh, Arlene M., *Latino Pentecostal Identity: Evangelical Faith, Self, and Society* (New York: Columbia University Press, 2003).

Sexton, Jay, *The Monroe Doctrine: Empire and Nation in Nineteenth-Century America* (New York: Hill and Wang, 2011).

Smith, James K.A., *Thinking in Tongues* (Grand Rapids, MI: William B. Eerdmans, 2010).

Spink, Kathryn, *Mother Teresa: A Complete Authorized Biography* (New York: Harper Collins, 1997).

Stanley, Susie, 'Shattering the Stained-Glass Window', in Reta Halteman and Kari Sandhaas (eds.), *The Wisdom of Daughters: Two Decades of the Voice of Christian Feminism* (Philadelphia, PA: Innisfree Press, 2001), pp. 83-86.

Steffan, Melissa, 'The Surprising Countries Most Missionaries Are Sent From and Go To', *Christianity Today* (July 25, 2013).

Stephenson, Christopher A., *Types of Pentecostal Theology: Method, System, Spirit.* (New York: Oxford University Press, 2013). http://www.questia.com/read/121501082. Accessed April 25, 2014.

Stephenson, Lisa, 'Prophesying Women and Ruling Men: Women's Religious Authority in North American Pentecostalism', *Religion* 2.3 (August 2011), pp. 410-26.

Stronstad Roger, *The Prophethood of All Believers: A Study in Luke's Charismatic Theology* (Cleveland, TN: CPT Press, 2010).

Synan, Vinson, *The Holiness-Pentecostal Tradition: Charismatic Movements in the Twentieth Century* (Grand Rapids, MI: William B. Eerdmans, 1997).

———. *The Century of the Holy Spirit: One Hundred Years of Pentecostal and Charismatic Renewal* (Nashville, TN: Thomas Nelson, 2001).

Tábora, Jesús Muñoz, *Folklor y turismo* (Tegucigalpa, Honduras: Editorial Guaymuras, 2002).

Tanja, Bastia, *Migration and Inequality* (New York: Routledge, 2013).

Torres-Tama, José, *Immigrant Dreams and Alien Nightmares* (New Orleans, LA: Dialogos Books, 2014).

Twelftree, Graham H., 'Prayer and the Coming of the Spirit', *Expository Times* 117.7 (April 2006).

———, *People of the Spirit: Exploring Luke's View of the Church* (Grand Rapids, MI: Baker Academic, 2009).

U.S. Department of State, Office of the Historian, 'United States Maritime Expansion Across the Pacific During the 19th Century: 1830-1860', https://history.state.gov/milestones/1830–1860/pacific-expansion. Accessed July 28, 2015.

UNESCO, 'International Migration and Multicultural Policies', http://www.unesco.org/most/migration/glossary_migrants.htm (accessed September 14, 2015).

UNICEF, 'Fast Facts on Adolescents and Youth in Latin America and the Caribbean', www.unicef.org/media/files/Fast_facts__EN.doc (accessed December 14, 2015).

United Nations Department of Economic and Social Affairs, 'Trends in International Migration', International Migration Report 2013 (Geneva: United Nations, 2013).

Vasconcelos, Jose, *La raza cosmica: misión de la raza Iberoamericana* (Barcelona: Espasa-Calpe, 1925).

Vilaça, Helena, Enzo Pace, Inger Furseth, and Per Pettersson, *The Changing Soul of Europe: Religions and Migrations in Northern and Southern Europe* (Burlington, VT: Ashgate, 2014).

Villafañe, Eldin, *The Liberating Spirit: Toward a Hispanic American Pentecostal Social Ethic* (Grand Rapids, MI: Eerdmans, 1993).

Villegas, Rodrigo Dominguez, 'Central American Migrants and La Bestia: The Route, Dangers, and Government Responses', Migration Policy Institute (September 2014). http://www.migrationpolicy.org/article/central-american-migrants-and-la-bestia-route-dangers-and-government-responses. Accessed August 3, 2015.

Vondey, Wolfgang, and Martin William Mittelstadt, *The Theology of Amos Yong and the New Face of Pentecostal Scholarship* (Leiden, Netherlands: Brill, 2013).

Walker, Ken, 'Kathryn Kuhlman: Healing Evangelist Ministered to Millions', *Charisma Magazine* (August 2015). http://www.charismanews.com/40-year-anniversary/50893-kathryn-kuhlman-healing-evangelistministered-to-millions. Accessed December 10, 2015.

Wallace, Bruce, 'The Latino Pentecostals', *Drew Magazine* (January 2013). http://www.drewmagazine.com/2008/09/the-latino-Pentecostals. Accessed May 12, 2014.

Walls, Andrew F., 'Mission and Migration: The Diaspora Factor in Christian Mission', in Chandler H. Im and Amos Yong (eds.), *Global Diasporas and Missions* (Oxford: Regnum Books International, 2014).

Wilson, Marie, *Closing the Leadership Gap* (New York: Penguin Books, 2007).

Winders, Jamie, 'Re-Placing Southern Geographies: The Role of Latino Migration Transforming the South, Its Identities, and Its Study', *Southeastern Geographer* 5. 2 (2011).

Wood, George, 'What George O. Wood Really Thinks About Pentecostals Speaking in Tongues', *Charisma Magazine* (April 25, 2014).

http://www.charismamag.com/spirit/church-ministry/20268-what-george-o-wood-really-thinks-about-Pentecostals-speaking-in-tongues. Accessed July 6, 2015.

Yale Law School, 'Monroe Doctrine', The Avalon Project: Documents in Law, History, and Diplomacy. http://avalon.law.yale.edu/19th_century/monroe.asp. Accessed October 10, 2015.

Yong, Amos, *The Spirit Poured Upon All Flesh: Pentecostalism and the Possibility of Global Theology* (Grand Rapids, MI: Baker Academic, 2005).

Yu, Bin, *Chain Migration Explained: The Power of the Immigration Multiplier* (New York: LFB Scholarly Publishing, 2008).

Zerpa, Ida, *Silent Invasion of the U.S.A.* (Buenos Aires: Libros en Red, 2006).

Zibechi, Raúl, 'Pentecostalism and South America's Social Movements', Upside Down World, October 15, 2008. http://upsidedownworld.org/main/international-archives-60/1529-Pentecostalism-and-south-americas-social-movements. Accessed March 10, 2014.

Zub, Roberto, *Protestantismo y participación política* (Managua, Nicaragua: CIEETS/UENIC, 2002).

Index of Biblical References

11.9-11	6	1.24	52	9.17	46
12.5-13	21	2.1-13	12	9.36-43	46
12.27	29	2.2-4	48	10.4	52
13.2	21	2.7	11	10.10	51
13.10-17	66	2.14-40	44	10.15	47
13.20-21	67	2.18	67	10.10	51
13.33-34	72	2.38	49	10.19	51
17-21	23	2.29-30	9	10.34-43	44
19.29, 37	32	2.33	51	10.46	51
21.15	51	2.41	31	11.15	49
21.12-19	70	2.46	11	12.1-3	
21.36	30	2.47	51	12.5	52
21.36	30	3.1	11	12.6-11	71
22.17	21	3.1-19	47	12.12	67
22.22	70	3.21, 22	17	13.2-3	51
22.31-32	17	4.8	46	13.9, 52	46
22.40-41	18	4.12	51	13.12	12
22.42	32	4.13-18	51	13.16-41	44
23.18	71	4.31	48	14	12
23.46	18	5.12	44	15	12
24.9	66	5.15	52	16	12
24.19	23	5.16	17	17	12
24.49	11	5.17-18	52	18	12
22.50	31	5.20	52	19	12
23.34-49	35	5.29	70	20.9-12	46
24.53	20	5.31	51	20.28	51
27.38	33	5.41-42	52	21.27, 28	12
28.20	28	6.1-7	67	22.17	11
28.33-35	28	6.3	71	22.1-21	44
		6.4	52	22.39-44	31
John		6.6	52	23.34, 46	33
13.34	41	6.8	47	26.2-23	44
14.13	6	6.9	51	26.56	33
15.5	5	6.10	71	27.34, 35	11
16.23	20	6.12	17	28.8	11
18.10	31	6.13-14	68		
21.17	31	7.2-52	44	**Romans**	
15.5	5	7.55	51	8.22	5
		7.56-60	71	8.26, 27	4
Acts		8.1-3	70	11.17	38
1.1	72	8.12	67	16.3	67
1.4	11	8.15-17	12		
1.5	49	8.29	52	**I Corinthians**	
1.8	11	9.1	69	1.27	86
1.9	23	9.1-22	71	10.12-13	31
1.14	67	9.10-18	51	11.23	15
1.21-22	25	9.11	12	14.12	4

Index of Authors

Made in the USA
Columbia, SC
18 May 2024